Mass Surveillance and
State Control

Mass Surveillance and State Control

The Total Information Awareness Project

Elliot D. Cohen

MASS SURVEILLANCE AND STATE CONTROL
Copyright © Elliot D. Cohen, 2010.
All rights reserved.

First published in 2010 by
PALGRAVE MACMILLAN®
in the United States – a division of St. Martin's Press LLC,
175 Fifth Avenue, New York, NY 10010.

Where this book is distributed in the UK, Europe and the rest of the world,
this is by Palgrave Macmillan, a division of Macmillan Publishers Limited,
registered in England, company number 785998, of Houndmills, Basingstoke,
Hampshire RG21 6XS.

Palgrave Macmillan is the global academic imprint of the above companies
and has companies and representatives throughout the world.

Palgrave® and Macmillan® are registered trademarks in the United States, the
United Kingdom, Europe and other countries.

ISBN: 978–0–230–10304–7

Library of Congress Cataloging-in-Publication Data

Cohen, Elliot D.
   Mass surveillance and state control : the total information awareness
project / Elliot D. Cohen.
         p. cm.
   Includes bibliographical references.
   ISBN 978–0–230–10304–7 (alk. paper)
   1. Privacy, Right of—United States. 2. Electronic surveillance—Social
aspects—United States. 3. Social control—United States. I. Title.
   JC596.2.U5C64 2010
   323.44'820973—dc22

                                                              2010013239

A catalogue record of the book is available from the British Library.

Design by MPS Limited, A Macmillan Company

First edition: October 2010

10 9 8 7 6 5 4 3 2 1

Printed in the United States of America.

Contents

Introduction

Warrantless Mass Surveillance in a Culture of Control

In George Orwell's famous novel, *1984*,[1] Big Brother kept 24/7 surveillance on all citizens of Oceana via a "telescreen" installed in every home, while the Ministry of Truth streamed in news and entertainment it deemed suitable for popular consumption. Should citizens harbor heretical thoughts, there was also always the Thought Police who, in the dark of night, would visit their homes in order to "vaporize" them, which included wiping out all traces of their past existence. The Ministry of Love was in charge of law and order, even though there were no longer any laws. And there was the "ultimate" enemy of state, Emmanuel Goldstein, whose diatribes against Big Brother were regularly broadcast, uniting citizens in hate and fear and in solidarity with Big Brother against this common enemy.

A Culture of Control

In *1984*, the tripartite slogan of "The Party" is, "WAR IS PEACE; FREEDOM IS SLAVERY; IGNORANCE IS STRENGTH." These three ideological perspectives characterize what in this book is called a *culture of control*. Such cultures are characterized by an unequal power structure where one individual or group dominates another; hence, power flows in only one direction. Examples of such a culture can be found in civilizations based on religious extremism. In such cultures, the enemy is the infidel who must be defeated or killed. Questioning one's faith or otherwise straying from it may even be punishable by death. One's allegiance must be to God (and hence to those who are His ministers). In such a culture, freedom consists in surrendering one's earthly possessions (often to a religious leader), thereby escaping the bondage of the flesh and of the material world, which is viewed as the source of all evil.

In the political sphere, despotic, fascistic states exemplify the idea of a culture of control. The Third Reich is a good example. Power was unilateral, war was waged against a common enemy in the name of national security; and all citizens were expected to have their views aligned with those of the Nazi party. Knowledge flowed only in one direction. The Nazis sought to know everything possible about those subject to their rule. They spied on everyone, including themselves. They wanted to know who were homosexual, Jewish, Gypsy, and who did not have allegiance to the Nazi party. On the other hand, citizens of the Third Reich were expected to believe the propaganda and lies that were disseminated by the Nazi government.

A Culture of Autonomy

In contrast to a culture of control is a *culture of autonomy*. Such a culture permits power to flow bilaterally. Questioning authority is viewed as a healthy way to resolve differences in living a satisfactory life in common. Diplomacy and friendship are to be favored over attempting to destroy or ostracize those who are not ideologically aligned. In contrast to a culture of control, a culture of autonomy thrives on the mutual exchange of information. There is also transparency between the governor and the governed, and communication flows freely both ways. This kind of culture is identified with the democratic state. It is the idea of a culture that is enshrined in the Declaration of Independence according to which a government derives its power from the consent of the governed for purposes of ensuring unalienable rights to life, liberty, and the pursuit of happiness.

Both cultures of control and autonomy are ideals that are never completely realized. In the real world, a culture of autonomy may resemble, to some extent, a culture of control. Thus, no government is entirely transparent; nor is it entirely open to the views of those who oppose it. Nevertheless, some cultures have moved far enough in one direction or another so as to be appropriately called a culture of control or one of autonomy.

What sort of culture presently exists in America?

America as a Culture of Control

In the past decade, since the 9/11 attacks, America has largely moved in the direction of a culture of control. The tripartite characteristics of such a culture are reflected in the conventional wisdom that "winning the war on terrorism" is the route to peace; "freedom is not free" and, therefore, requires sacrifice, such as giving up civil liberties for the sake of safety (including relinquishing our right to privacy); and questioning authority, especially when it comes to national security, is unpatriotic and even treasonous.

Not unlike Orwell's Oceana, we are presently a nation under surveillance, a nation whose corporate mainstream media is largely under the influence of the government. While we do not yet have thought police (we do not yet have the technological means), we have indeed been known to "disappear" citizens deemed to be national security threats. Since the inception of the Bush administration in 2000, the rule of law has been severely compromised by the passage of "laws" enacted in the interest of "national security," that contravene the Bill of Rights of the United States Constitution. This legislation includes laws that permit mass warrantless spying on Americans' electronic communications without adequate judicial oversight. In this climate of fear, we have become a nation in the midst of an all out "war on terror," not against Emmanuel Goldstein, the dreaded "Jew," but this time against Arabs, whose associations and/or ideological ties with al Qaeda or other terrorist groups must never be put past suspicion. Indeed, as discussed in Chapter 3, new FBI laws now permit the FBI to engage in racial profiling in order to hunt for terrorists!

This brief characterization of America today is not a ruse. It is not an exaggeration. Nor is it another slippery-slope argument that lacks empirical evidence. It is a reality.

Will the Obama administration help move us away from a culture of control and more in proximity to one of autonomy? There are insidious roots of state control that have not yet been called into question by this administration, and much will depend on whether its actions will comport with its rhetoric of "change." A main purpose of this book is to help create the momentum for such real change.

Total Information Awareness

In 1597, Sir Francis Bacon said, "knowledge is power." The American government has adopted this insight as the basis for research and development of a technologically driven system of "Total Information Awareness" (TIA). In the aftermath of the September 11, 2001, attacks on the World Trade Center and the Pentagon, in the name of "national security," it began research and development of a vast database containing the personal information of every American citizen. This technology also included high-powered search engines using secret matching criteria to parse through this personal information. Deploying this technology, beginning as early as 2004, the Bush administration had been secretly monitoring the e-mail messages, Internet searches, and phone conversations of millions of Americans without their knowledge, the approval of Congress, or a warrant issued by a judge.

In assessing the constitutionality of this program, it is instructive to look carefully at what the Fourth Amendment of the United States Constitution states:

> The right of the people to be secure in their persons, houses, papers, and effects, against unreasonable searches and seizures, shall not be violated, and no Warrants shall issue, but upon probable cause, supported by Oath or affirmation, and particularly describing the place to be searched, and the persons or things to be seized.

No warrants were issued! No probable cause was given! No details about the place to be searched or the persons or things to be seized, were presented to a court in application for a search warrant! Every American was instead treated as a terrorism suspect.

In 2008, Congress passed the Foreign Intelligence Surveillance Amendments Act to amend the 1978 FISA (Foreign Intelligence Surveillance Act), which had required a search warrant for any electronic communication passing through a U.S. switch. Effectively, this new legislation gutted the 1978 Act and gave the green light to continue warrantless surveillance of millions of Americans. And soon-to-be President Barack Obama (then an Illinois Senator) voted for it.

A Plea for Constructive Change

This book will carefully examine the dangerous currents toward a controlled Orwellian culture now in the air. The TIA Project cannot be severed from the political, legal, social, economic, technological, and ideological climate that now supports it. These factors include:

- The passage of laws permitting egregious violations of human rights;
- federal courts—from FISA to the Supreme Court—falling asleep at the wheel;
- a "war on terror" used to promote the politics of fear and to justify increasingly greater abridgments of privacy;
- psychological manipulation aiming at mass, blind conformity, lock-step politics, and jingoism;
- corporate media consolidation, telecom mergers, and media-government quid pro quo;
- the consequent clogging and censoring of the arteries of mass communication;
- widespread and systematic injection of government propaganda into the mainstream media news hole;

- private data warehousing and mining companies working cooperatively with the U.S. Department of Defense to amass personal data on all of us;
- the military-industrial revolving door incestuously sustaining TIA technological development;
- corporate lobbies in Congress and the Federal Communications Commission seeking to undermine net neutrality;
- government monitoring of the internet;
- Defense Department sponsorship and use of social media to support its clandestine agenda;
- research and development of chilling late generation, privacy-eviscerating surveillance technologies;
- deployment of real time surveillance subsystems including video surveillance cameras in private zones;
- Secret Services death squads operating underneath the radar of Congress;
- a nationalistic, neoconservative ideology hell-bent on establishing and maintaining U.S. geopolitical supremacy;
- corporate globalization, breakdown of trade barriers, and the blurring of lines between political and corporate power, leaving a trail of exploitation of the world's labor force, destruction of the environment, and centralized means of world power and control in the hands of the superrich.

These are some of the factors that are indissolubly fused to the steady creep of a culture of control at the center of which is the TIA project. Accordingly, this book looks at all of these factors, among others, with an eye toward constructive change. It is, thus, a plea for activism regarding the climate of control that has been spreading like a cancer in this nation and throughout the world, especially in the past decade.

We cannot expect this degenerative process to remit if we sit by idly and permit it to fester and grow. Hence, this book appeals to Americans and the greater world community to form coalitions of groups for the survival of the free world. Again, this is not an illusion. The dangerous trends flagged in this book are supported by empirical evidence. But if some insist that the alarm sounded here is an overreaction, then the response must be that it is better to be safe than sorry, given the incredible importance of the stakes.

1

Post-9/11 America's Culture of Control

The September 11, 2001, attacks on American soil were a decisive marker in the shift toward a culture of control in America. This does not mean that many of the seeds of this shift were not already planted. They were. The lesson of the Nixon administration had begun to fade, along with the Watergate break-in and the unlawful, warrantless wiretapping of private citizens. The 1996 Telecommunications Act, signed by William Jefferson Clinton, raised media-ownership caps of the already gigantic media corporations, thereby allowing further consolidation and, hence, less-independent sources of news and information for public consumption. The collapse of the Soviet Union in 1991 provided the occasion for right-wing, militant extremists from the George H. W. Bush administration to launch an aggressive campaign aiming at change in the balance of power toward American geopolitical dominance.[1]

Restriction of Civil Liberties: The PATRIOT Act

In this context, the 9/11 attacks provided a pretext for restricting civil rights, especially privacy and the right to be kept informed. In particular, the U.S. PATRIOT Act was approved by Congress without careful examination or discussion and was signed into law by George W. Bush on October 26, 2001.

Section 213 of the PATRIOT Act, the so-called "sneak and peek" provision, allowed law enforcement officers to search the homes or businesses of private citizens without their knowledge or permission.

Section 218 of the Act eliminated an important protection established in 1978 under the Foreign Intelligence Surveillance Act (FISA) against warrantless surveillance of American citizens and violation of their Fourth Amendment rights. In particular, Provision 104(7)(B) of 1978's FISA required that *the purpose* of conducting a warrantless electronic surveillance was to obtain foreign intelligence information.[2] The PATRIOT Act changed the language of this provision to say that *a significant purpose* of such surveillance was to obtain foreign intelligence.[3] This provided a loophole for law enforcement to gather evidence for criminal investigations without having or showing probable cause pursuant to the Fourth Amendment.[4]

Section 215 of the PATRIOT Act gave the Federal Bureau of Investigation (FBI) the power to access the "tangible things" of private citizens including their "books, records, papers, documents, and other items" through the issuance of National Security Letters (NSL). These letters did not require a court order. All the FBI had to claim was the surveillance was being conducted "to protect against international terrorism or clandestine intelligence activities." No evidence needed to be produced to show that the subjects in question were "agents of a foreign power" as previously required. Further, those forced to turn over the information were placed under a gag order preventing them from disclosing the search to anyone else. As a result, the subjects of the search could have their personal records examined by government without being able to find out about it and therefore obtain redress against illegal searches.[5] Unfortunately, Section 15, as well as other questionable provisions of the PATRIOT Act, has been reauthorized under the Obama administration.[6]

God as a Political Weapon of Mass Conformity

Under the George W. Bush administration, fundamentalist Christian values were mixed with politics in an effort to transform America into a theocratic state in contravention of the First Amendment right to freedom of religion. It is this theocratic line that now attempts to teach "intelligent design" as science, and to add an amendment to the U.S. Constitution proclaiming marriage to be exclusively between a man and a woman.

Under the George W. Bush administration, reverence for life equated to an absolutistic and inflexible "culture of life." Personhood was redefined to include unimplanted human embryos that would never act, think, or feel. The result was to thwart and delay the progress of stem cell research in America and therewith the promise of saving millions of actual human lives. To his credit, President Obama has recently overturned Bush's ban on stem cell research, but the "culture of life" that his administration helped to fortify (including its adherents in Congress) is still active in attempting to exercise political control over the direction of such research.

The Terry Schiavo case is a good example of how such a "culture of life" is part of a culture of control. Terry Schiavo was a patient on a feeding tube in a persistent vegetative state. Using her misfortune to advance its political agenda, the Bush administration attempted to short-circuit decades of settled Florida law by passing federal legislation interfering with the removal of her feeding tube. After fourteen unsuccessful appeals, when Schiavo's feeding tube was finally removed, Florida Governor Jeb Bush, the President's brother, sent state police to Schiavo's hospice to seize her and have her feeding tube reinserted. Confronting local police who were ordered by a judge to guard her, the state police finally backed off.[7] Subsequently, when an autopsy was performed, it was learned that Schiavo's upper brain had liquefied.

Religious fanaticism of this kind threatens democracy not because of the views it entertains but because it seeks to silence public debate and unbiased exploration of controversial moral issues, and attempts to control others by imposing its views on them. During the Bush administration, ethicists who worked at publicly funded institutions, such as the National Institutes of Health (NIH) were "free" to do research on the cutting edge—to explore issues like cloning and stem cell research as long as the conclusions they drew squared with those held by the White House. Federal agencies, such as the Environmental Protection Agency (EPA), were overseen by "gatekeepers" who reported directly to the president. In this contrived context, scientists were muzzled. As such, Americans could not expect federal agencies to tell them the truth about such genuine concerns as global warming.

Fear and Hate Mongering

The rallying cry of the Bush administration was that of giving up civil liberties for the sake of peace and security. American support for the war in Iraq was largely a product of such fearmongering rather than the higher reflective powers of a democratic nation. Thus, Saddam Hussein was a pretext used by the Bush administration to stir up support among Americans for the invasion of Iraq. And when the Bush administration fabricated a link between Hussein and the 9/11 attacks, most Americans came on board; and most were also willing to consent to having their electronic communications warrantlessly wiretapped for the sake of averting the next terrorist attack.

Manipulation of Mainstream Media and Telecoms

But it is not just the average American who is subject to being manipulated; the mainstream media is, and has been so subject. Giant media corporations have come largely under government influence or control. To a considerable extent, this is due to consolidation. A relatively few number of companies now control all of cable and network TV (News Corp, General Electric,

Viacom, Disney, and Time Warner being the prominent conglomerates). These companies also have joint ventures with the telecom companies such as AT&T and Comcast. All of these companies are beholden to the government for media ownership caps, mergers, tax breaks, military contracts, and other means of expanding their bottom lines. They also have lobbies in Congress and the Federal Communications Commission (FCC) and are, therefore, disinclined to report news that strains their relationship with the government. A classic example of this is the lead-up to the Iraq war. Even the *New York Times* was relegated to quoting government spokespersons in making the case for the Bush administration to go to war in Iraq.

An instructive example of what can happen to a company that refuses to cooperate with government is that of Qwest Communications, which refused to assist the Bush administration in its warrantless surveillance program.[8] According to the former CEO of Qwest, Joseph P. Nacchio, the Bush administration had withdrawn lucrative government contracts due to Qwest's refusal to comply with the directive to cooperate in its program. Qwest had entered into two classified government contracts and in 2000 and 2001, Nacchio participated in discussions with high-ranking government officials about the awarding of other similar contracts; but Qwest's refusal to participate in the program of warrantless surveillance, claimed Nacchio, led the Bush administration to cancel these contracts.

The Net Neutrality Crisis

If the abuses of power perpetrated by the Bush administration teach us anything, it is that we cannot afford to place our blind trust in any government administration. But this means that we need a vigilant media to keep us informed. Unfortunately, the mainstream corporate media has been asleep at the wheel; and given its insatiable drive for profit maximization, and its reliance on the government to feed this appetite, there is presently no good reason to think that it will perform better in the future.

So we might conclude that the free and open architecture of the Internet provides the answer to our need to be kept informed. Unfortunately, as will be discussed in Chapter 7, the Internet is also in clear and present danger of becoming another branch of the corporate, mainstream media. Currently, there are powerful telecommunication companies such as Comcast seeking to turn the free and open architecture of the net into a "pay for play" system according to which only companies that have deep pockets would be able to afford an Internet presence. Consequently, these companies, which include the major cable and broadcast media corporations, would have the ability to control, censor, and otherwise manipulate the flow of information through the Internet pipes. This would mean the end of net neutrality and a brave new world of Internet control.

The Supreme Corp Decision

On January 21, 2010, in a vote of four to five, the Supreme Court handed down a decision in *Citizens United v. Federal Election Commission*[9] that gave corporations the right to finance the advertising campaigns of the political candidates of their choice. This decision portends serious consequences for the survival of mainstream media and Internet as democratic forums.

Powerful corporations already influence political outcomes. In the aftermath of the Court's decision, telecom and cable lobbies in Congress, to usurp net neutrality, will predictably be brought directly into the arena of the boardrooms of corporations like Comcast and AT&T, which will decide how much financial backing to give to a candidate in a congressional election (or even in a presidential election) based on the candidate's willingness to support legislation sanctioning a pay-for-play Internet. Similarly, giant media companies like News Corp and Time Warner will pay for the candidates who are willing to support tax breaks, corporate-friendly antitrust laws, and other legal changes calculated to massage the corporate bottom line. Similarly, private military contractors, such as Lockheed Martin and Boeing, will support candidates willing to escalate and fight wars, thereby offering lucrative defense contracts. In all these cases, it will simply be a matter of corporate cost-benefit analysis likely to determine who will ultimately be elected to office.

Clearly, contributions to campaigns made by individuals, unions, and political action committees will invariably wane in comparison to those amounting to billions of dollars that giant corporations will pump into the campaigns of politicians who are willing to support their business interests. The outcome is predictable. Politicians who have been bought by these corporations will win elections. The government will be by the corporations and for the corporations. There will be "free-market" capitalism but no democracy.

Curiously, the Court's decision was based on the ideology that every person has a right to free speech and that, therefore, so do corporations. According to this perspective, the Court's decision should thus be lauded as a move toward a culture of autonomy and away from one of control. However, nothing can be further from the reality.

It is settled law that people should not be free to sell themselves into slavery. Such granting of freedom would be contrary to respecting freedom in the first place; for people should not be free to sell their freedom.

Freedom for the sake of relinquishing freedom is self-defeating and not really freedom at all. The situation is similar in the case of granting corporations a right to freedom of political speech. The granting of such a right destroys political free speech, because it creates an unfair advantage for the corporations who wield unparalleled money and power. Instead of enhancing the autonomy and freedom of citizens of a state, it forecloses it, and makes elections into a farce.

Further, corporations are not *natural* persons. Legal personhood is a legal fiction. Real people, not fictitious ones, have a right to free political speech. While it is true that corporations are composed of real persons, this does not make corporations real persons. What's true of the part is not necessarily true of the whole. From the fact that the individuals who work for a corporation have a right to political free speech, it does not follow that the corporation itself has a right to political free speech. The Court's reasoning was flawed and the decision sets a dangerous precedent for the future survival of democracy in America. Dissenting, Justice John Paul Stevens stated,

> In the context of election to public office, the distinction between corporate and human speakers is significant. Although they make enormous contributions to our society, corporations are not actually members of it. They cannot vote or run for office. Because they may be managed and controlled by nonresidents, their interests may conflict in fundamental respects with the interests of eligible voters. The financial resources, legal structure, and instrumental orientation of corporations raise legitimate concerns about their role in the electoral process. Our lawmakers have a compelling constitutional basis, if not also a democratic duty, to take measures designed to guard against the potentially deleterious effects of corporate spending in local and national races.[10]

Changing the Rhetoric but not the Policy

At the time of this writing, it remains to be seen how the Obama administration will confront such expanded corporate power to influence political outcomes. So far, the Obama administration *appears to be* less inclined than the Bush administration to cave to corporate pressures, such as that of the telecoms to end net neutrality; and it has explicitly denounced the Citizens United ruling as "a major victory for big oil, Wall Street banks, health insurance companies and the other powerful interests that marshal their power every day in Washington to drown out the voices of everyday Americans."[11] Indeed, this administration has meticulously fashioned its rhetoric around a culture of autonomy, especially talk about "the rule of law."[12] Thus, in his May 21, 2009, speech President Obama proclaimed,

We are indeed at war with al Qaeda and its affiliates. We do need to update our institutions to deal with this threat. But we must do so with an abiding confidence in the rule of law and due process; in checks and balances and accountability. For reasons that I will explain, the decisions that were made over the last eight years established an ad hoc legal approach for fighting terrorism that was neither effective nor sustainable—a framework that failed to rely on our legal traditions and time-tested institutions, and that failed to use our values as a compass.[13]

Indeed, a culture that upholds "the rule of law," "due process," "checks and balances," and "accountability" is a good candidate for a culture of autonomy. This is just what we hope America will aspire to be. Unfortunately, even very oppressive cultures have touted the importance of these ideals but, in practice, defined them to suit their oppressive agendas. What matters are the actual practices, laws, and policies that are instituted in the name of freedom and democracy.

Here is an example of how the Obama administration has created the false appearance of real change toward a culture of autonomy. On March 13, 2009, in a federal district court filing, the Obama Justice Department eliminated the category of "unlawful enemy combatant," which the Bush administration had built into the 2006 Military Commissions Act for purposes of detaining suspected terrorists without due process. Two months later, in his May 21 speech cited above, Obama announced a replacement system that changed the language but not the concept.

According to the old definition of "unlawful enemy combatant" included in the 2006 Military Commissions Act, an unlawful enemy combatant was "a person who has engaged in hostilities or who has purposefully and materially supported hostilities against the United States or its co-belligerents who is not a lawful enemy combatant . . . "[14] In other words, if the government suspected that an individual posed a threat to national security, this individual could be detained as an "unlawful enemy combatant."

Now, instead of branding suspects as "unlawful enemy combatants," Obama proposed their "prolonged detention" by which "al Qaeda terrorists and their affiliates . . . that we capture—like other prisoners of war" could be "prevented from attacking us again." That is, "prisoners of war" who allegedly could not be prosecuted for their past crimes but who allegedly posed a future threat to national security could be detained for a "prolonged" period of time.

Since such "prisoners of war" were suspected terrorists, and since the "war on terrorism" has no definable end, what "prolonged" here could possibly mean boggles the imagination. Would they ever be released or would they die in prison for crimes they have not yet committed? Moreover, if they really could not be prosecuted, they could also not be accorded the right of habeas corpus unless this meant being charged with the potential to commit a future hostile act against America. All this, and Obama still contended that his administration had begun to reshape detention policies "to ensure they are in line with the rule of law."

But just how Obama could have squared preventively detaining individuals for crimes they haven't yet committed with the rule of law is beyond comprehension. For law is inherently retrospective. It looks back for purposes of holding people criminally or civilly liable for their past actions. It does not look forward to future acts not yet committed. Obama's new "legal" category set a dangerous precedent for incarcerating someone for crimes they hadn't yet committed. This raised the Orwellian specter of the "Thought Police" who come in the dead of night to take away dissidents.

As will be discussed in Chapter 3, President Obama, even as a Senator, had supported legislation that permitted Bush's program of warrantless spying on the personal electronic communications of American citizens. So, while the government did not yet have the capacity to read minds, it now had an incredible power to intrude into private communications. Viewed in this light, it is not such a stretch to imagine being preventatively imprisoned for saying something over a wire that the government thought was "hostile against the United States."

Unfortunately, in the decade following the 9/11 attacks, America had been placed on a path toward increasing levels of government control. Entering into an environment that had been substantially divested of the legal safeguards undergirding due process, checks and balances, the rule of law, accountability, and working in tandem with a Congress that had been largely complicit with this degeneration of democracy, the Obama administration has the formidable duty to restore what has been so severely compromised.

In an effort to placate those who were complicit, a very real danger is that Obama may facilitate the dangerous precedents set by his predecessor. Thus, while the rhetoric has now been softened, the potential for the same climate of control still exists in the American culture. And it will take more than change in rhetoric to rebuild what was torn down. In fact, the change in rhetoric may merely help to conceal a ripening cultural of control.

Indeed, if the Obama administration's rhetoric forms the basis of our trust, then we may be less inclined to hold its feet to the fire when it violates international law by launching deadly military strikes inside sovereign nations,[15] refuses to prosecute the architects of an illegal program of torture,[16] forecloses the rights of citizens to sue the government for unlawfully spying on them,[17] or perpetrates other violations of law, especially when they are undertaken in the name of "peace," "national security," and "freedom."

Militarism and Mind Control

Unquestionably, the period that ensued after the 9/11 attacks has been one of movement toward a militaristic state. Driven by an ideology that seeks power and control through military strength, we have been embroiled in two simultaneous wars under the banner of a geographically and temporally boundless "war on terror." The culture of America has changed dramatically as a result. This has been a period of "enhanced interrogation," "extraordinary rendition," and the cancellation of habeas corpus. As such, the trend toward militarism has left its taint on our image and self-image, as a people, and as a nation of laws and morals.

This militaristic trend has important roots in the neoconservative organization that emerged in 1997 known as the Project for the New American Century (PNAC). This project's members included many of the soon-to-be members of the Bush administration, including Richard Cheney, I. Lewis "Scooter" Libby, Donald Rumsfeld, Paul Wolfowitz, Richard Pearle, John Bolton, and William Kristol. Its primary goal was to help "to preserve American preeminence through the coming transformation of war made possible by new technologies." That such technologies included *mind control* is past doubt. Thus, PNAC speculates about the new military:

> Future soldiers may operate in encapsulated, climate-controlled, powered fighting suits, laced with sensors, and boasting chameleonlike "active" camouflage. "Skin-patch" pharmaceuticals help regulate fears, focus concentration and enhance endurance and strength. A display mounted on a soldier's helmet permits a comprehensive view of the battlefield—in effect to look around corners and over hills—and allows the soldier to access the entire combat information and intelligence system while filtering incoming data to prevent overload.[18]

PNAC's above depiction of military transformation is a lamentable prelude to a burgeoning culture of control: the human person as a self-determining agent who possesses free will is transformed into a (literal) killing machine.

But PNAC was not just speculating. Six days after the 9/11 attacks, on September 17, 2001, the Defense Advance Research Project Agency (DARPA), under the Bush administration's Department of Defense, issued the following memo:

> The Defense Sciences Office is interested in new proposals in BRAIN MACHINE INTERFACES. This new program represents a major thrust area for DSO that will comprise a multidisciplinary, multipronged approach with far reaching impact. Brain Machine Interfaces: The brain takes inputs and generates output through the electrical activity of neurons. DARPA is

interested in creating new technologies for augmenting human performance through the ability to non-invasively access these codes in the brain in real time and integrate them into peripheral device or system operations.[19]

While there can be invaluable uses of such technologies, for example, in restoring movement to paralyzed limbs resulting from trauma or disease, it is clear that the Department of Defense was not interested in medical applications. Instead, its goal was to peripherally, remotely control the thoughts, emotions, and actions of soldiers on the battlefield, thereby giving them a decisive advantage over their opponents.

Thus, according to the DARPA Brain Interface Program Manager, Alan Rudolph, the focus would include:

> Demonstrations of plasticity from the neural system and from an integrated working device or system that result in real time control under relevant conditions of force perturbation and cluttered sensory environments from which tasks must be performed (e.g., recognizing and picking up a target and manipulating it)[20]

In other words, soldiers would not experience the usual fears and sensory confusions that occur in the high-stress arena of the battlefield. Instead, as a result of brain machine interfaces, they would be capable of engaging in warfare with the same temperament as, say, taking an afternoon stroll.

While such technology is still in its infancy, work for the DARPA program has been undertaken at such places as MIT, and it has resulted in the ability to remotely control the movement of a monkey's arm as well as to glean enough information from its brain to predict in advance its next action.[21] The Orwellian idea of the "Thought Police" is, thus, not so far in the offing, especially if we continue on the path of militarism and mind control.

Along similar lines, in 2002, DARPA announced that it was "tinkering with a soldier's brain using magnetic resonance" to create a sense of being well-rested even after being deprived of sleep for as much as seven consecutive days and nights. According to DARPA officials, "Eliminating the need for sleep during an operation . . . will create a fundamental change in war fighting and force employment."[22]

The idea of using mind control for military purposes is not new to American history. For example, the MK-ULTRA Project conducted by the Central Intelligence Agency (CIA) in the 1950s and 1960s consisted of experiments on unwitting and unconsenting subjects with mind-controlling drugs for purposes of producing a "Manchurian candidate." But with the advance of digital technologies, what was then science fiction has now become a real, and chilling, possibility.

The Total Information Awareness Project

At the center of America's trend toward a controlled society is a project begun in the early years of the Bush administration originally called, "Total Information Awareness" (TIA). The TIA project represents another formidable move by DARPA toward a culture of control. As will be discussed in the next chapter, this project involves construction of a vast database of personal information (from movie rentals and credit card purchases to phone and e-mail conversations) and a network of integrated technologies for trolling through it. The Orwellian nightmare has now become the American reality.

2

The Total Information Awareness Project

The control of information is the cornerstone of a controlled society. For any government bent on controlling its subjects, this control is double-edged. First, the government must know everything it can possibly know. Second, everyone other than the government must not know what the government knows. As Niccolo Machiavelli expressed, "Thus it happens in matters of state; for knowing afar off (which it is only given a prudent man to do) the evils that are brewing, they are easily cured. But when, for want of such knowledge, they are allowed to grow so that everyone can recognize them, there is no longer any remedy to be found."[1]

The Orwellian/Machiavellian formula for control is, therefore, to know all and keep everyone else, especially one's enemies, in a state of ignorance or (better yet, for the purposes at hand) a state of misinformation. This was exactly the approach taken by the Bush administration in the aftermath of the 9/11 attacks, and the double-edged edifice of control it established is still alive and flourishing.

The Office of Strategic Influence

In Orwell's *1984*, the "Ministry of Truth" (otherwise known as "Minitruth") determined what was to count as news and information for the citizens of Oceana. After the 9/11 attacks, on October 30, 2001, the Defense Advanced Research Projects Agency (DARPA), a branch of the Department of Defense, established the "Office of Strategic Influence" (OSI) (otherwise known as the "Office of Disinformation") for similar purposes. When its existence became public in late February 2002, it was poorly received and was reported to have been closed down, but, as confirmed on November 18, 2002, in a media interview with then Secretary of Defense, Donald

Rumsfeld, the office continued to operate under a different name. Said Rumsfeld, "And then there was the office of strategic influence. . . . I went down that next day and said fine, if you want to savage this thing fine I'll give you the corpse. There's the name. You can have the name, but I'm gonna keep doing every single thing that needs to be done and I have."[2]

Headed by Air Force Brigadier General Simon P. Worden, the official purpose of the OSI was to disseminate false information to America's foreign "enemies," especially Islamic nations, by spreading disinformation through their media networks, the Internet, and covert operations. For such purposes, the Pentagon hired the Rendon Group, an international communications firm, and paid it US$100,000 per month. In fact, while the United States was allegedly fighting a war in Iraq for purposes of liberating Iraqis and spreading freedom and democracy, the Rendon Group, under the direction of John W. Rendon, Jr., was also busy attempting to control the Iraqi media by feeding it pro-American propaganda.

However, these surreptitious attempts to control information did not stop at infiltrating foreign media. At this time, the Bush administration was also aggressively disseminating prowar and pro-Bush propaganda into the American mainstream media. In fact, the Bush administration paid millions of tax-payers' dollars to produce and disseminate phony news favorable to its policies and image. Such government propaganda was produced and reported by public relations specialists, not by journalists, and it was passed off by the corporate mainstream media as real news. The famous footage of the statue of Saddam Hussein in Baghdad being toppled at the beginning of the Iraq war (a scene that was repeatedly aired on all major cable and broadcast news networks) is a prime example of a staged event.

Sadly, the willingness of the corporate media to self-censor as well as disseminate government propaganda for a price shows the serious danger in trusting these behemoth organizations to keep us informed. Much like the news organ of Orwell's Oceana, the mainstream media cannot serve to expose government lies and deception when it is, itself, the disseminator of this misinformation.

The Information Awareness Office and the Total Information Awareness Project

But, the spread of disinformation was only one side of the government's equation for realizing and maintaining a culture of control. In January 2002, DARPA established the "Information Awareness Office" (IAO) to direct the "Total Information Awareness" (TIA) project. The IAO's mission was to "imagine, develop, apply, integrate, demonstrate and transition information technologies, components and prototype, closed-loop, information systems that will counter asymmetric threats by achieving *total information awareness*." In other words, it sought to create a giant network of integrated computer technologies for intercepting, storing, searching, monitoring, reading, and analyzing all private, computerized records of 300 million Americans (not to mention the electronic traffic generated by millions of foreign users).

The project was largely the brainchild of John Poindexter, a former Reagan National Security advisor who, in 1990, had been convicted of multiple felonies in the Iran-Contra scandal, which were later reversed. Poindexter, along with a Hicks & Associates[3] executive, Brian Sharkey, proposed the idea of the TIA project to the Department of Defense soon after the 9/11 attacks, and was named the director of the IAO.

Here was a case of reality imitating fiction. Just as, in Orwell's *1984*, the omnipresent face of Big Brother with a caption that read, BIG BROTHER IS WATCHING YOU, the logo of the IAO showed an all-seeing eye with the Latin caption, "scientia est potentia," meaning "knowledge is power."

The IAO and its TIA project first came to public light largely as a result of an article printed in the *New York Times* in February 2002.[4] The article stated, "One component of the new computer information systems that is being emphasized by Mr. Poindexter's new office are 'data mining' techniques intended to scan through vast collections of computer data, which may include text, images, sound and other computer data, and find significant patterns." However, the *Times* article did not include details about the nature of the project. On November 21, 2002, the American Civil Liberties Union launched a campaign against TIA. It stated,

> Recent news reports have revealed the development of a new federal program dubbed "Total Information Awareness." The program will create a computer system that will search through a vast centralized database that contains information about your purchases, your medical history, your school records, and more. Help stop this domestic spying program.[5]

Clearly, the details of the project omitted by the *Times* in its article (namely, the kind of information to be searched) presented a chilling picture of the breadth of the TIA project. It was truly intended to be a *total* information awareness project—more exactly, total *government* awareness.

Amid the public outcry from civil libertarians, the TIA project was supposed to have been defunded by Congress in 2003, but instead its core technologies were transferred from the Department of Defense to Advanced Research and Development Activity (ARDA), a branch of the National Security Agency (NSA). Subsequently, ARDA itself was transferred from the NSA to the Disruptive Technology Office, which is directed by the Director of National Intelligence. As will be discussed in Chapter 3, this is significant because under new legal provisions established at the end of the Bush administration, all intelligence operations (including those of the FBI and CIA) have been centralized under the Director of National Intelligence, thus giving to a single individual both the eyes and ears of "Total Information Awareness" as well as the legal authority to use them to warrantlessly spy on Americans.

The TIA Technologies

The TIA technologies consisted of an integrated system of technologies that would engage the following levels of operation:

Detect → Classify → ID → Track → Understand → Preempt

Key components of the original technologies in this integrated system included the following:[6]

Genysis: technology that builds ultralarge, all-source information repositories, that is, permits the storing and organizing of vast amounts of data.

Evidence Extraction and Link Discovery: technologies for automated discovery, extraction, and linking of sparse evidence contained in large amounts of classified and unclassified data sources. These technologies extract data from multiple sources (such as text messages and Web pages); detect instances of patterns consisting of financial transactions, communications, travel, medical, housing, education, transportation, etc.; and have the capacity to learn patterns consisting of persons, organizations, etc.

Scalable Social Network Analysis: technologies for finding patterns that exemplify key characteristics of terrorist groups and for distinguishing these populations from other types of societal groups. In order to distinguish possible terrorists from innocent civilians, this requires that information also be gathered on the social interactions of the masses of innocent people. This means that the latter group must be placed under surveillance and subjected to analysis along with the former group.[7]

Human ID at a distance: automated biometric identification technologies to detect, recognize, and identify humans at great distances, which provide "critical early warning support for force protection and homeland defense against terrorist, criminal, and other human-based threats." Such biometric ID technologies require a searchable database. In fact, in February 2008, at a cost of one billion dollars per year, the FBI awarded a ten year contract to Lockheed Martin to develop a giant database of biometric data including fingerprints, iris scans, and DNA, which the FBI refers to as the "Next Generation Identification" (NGI).[8] The goal is to have such personal data from every human being on file.

Effective Affordable Reusable Speech-To-Text: speech-to-text (automatic transcription) technology, which will focus on "natural, unconstrained human-human speech from broadcasts and telephone conversations in multiple languages." Such technology is necessary to construct a massive dragnet surveillance of telephone and Voice/IP communications by translating audio signals into text and then utilizing natural language filters to capture predefined words and phrases.

Genoa II: cognitive (learning) support technology that allows humans and machines to "think together" in real-time about complicated problems; overcome human biases and limitations; clarify complicated and uncertain situations; and create dynamic, adaptable, peer-to-peer collaborative networks.

Translingual Information Detection, Extraction, and Summarization: "advanced language processing technology to enable English speakers to find and interpret critical information in multiple languages without requiring knowledge of those languages."

Communicator: "dialogue interaction" technology that enables warfighters to talk with computers, such that information will be accessible on the battlefield or in command centers without ever having to touch a keyboard." The obvious next step here is to combine such software with remote-control brain machine interfaces, such as those discussed in chapter 1.

Wargaming the Asymmetric Environment: predictive technology to better anticipate and act against terrorists by identifying predictive indicators of attacks by specific terrorists by examining their behavior in the broader context of their political, cultural, and ideological environment. Such technology would necessarily screen on the basis of personal data such as race and religion.

Future markets applied to prediction: technology to help predict political instability, threats to national security, and other major events in the near future.

The Information Awareness Prototype System

DARPA's Information Awareness Prototype System was the main "brain" of the TIA system for integrating all of the above information extraction, analysis, and dissemination technologies. According to DARPA, to perform its function, this integrated TIA system had to have three core elements: (1) architectures for creating a vast database; (2) new and innovative methods for populating this database; and (3) new means for analyzing and correlating information in the database in order to derive actionable intelligence. In fact, such a functionally integrated TIA system was deployed by the NSA to spy on the telephone and e-mail conversations and Internet activities of millions of Americans.

The National Security Agency's Deployment of the TIA System

The day after President Bush left office, Russell Tice, who was an NSA intelligence officer until 2005, appeared on MSNBC's Countdown with Keith Olbermann and alleged that the NSA surveillance program had routinely parsed through all faxes, phone calls, email exchanges, and Internet searches of every American. "It didn't matter whether you were in Kansas, in the middle of the country, and you never made foreign communications at all," he stated. "They monitored *all* communications." According to Tice, the NSA had kept a file on every American citizen, and each such file contained not only communications data but also credit card information and other financial data (as consistent with the use of evidence extraction and link discovery software). What is more, he said that the NSA had expressly targeted U.S. journalists for purposes of collecting their data.

In 2006, a former AT&T technician, Mark Klein, alleged that the NSA was conducting a massive dragnet of all electronic communications of American citizens starting in 2003. Klein had carefully documented his claims, which included photographs and diagrams describing the surveillance equipment installed at the San Francisco AT&T hub where Klein had worked.[9] Klein maintained that the NSA had built a secret room and housed computer equipment in it that included a "Semantic Traffic Analyzer [a form of evidence extraction and link discovery software] that could sift through large amounts of data looking for preprogrammed targets." This piece of equipment was a Narus ST 6400, produced by Narus,[10] a private technology development company with connections to DARPA and the NSA.[11]

This computer equipment was connected by fiber optic splitters that tapped into the circuits through which messages throughout the nation and the rest of the world flowed. This meant that all messages, both domestic as well as international were being copied and parsed by the NSA according to predefined, secret definitions.

The Risk of False Positives

The IAO had originally budgeted for the development of software that was intended to build into the TIA system privacy and security protections. However, when the project was transferred to the NSA, the development of this technology was halted. However, notwithstanding whether the government has developed or is in the process of developing privacy safeguards, it is clear that the software has the inherent potential for egregious violations of the right to privacy.

This is due to the nature of natural language itself. By its nature, natural language is imprecise, nuanced, and it is not possible to develop syntactical rules or algorithms that flawlessly interpret (semantic) meaning. To overcome this problem, scientists would have to create a machine that had the capacity to think; and there is an ongoing philosophical debate as to whether this is even possible.[12] While computers are quite good at manipulating symbols, the problem lies in the interpretation of these symbols so that they take on meaning. Because the meaning of a string of symbols (words, sentences, paragraphs, and larger expanses of text) is a function of context, which includes intonation, body language, sarcasm, and a host of other aspects of language not easily captured in an algorithm, natural language filters are inherently subject to error.

In any event, given the current state of technology, *all* Americans, regardless of whether or not they think they have "nothing to hide," should be concerned about the possibilities of "false positives." Indeed there have been cases of individuals who were not guilty of any crimes but were nevertheless renditioned and tortured under the Bush administration; and this occurred under the watch of Bush's electronic surveillance program.

Here, the case of telecommunications engineer, Maher Arar is instructive. In 2002, Arar, who lived in Ottawa, was detained by U.S. officials at the John F. Kennedy International Airport in New York on his way back home from a vacation in Tunis. Subsequently, he was "renditioned" to Syria where he was tortured. The U.S. had falsely suspected Arar of being associated with al Qaeda. How did this happen?

The Royal Canadian Mounted Police had been investigating Abdullah Almalki for connections to al Qaeda, which investigation was broadened to include Arar, an acquaintance of Almalki. Somehow, the U.S., which was likely complicit in the investigation, had gotten hold of a rental lease from 1997, on which Almalki had signed as a witness for Arar. In fact, Arar had asked Almalki's brother, Nazih, to witness the lease, but because Nazih was unable to come, he sent Almalki. This was the "smoking gun" the United States used to justify the rendition and torture of Arar.

Evidence extraction and link discovery technology have an uncanny power to pick up circumstantial connections not unlike the one that was used against Arar.[13] In fact, given the incredibly large amount of data such technology can analyze it is inevitable that it will find circumstantial connections that yield false positives. This means that one might have been guilty of no more than having been in the wrong place at the wrong time, or having lost one's cell phone, or having sent an e-mail using a poor choice of words, or having gone on a "subversive" Web site, or of having the same name as a terrorist suspect.

The Inherent Defect of TIA Algorithms

Algorithms used to identify terrorists generally look for anomalous behavior, that is, behavior that does not fit the usual case. This means that anyone who is a nonconformist can be a terrorism suspect. This is an affront to a culture of autonomy in which there is freedom of expression.[14]

Further, reliance on anomalous cases, without patterns of behavior that uniquely characterize terrorists, is fraught with the probability of error. Thus, any terrorist could circumvent such an algorithm by feigning "typical" American patterns of Internet use, phone calling, doctor visits, purchases, travel, reading, and so on.[15] Indeed, this is a core idea behind so-called "sleeper cells," namely to present the appearance of being as "normal" as possible. As Jeff Jonas and Jim Harper suggest, "Treating "anomalous" behavior as suspicious may appear scientific, but, without patterns to look for, the design of a search algorithm based on anomaly is no more likely to turn up terrorists than twisting the end of a kaleidoscope is likely to draw an image of the Mona Lisa."[16]

A telling example of the inefficacy of such search engines is the case of the 2009 Christmas-day terrorism plot. On December 25, Umar Farouk Abdulmutallab, a Nigerian citizen, attempted, albeit unsuccessfully, to blow up Northwest flight 253 when it was getting ready to land in Detroit. He had boarded a plane in Nigeria with only carry-on luggage and a one-way ticket to America. More than one month prior to the incident, Abdulmutallab's father, a prominent Nigerian banker, warned officials at the United States Embassy in Nigeria that his son had gone missing and that he suspected that he was involved with Yemini-based religious extremists. The NSA had also intercepted telephone communications between Anwar al-Awlaki, a radical Yemen Cleric with links to al Qaeda,[17] and Abdulmutallab. It also had intelligence suggesting that al Qaeda in Yemen was planning to use an unidentified Nigerian in an attack during the holiday season. Further, Abdulmutallab had been denied a visa to enter Britain, but he had a valid visa to enter the United States.[18] However, while Abdulmutallab was subsequently added to a list of 550,000 other individuals with alleged terrorist connections, he was not added to a No Fly List[19] Neither the aforementioned information nor any other information in the federal government's vast system of databases managed to set off an alarm. Instead, it was a passenger onboard the plane who noticed and managed to stop Abdulmutallab's attempt to ignite the explosives he had hidden in his underwear.

The Obama administration claimed that failure to flag Abdulmutallab in advance was a result of "systemic and human failure." According to a summary of the preliminary, redacted White House Review of the December 25, 2009, Attempted Terrorist Attack,[20] a significant part of the system failure was a misspelling of Abdulmutallab's name, resulting in failure to correlate the information provided by Abdulmutallab's father with the fact that he had a valid U.S. visa. According to this report, had the said information been so correlated, this would have resulted in the revoking of Abdulmutallab's visa and, hence, his placement on the No Fly List. Lame as this explanation appears (there is relatively inexpensive software that can adjust for spelling errors), system failure cannot be eliminated in any system that must fish through a vast sea of data. As the White House Review itself admitted, "the information that was available to analysts, as is usually the case, was fragmentary and imbedded in a large volume of other data."[21] Add to this fact that there are no clear, unequivocal criteria for constructing algorithms to always distinguish between terrorists and nonterrorists, and it is apparent why such a system will be inherently subject to failure.

Plainly, there is no technological means of eliminating the possibility of a terrorist attack. Those who expect as much are demanding perfection in an imperfect world. A more sober question is whether the degree of protection that might possibly be gained through the use of TIA technologies is worth the abridgement of civil liberties arising out of such use.

Adding Full-body Scanning Technology

The Abdulmutallab event was a catalyst for interest in "tightening up" security on airlines by adding still further technologies that scan passengers' entire bodies. Such full-body scanners have already been deployed at major U.S. airports, and the number and expanded use is planned to increase.[22]

In fact, in the aftermath of the Abdulmutallab event, the Obama administration instituted a policy according to which "every individual flying into the U.S. from anywhere in the world traveling from or through nations that are state sponsors of terrorism or other countries of interest will be required to go through enhanced screening." These nations include Cuba, Iran, Sudan, Syria, Afghanistan, Algeria, Iraq, Lebanon, Libya, Nigeria, Pakistan, Saudi Arabia, Somalia, and Yemen. According to the Transport Security Administration, "enhanced screening" could include full body pat-downs, but it "could also include explosive detection technology or advanced imaging technology where it's available."[23]

This trend toward using full-body scanners moves us further in the direction of violating privacy.[24] The images produced by such body-scanning technologies display the private parts of those who are scanned. When human beings become objects to be routinely (technologically) disrobed and examined by others, one must weigh the price paid in respect for persons against the possibility of discovering an explosive hidden underneath someone's clothing. Further, as this kind of technology becomes more advanced and more prevalent, it is not unlikely that the next move in "fighting the war on terror" will be to make these digital images permanent contributions to the files maintained on each of us in the grand TIA system.

Low Tech, Privacy-respecting Solutions Instead

According to the 1978 FISA (now replaced by the 2008 FISA Amendments Act), a federal agency could have begun immediate surveillance of Abdulmutallab, on an emergency basis, once the information conveyed by his father was received and it became evident that he was high risk to commit a terrorist act. The government would then have had 72 hours to apply for a court warrant. In the interim, this would have provided ample legal machinery to have stopped Abdulmutallab before he boarded a plane with an explosive. And, it would not have involved violation of the privacy of millions of American citizens through deployment of a system of TIA technologies.

The systemic failure that Obama pointed to was, therefore, not the problem. Rather, it was failure to take precautions against risks that could reasonably have been foreseen without the use of such a system of intrusive technologies, including ones that scan human bodies. The real tragedy here is that billions had been spent on the systematic evisceration of constitutional rights.

It is also noteworthy that it took a passenger onboard the flight to stop Abdulmutallab from detonating his bomb. A federal marshal onboard the plane, for security purposes, would have provided increased probability that such attempts at terrorism would be thwarted. The fact that a passenger had to be the one to stop Abdulmutallab speaks volumes about the need for having federal marshals onboard all domestic and international flights. It is bewildering why this low-tech, second line of defense against foiling terrorist plots was not implemented after the 9/11 attacks, for it is not unreasonable to suppose that had federal marshals been onboard the hijacked airliners, the fatal attacks *might* have been stopped.

Abridgement of the Fourth Amendment

Technological problems aside, warrantless, wholesale spying operations were never legal in the first place. Nor should they have been, because they are inconsistent with the Fourth Amendment, which forbids unreasonable searches and seizures without a warrant or probable cause. If *any* search or seizure is "unreasonable" then surely it is a massive dragnet that spies on the most intimate details of a person's life without probable cause and without the person's informed consent.

Bush's warrantless surveillance program was in clear violation of the 1978 FISA, which was in effect at the time the program was implemented. This is because, pursuant to this law, messages passing through U.S. switches could not be tapped without a court warrant. Unfortunately, as will be discussed in Chapter 3, this inherently unconstitutional program was subsequently turned into law, at first in the form of the 2007 Protect America Act, and later in the form of the 2008 FISA Amendments Act. These laws have given an air of legitimacy to what should never have been legal in the first place.

Abridgment of the First Amendment

But it is not *just* the right to privacy afforded by the Fourth Amendment that is being abridged through government deployment of TIA technologies—especially those that monitor electronic communications. The fact that journalists may be spied on by the government when they discuss their stories with their sources over the phone, via e-mail, or through other electronic communications devices portends grave consequences for First Amendment rights. This is because the First Amendment protects not only the exercise of free speech but also the gathering of information. TIA chills off the possibility of newsgathering. What source would reveal his complicity in illegal activities if he knew the government was spying on him and could use this information to prosecute him? And what informant would not be reticent to speak openly about the illegal activities of the government if he knew that the perpetrator of these crimes (a high government official, for example) was listening in? Moreover, insofar as it is journalists or their news agencies that are targets of TIA technologies, this allows government to "read the headlines" before they are even printed. In this case, a story about government activities (including illicit or corrupt ones) could be anticipated, altered, or censored (by government) before it sees the light of day. As will be discussed in Chapter 6, this form of "information warfare" is not merely possible; it is a reality.

Potential for Election Fraud

Consider also the leverage a current government administration (Republican or Democrat) could have over the opposing party during a national election campaign if it had the ability to place the party officers under TIA surveillance. So, if the Bush administration spied on journalists, perhaps it also spied on its democratic opponents, say during the 2004 presidential election. But even if the Bush administration did not reap such an unfair advantage through the use of TIA technologies, this does not mean that a subsequent administration that had access to this technology would not so use it.

Taking this possibility further, once the TIA architecture has been installed, as it has been within the secret confines of telecom companies, it is also possible to add software that reconfigures precinct votes as they are transmitted and passed through an AT&T hub on their way to the main tabulation center. Again, even if the Bush administration did not engage in such an egregious and insidious form of election fraud, the fact is that, given the TIA platform, it is always possible that a subsequent administration will take such liberty. In this case, the TIA project will have put the final nail on the coffin of democracy in America.

Further, if journalists and politicians can be targeted, then why not Middle Easterners, or gays, or Jews, or liberals, or feminists, or some other group that has been vilified and branded as "the enemy"? As will be discussed in the next chapter, the "legal" green light has already been given for such egregious discrimination.

Legal Pretexts for Continuing the TIA Project*

In its last months, the Bush administration made changes to spy laws that have given a veneer of legality to the TIA Project and helped to ensure its survival into subsequent government administrations. These changes have undermined the Fourth Amendment, eviscerated the right to peacefully assemble, and sullied Equal Protection. There were at least three major legal reforms by the Bush administration between the months of July and October 2008 that were largely responsible for these constitutional abridgements:

1. On July 10, 2008, with the approval of Congress (including that of soon-to-be President Obama), President Bush signed into law the FISA Amendments Act of 2008 (H.R. 6304),[1] which downgraded the role of the FIS Courts and gave giant telecom corporations both retroactive and retrospective legal immunity, thereby building a legal shield around Bush's unlawful past program of warrantless, mass surveillance; and, effectively, permitting it to operate, in the future, outside the radar of the judiciary.
2. On July 31, 2008, President Bush placed on the White House Web site an amended version of Executive Order 12333,[2] a directive that was first issued in 1981 by the Reagan administration. The newly amended version established the Director of National Intelligence (DNI) as the "head of the intelligence community." The Order also gave the Attorney General (AG) the power to spy on persons inside the United States as well as U.S. citizens abroad without a warrant.
3. On October 1, 2008, the latest assault on privacy and the rule of law came in the form of revised FBI rules that permit racial profiling as a basis for spying on Americans.[3]

Each of these changes has created a cumulative thrust toward a breakdown of checks and balances against abuses of government power in America. These laws have set the stage for continuing the TIA project begun during the Bush administration and for moving America further down the road of a culture of control. In this chapter, the significance of each will be discussed chronologically.

H.R. 6304

From 2001 to 2007, the Bush administration conducted mass surveillance of the e-mail and telephone calls made by American citizens. All electronic messages passing through switches in the United States, regardless of whether they were international or domestic communications, were systematically intercepted and screened by the National Security Agency (NSA). Technologies, which were installed at major hubs of telecommunication companies throughout the nation, copied and deposited all electronic messages into a giant NSA computer network. The NSA then employed complex algorithms to parse through these messages, using matching criteria such as key words, phone numbers, and dates, and linking these data to further data—anything from credit card and bank records to movie rentals.

H.R. 6304 does not, on the face of it, require that these complex algorithms used to parse through electronic messages be examined and approved by a FIS Court. The role of the FIS Court appears to have been limited by this Act to approving the general design of the software used in conducting intelligence acquisitions. This consists of reviewing the authorizations made by the Attorney General and Director of National Intelligence to see if this general design satisfactorily conforms to "minimization procedures," that is, that it takes reasonable precautions to avoid targeting American citizens. However, without access to the algorithm itself, as well as to the actual source code and a representative sampling of the data that ultimately get caught in its electronic net, there is no way to confirm that the actual procedures pass legal muster and are constitutional.

The Act does require that the certification sent to the FIS Court include the procedures adopted in accordance with subsections (d) (targeting procedures) and (e) (minimization procedures).[4] However, if this requirement is to have teeth, then it would have to be interpreted very strictly to include *demonstrable evidence* that the algorithm satisfies the said standards. Otherwise, the new rule is tantamount to a blank check to invade the privacy of every American citizen.

For example, according to H.R. 6304, an acquisition "may not intentionally target a person reasonably believed to be located outside the United States if the purpose of such acquisition is to target a particular, known person reasonably believed to be in the United States."[5] This proscription against reverse targeting provides a potentially important protection. However, it means very little unless there is a way of proving that the procedures adopted do not reverse target particular Americans. Unfortunately, the Act does not appear to provide any way of verifying this, because it does not require that the government provide particular names, addresses, places, and other details. For instance, the Boolean command "If $x > 0$ and $y > 0$ then Flag Message" takes on meaning only if the variables x and y are given a physical interpretation. Thus, there would be serious breaches of both First and Fourth Amendment rights if these physical interpretations were "x = Name of American Journalist" and "y = Name on Government Enemies List." Without such particular knowledge, the FIS Court is impotent.

What this means is that, if constructive reform of the current FISA laws is to take place during the Obama administration, or subsequent administrations, the FIS Court must require such particular knowledge and it must avail itself of independent expert witnesses who have the mathematical and scientific expertise to adequately assess the software being used by the government to conduct its surveillance activities. It also means that the program needs to be under constant and careful watch by a vigilant judiciary. This would involve periodic audits to make sure that the software being used is actually the software for which a certification has been granted by the FIS Court.

Unfortunately, even with such a safeguard in place, H.R. 6304 is unsatisfactory. This Act also provides *both* retroactive and future civil immunity to all telecommunication companies for assisting government in conducting warrantless spying on Americans. Not only does H.R. 6304 grant immunity from civil action to telecoms that participated in the president's surveillance program during the period beginning on September 11, 2001, and ending on January 17, 2007,[6] it also unconditionally releases these companies from any *future* liability (presumably both civil and criminal). For it unqualifiedly states, "No cause of action shall lie in any court against any electronic communication service provider for providing any information, facilities, or assistance in accordance with a directive issued pursuant to paragraph (1)."[7]

The Act also preempts state investigations into the allegedly illegal activities of these companies in assisting the intelligence community, and from requiring through regulations or other means disclosure of information about such assistance. The courts as well as the states are, therefore, barred from fulfilling their respective roles in protecting the public from encroachment of civil liberties by federal agencies, and by the telecommunication companies working in concert with these agencies.

These provisions of H.R. 6304 were in response to several civil suits filed on behalf of American citizens against AT&T and other telecom companies for violations of their Fourth Amendment rights for allegedly having cooperated with the NSA in systematically intercepting and screening both international and domestic electronic communications of American citizens passing through switches in the United States.

Pursuant to H.R. 6304, inasmuch as American citizens can no longer file suit against the telecom companies for past or future violations of their Fourth Amendment right to privacy, it has to be questioned how much of the Fourth Amendment still remains intact. Thus, there is now, under the Obama administration, urgent need of enacting changes in FISA that reinstate safeguards placing the government under careful judicial watch. Without such oversight of government surveillance activities, American citizens are vulnerable to having their privacy unlawfully abridged. And with retroactive and future immunity given to the telecoms, Americans are left with no available legal recourse to seek redress for these violations—or even to know or find out that they are being so violated.

Unfortunately, while Obama campaigned against the 2008 FISA Amendments Act on the grounds that it gave telecom companies retroactive immunity, he still voted for it. In December 2007, he released a statement saying that he "unequivocally opposes giving retroactive immunity to telecommunications companies. . . . Granting such immunity undermines the constitutional protections Americans trust the Congress to protect. Senator Obama supports a filibuster of this bill, and strongly urges others to do the same."[8] And in February he reaffirmed his position by stating, "There is no reason why telephone companies should be given blanket immunity to cover violations of the rights of the American people."[9]

Yet Obama voted for the law anyway, and he also voted against a fillibuster. He said, at the time, that it was a "close call," but that the legislation made sure that the president "can't make up rationales" for wiretapping without warrants. And he maintained that the legislation met his "basic concerns"[10] despite the fact that one of these basic concerns was clearly that of granting retroactive immunity to the telecom companies, which, he said, "undermines the constitutional protections Americans trust the Congress to protect." The question now is whether Americans can trust the President to protect these constitutional rights when, as a Senator, he voted against them.

Why was the 1978 FISA challenged in the first place? Proponents of FISA reform during the Bush administration argued that such reform was necessary because of changing technology. In 1978, most foreign intelligence was gathered overseas by tapping communications that, themselves, occurred outside the United States. However, today much of the world's electronic communications pass through fiber-optic networks ("switches") located in the United States, even in cases where both parties to the communication are located outside the country. Because the 1978 FISA was understood to require the government to obtain a court warrant whenever the communication was routed through the United States, this meant that such foreign communications also required a warrant. So, proponents of FISA reform argued that existing law needed to be changed in order to permit warrantless surveillance of foreign communications routed through the United States.

Unfortunately, proponents of this argument effectively opened up the floodgates to engage in mass, warrantless surveillance on the pretext of catching such foreign communications routed through the United States. But this argument never justified such a slippery slope, that is, intercepting millions of domestic as well as foreign communications without a warrant. Nor did such a rationale justify screening everyone's communications in order to hunt for patterns of behavior suggestive of terrorists or terrorist plots using link and analysis software. At most, it justified intercepting only a select few foreign communications passing through U.S. switches when these were deemed necessary for purposes of gathering actionable intelligence. In short, even if the 1978 FISA required amending due to technological changes, such a rationale could never have supported mass, warrantless surveillance.

Executive Order 12333

Executive Order 12333, which was created in secrecy and without approval of Congress, brings the entire intelligence community under the DNI (presently Dennis Blair), including the Central Intelligence Agency (CIA), the Federal Bureau of Investigation (FBI), and the National Security Agency (NSA). All heads of these and other agencies of the intelligence community are required under the Order to "Provide the Director access to all information and intelligence relevant to the national security or that otherwise is required for the performance of the Director's duties"[11] The DNI is then in turn, "subject to the authority, direction, and control of the President."[12] Thus, there is now by fiat of this Order a unilateral executive authority and control over the acquisition and use of foreign intelligence. The CIA, which had previously largely set the agenda for the gathering of foreign intelligence is now directly under the direct authority of the DNI.

The NSA, which, as discussed above, had conducted Bush's warrantless, mass surveillance program, beginning in 2001, is now also directly under the authority of the DNI and, ultimately, the President. This means that, in the current climate of eviscerated FIS Court oversight, clandestine operations such as mass surveillance of e-mail and phone conversations of millions of Americans are also directly under the control of the DNI. This is especially problematic because, as explained above, H.R. 6304 does not require the DNI or AG to disclose details (names, places, times, etc.) of those who are being spied on. Since the role of the FIS Courts has now largely been limited to reviewing the authorizations made by the AG and DNI to see if procedures are in place that "minimize" the targeting of American citizens, the combined thrust of H.R. 6304 and Executive Order 12333 has been to place all intelligence activities under the control of the DNI while simultaneously removing primary judicial checks and balances on his or her power and authority, and, therefore, granting unprecedented power and authority to the president, to whom the DNI is directly accountable, under this new Executive Order.

> In addition, according to Order 12333, the AG has the power to approve the use for intelligence purposes, within the United States or against a United States person abroad, of any technique for which a warrant would be required if undertaken for law enforcement purposes, provided that such techniques shall not be undertaken unless the Attorney General has determined in each case that there is probable cause to believe that the technique is directed against a foreign power or an agent of a foreign power.[13]

This would not be so bad if this power to conduct surveillance of American persons was overseen by a FIS Court as it was according to the 1978 FISA. However, according to the newly revised Order, "The authority delegated pursuant to this paragraph, including the authority to approve the use of electronic surveillance as defined in the Foreign Intelligence Surveillance Act of 1978, as amended, shall be exercised in accordance with that Act."[14] Unfortunately, as discussed, H.R. 6304 had already eviscerated the authority of the FIS Courts.

The New FBI Rules

Coming on the heels of the FISA Amendments Act and Executive Order 12333 are the revised FBI guidelines signed into law on October 1, 2008, by Attorney General Mukasey. These rules purportedly allow the FBI to use *racial* criteria in conducting its terrorism investigations. This means that computerized searches could insert racial matching criteria—for example, keywords and names associated with Middle Easterners—into the algorithms used to hunt for terrorists among the electronic profiles of millions of Americans amassed by the federal government. With this new law in place, not only is such *digitized racial profiling* not subject to direct

FIS Court inspection pursuant to H.R. 6304, it is also legal. Chillingly, this seems to be reminiscent of the Nazis who, with the aid of IBM, used early punch card computer technology to keep tabs on Jewish people.

On September 17, 2008, the Senate Judiciary Committee held a hearing on the new rules. However, despite the fact that they had been challenged in the preceding month by several senators, including Dick Durbin (D-IL), Russ Feingold (D-WI), Edward Kennedy (D-MA), and Sheldon Whitehouse (D-RI), Mukasey failed to provide the Committee with a copy of the new rules as requested. "This hearing," said Judiciary Committee Chairmen, Patrick Leahy, "could have been more productive in addressing those concerns if the Department of Justice had agreed with my request and Senator Specter's request to provide copies of the proposed guidelines."[15]

In addition to permitting racial profiling, these new guidelines allegedly permit the FBI to undertake surveillance without probable cause, based on the vague grounds of a perceived "threat." They also allegedly permit the use of intrusive investigative techniques such as undercover interviews, the use of informants, and physical surveillance to investigate individuals planning a public demonstration, an activity that is supposed to be protected by the First Amendment.

The Slippery Slope

Accordingly, the sequence of recent spy laws appears to have caused a slippery slope of ballooning stages in the undermining of privacy and the rule of law in America. H.R. 6304 has set the stage for this decline by short-circuiting judicial oversight by FIS Courts of warrantless, federal surveillance of American citizens, and by blocking and sealing off any realistic legal means, as through civil suits and state investigations, of exposing and remedying such violations of civil liberties. Executive Order 21333 has capitalized off of these breakdowns in checks and balances, creating by fiat, a unilateral executive authority and control over the warrantless surveillance of American citizens at home and abroad. Thus, the President, acting through the AG and DNI, now wields this awesome power virtually unchecked by the courts and by the states.

As a result of these expanding assaults on the rule of law, the die has been cast for one of the most egregious and brazen government abuses of equal protection: *legalized* discrimination on the basis of race. This travesty of justice is now possible because the justice system of checks and balances that is supposed to protect Americans from such an encroachment on their constitutional rights has been eviscerated and no longer has the legal teeth to prevent it. Down the slippery slope, unless there is disruption of this degenerative trend by the Obama administration, or subsequent administrations, there may eventually be little or nothing left to distinguish America from the oppressive societies that it is supposed to be defending against.

*Acknowledgment: This chapter is an expanded version of "What Constitution: How Racial Profiling and Other Unlawful Activities Became Law," The American Trial Lawyer (Winter 2009).

4

The Foreign Intelligence Surveillance Court of Review: Purveyor of "DoubleThink"

In Orwell's Oceana, when the Party said something was true, it did not matter what evidence existed to the contrary. All such evidence was cleansed by changing history or simply by thinking that the contradictory facts were misremembered. The Foreign Intelligence Surveillance Court of Review (FIS court), which has the power to review petitions made by telecommunications companies, now seems to have become afflicted with such "doublethink." This is because this Court has recently set the dangerous precedent of taking the word of government officials, indeed taking it on "faith," that they would not infringe the constitutional right to privacy of millions of Americans. This is the case, although there is a body of contradicting evidence. Instead of considering this evidence (or even dignifying the possibility of such evidence), the Court cleansed away the contradiction simply by ignoring it. The legislative branch of government has not to date considered the dangerous dynamics of having approved legislation that exempts telecommunication companies from the usual criminal and civil liability in order to make them accomplices to mass, warrantless spying on millions of Americans.

The telecom companies' participation in such a program is now "legally" coerced. According to the FISA Amendments Act of 2008, the Attorney General (AG) and Director of National Intelligence (DNI) may direct a telecom company to "immediately provide the Government with all information, facilities, or assistance necessary to accomplish the acquisition [of foreign intelligence]."[1] While a telecom company can appeal the decision to the Foreign Intelligence Surveillance Court of Review, the Court may grant the petition "only if the judge finds that the directive does not meet the requirements of this section, or is otherwise unlawful."[2] However, as will become apparent, a dangerous precedent has already been set by the Court to deny such a petition.

In fact, there is cause for serious concern, if not alarm, that primary as well as appellate FIS courts can no longer be relied on to provide the necessary judicial oversight. First, as was discussed in Chapter 3, the ability of the FIS courts to conduct judicial oversight of government surveillance activities has been largely reduced to approving certifications made by the DNI and the AG that adequate minimization standards are in place; second, the FIS Court of Review has become complacent with walking lockstep with the executive branch; and third, the Fourth Estate has been remiss in its reporting of this breach of public trust.

Compelled to Spy: The Case of Qwest Communications

On August 22, 2008, the three-member FIS Court of Review granted a motion by the Bush administration compelling a telecommunications company (whose name was redacted from the opinion) to participate in the National Security Agency (NSA) warrantless surveillance program.[3] The decision was made public five months later, on January 15, 2009, just five days before Barrack Obama was sworn in as the forty-fourth President, but the story was buried in the *New York Times* on page A13 and never received adequate coverage by mainstream media.[4]

The company in question, Qwest Communications, had refused to comply with the Bush administration's directive on the grounds that the program would have been in violation of the Fourth Amendment rights of its customers. The directive was issued pursuant to an amendment to the 1978 FISA called the Protect America Act (PAA), which became law on August 5, 2007, and sunset February 16, 2008. The Court concluded that the directive, which was issued at the time the PAA was in force, was lawful.

Ironically, just six days after the Court publicized its decision, and one day after Bush left office, former NSA officer Russell Tice claimed that the surveillance program had routinely parsed through all faxes, phone calls, e-mail exchanges, and Internet searches of every American. As was discussed in Chapter 2, according to Tice, the NSA had also expressly targeted U.S. journalists.

But even before Tice came forward, as early as November 2007, a former AT&T technician, Mark Klein, claimed that the NSA was conducting a massive dragnet of all electronic communications of American citizens. As was also discussed in Chapter 2, Klein had carefully documented his claims. This documentation included photographs and diagrams describing the surveillance equipment installed at the San Francisco AT&T hub where Klein had worked.

Nevertheless, the FIS Court of Review did not address the constitutional challenge raised by the possibility of such mass spying on Americans. On August 22, 2008, it concluded that, "the risks of error and abuse are within acceptable limits and effective minimization procedures are in place . . . we hold that the surveillances at issue satisfy the Fourth Amendment's reasonableness requirement."[5] Yet, given the massive dragnet described by Klein, it was unclear how it could have been so unequivocally concluded that the risks of error and abuse were within acceptable limits.

A determination of risk of abuse and error in such a technical context would have had to have been made on the basis of testing of particular natural language parsing software to confirm that the algorithm being used does not target Americans and does not have a significant probability of yielding false positives—that is, singling out Americans in error. Given the veracity of Tice's claim that the NSA was deliberately targeting journalists, such a "minimization standard" was not satisfied.

Accordingly, assessment of whether minimization standards are met cannot be made in these highly specialized circumstances without the expertise of independent evaluators who report their findings to the Court. Insofar as such an oversight requirement was not part of the PAA, it is not reasonable to maintain, as did the FIS Court of Review, that "the risks of error and abuse are within acceptable limits and effective minimization procedures are in place." And, therefore, the Court's conclusion that "the surveillances at issue satisfy the Fourth Amendment's reasonableness requirement" cannot reasonably be held.

Had the PAA been superseded by stricter standards, the Court's decision might have been less significant. However, this was not the case. On July 10, 2008, President Bush signed into law the FISA Amendments Act, which replaced the PAA. Like its predecessor, this replacement Act eviscerated the earlier 1978 FISA by reducing the role of the FIS Courts to one of certifying that the standards put in place by the Attorney General and National Director of Intelligence complied with "minimization standards"—that is, had sufficient safeguards in place so as not to violate the Constitutional rights of American citizens.[6] Unfortunately, the FIS Courts were required by the Act to make this determination on the basis of the certification itself rather than on the basis of details such as names, addresses, and persons of those who were explicitly being targeted. In other words, the system placed the AG and NDI on the honor system rather than subjecting these government officials to a rigorous judicial process.

The Court effectively affirmed this honor system when it asserted,

> The petitioner suggests that, by placing discretion entirely in the hands of the Executive Branch without prior judicial involvement, the procedures

cede to that Branch overly broad power that invites abuse. But this is little more than a lament about the risk that government officials will not operate in good faith.[7]

The fallacy inherent in the Court's above reasoning betrays the very reason for having a system of courts in the first place. The 1978 FISA put in place the FIS Courts, precisely because it was not enough to trust that the Executive Branch would operate in "good faith." These Courts were put in place to give reasonable assurance that the Executive Branch would not abuse its powers in the first place. That is what made it a system of *checks* and balances. It was supposed to check, not simply have "faith." Indeed, if the Founding Fathers trusted that government would act in "good faith," they never would have put in place a judiciary and a legislative branch to constrain the Executive Branch. Nor would they have looked to the press as a "Fourth Estate," which added a fourth and vital layer of checks against government abuse of power.

Thus enter media organizations such as the *New York Times,* which are entrusted with the awesome power of reporting the news in order to guard against abuses of power. When a Court cedes its constitutional charge of checking for abuses of power of government, it is up to the press to let the people know. Unfortunately, this did not happen in the case in point.

The *Times* story opened, "In a rare public ruling, a secret federal appeals court has said telecommunications companies must cooperate with the government to intercept international phone calls and e-mail of American citizens suspected of being spies or terrorists."[8] But what about interception of *domestic* phone calls and e-mail, never mind international ones? And what about mass trolling and data mining of *all* American citizens' electronic communications, never mind just those "suspected of being spies or terrorists"? The *Times* did not even broach the claims of Tice, Klein, or any other whistleblower (there *were* others). Nor did it mention that the redacted name of the telecom company was that of Qwest.

Mention of Qwest in connection with the Court ruling would have added substance to the story; but this would have been the tip of a glacier. According to the former CEO of Qwest, Joseph P. Nacchio, the Bush administration had withdrawn lucrative government contracts due to Qwest's refusal to comply with the directive to cooperate in its warrantless surveillance program. Qwest had entered into two classified government contracts in 2000 and 2001; Nacchio participated in discussions with high-ranking government officials about the awarding of other similar contracts; but Qwest's refusal to participate in the program of warrantless surveillance led the Bush administration to cancel these contracts.

According to Nacchio's account, the Bush administration had approached Quest and other telecom companies to assist in a warrantless surveillance program on February 27, 2001, almost seven months prior to the September 11, 2001 attacks, thus calling into question the Bush administration's persistent attempt to justify the need to institute the program *after* the 9/11 attacks *because* of them. Unfortunately, Nacchio had been (conveniently?) charged with insider trading, which appeared to have created misgivings about the veracity of his account. But given the gravity of such charges of government abuse and corruption, the mainstream media had an obligation as Fourth Estate to conduct a thorough investigation and to bring the facts to light. Unfortunately, this never happened.

In any event, because the prosperity and even survival of giant telecom companies depends upon government, these companies are currently in both a legal and financial stranglehold by the federal government. It is, therefore, predicable that these companies, acting to expand or protect their bottom lines, will, in the future, assist the government in regularly conducting mass spying operations on millions of Americans. Moreover, since controversial provisions have been included in the 2008 FISA Amendments Act, which grant retroactive and future legal immunity to telecoms, American citizens are now barred from filing suits against these companies for assisting the government in spying on them.

In addition, in April 2009, the Obama Justice Department has gone even further than the Bush administration in closing off avenues for citizens to seek redress for violation of their Fourth Amendment rights. This Justice Department filed a motion to dismiss and for summary judgment in the District Court of the Northern District of California against the Electronic Frontier Foundation, a civil rights organization that filed suit against the U.S. government for unlawful spying on American citizens. According to this motion, the United States Government has "sovereign immunity" against lawsuits pursuant to Section 223 of the Patriot Act, which holds that the federal government incurs liability for which it can be sued only if there is "willful disclosure" of the information obtained through surveillance; and this is true, argued the Obama Justice Department, even if the acquisition of the said information was obtained through the intentional commission of an illegal act.[9] Therefore, it appears that there is presently no significant possibility that American citizens will have legal recourse against such mass spying operations.

There are two possibilities that could change the present legal landscape: (1) a Supreme Court ruling that declares the 2008 FISA unconstitutional; and/or (2) an act of Congress that expands the role of the FIS Courts to include greater judicial oversight over the executive branch in conducting surveillances involving American citizens.

The Obama administration has thus far not expressed any intention of moving in this second direction; and the mainstream media has placed no pressure on it to revisit the matter in light of apparent abuses of executive power. When news media such as the *New York Times* fail to do their job of vigilantly investigating and publicizing government corruption, there can be no reasonable expectation that such an awesome power to spy on even the most intimate and private conversations of millions of Americans in the name of "national security" will not continue to be systematically abused in the future.

The 2008 FISA Amendments Act also preempted legal recourse by American citizens to file suit against telecommunication companies for unlawful searches and seizures of their electronic communications (phone and e-mail messages as well as Internet searches). It did this by granting both retrospective and prospective civil and criminal immunity to telecom companies that cooperated with the Bush administration and future administrations in a program of warrantless surveillance.[10]

Further, while, as already mentioned, the Act permitted telecom companies to appeal the directives of government to participate in such a program by appealing to the FIS Court of Appeals, the decision by this Court at the tail end of the Bush administration set a dangerous precedent for applying this option.

The Court held that national security was an overriding reason for requiring the telecom company to participate in the NSA's warrantless surveillance program. However, according to an Oct 13, 2007, *Washington Post* story, former chief executive of Qwest, Joseph P. Nacchio, said that, at a meeting on February 27, 2001, the Bush administration had attempted to enlist telecom companies in an NSA program of warrantless surveillance, which was seven months prior to the September 11, 2001 attacks.[11] This contradicts Bush's claim to have implemented the NSA warrantless surveillance program in response to the 9/11 attacks. Moreover, the FISA Amendments Act signed into law on July 10, 2008, states that the program was authorized by the President "during the period beginning on September 11, 2001."[12]

There is a fundamental difference between having "faith" in the executive branch to do its job and having faith that the judicial branch will do its job of keeping a watchful eye on the executive branch. The Court is correct that there is assumption of risk that government officials might not operate in good faith, even in cases where warrants are issued. However, to argue that faith at the level of the judiciary warrants faith at the level of the executive is to already surrender a system of checks and balances. Because there can be no risk-free system of justice does not warrant surrendering judicial oversight of one branch of government by another.

In fact, a system of checks and balances is not unilateral. A court that oversteps its boundaries is still subject to judicial review by an appellate court. Thus, a system of checks and balances also includes checks and balances for appellants who believe that the court may have failed to operate in good faith. This reciprocity of a system of checks and balances is essential to the operation of such a system of justice. The faith that is appropriately reposed is, therefore, not in any one branch of government to operate in good faith but rather in a system of checks and balances to protect against abuses of state power wherever they may occur.

5

The Military-Industrial Information Network

As was discussed in the previous two chapters, the system of checks and balances that prevents wholesale, warrantless surveillance of electronic communications has been eviscerated. Still, one might suppose that the government needs a court warrant to collect other private and personal information of American citizens. However, such a supposition is false.

Much of the personal data collection that feeds the government's Total Information Awareness (TIA) project is not *directly* obtained by government. Instead, data such as credit card purchase histories, medical records, bank records, airline ticket information, car rentals, and utility bills (among other digitized information) is collected by companies who are not subject to the same legal constraints as the federal government. The government then, in turn, contracts with these companies to tap into their massive databases. In this way, government is able to circumvent privacy protections such as court warrants.

Data Warehousing and Data Mining

The private sector is therefore helping the federal government to actualize two essential, integrated functions of the TIA system: data warehousing and data mining. Data warehousing involves collecting data and organizing it into databases. Data mining involves development and use of tools to analyze such data once it has been collected and organized into databases, and to make predictions based on these analyses. According to a January 2006 report of the Congressional Research Service,

> Data mining involves the use of sophisticated data analysis tools to discover previously unknown, valid patterns and relationships in large data sets. These tools can include statistical models, mathematical algorithms, and machine

learning methods (algorithms that improve their performance automatically through experience, such as neural networks or decision trees). Consequently, data mining consists of more than collecting and managing data, it also includes analysis and prediction.[1]

The processes of data warehousing and data mining have become lucrative businesses for private military contractors. One data warehousing company that played a major role during the Bush administration in aiding implementation of the TIA project was ChoicePoint, Inc.[2] After the September 2001 attacks, it shifted its focus from commercially available products to homeland defense.[3]

ChoicePoint maintained a revolving door with former or soon-to-be Bush administration officials. For example, some of its officers or business associates included Deputy Secretary of State (and PNAC member) Richard Armitage;[4] U.S. Attorney General John Ashcroft;[5] Deputy Director of the National Security Agency, William Crowell Jr.; FBI Executive Assistant Director of Counterterrorism and Counterintelligence, Dale Watson; and Assistant Attorney General (and author of the USA Patriot Act), Viet Dinh.[6] These close ties with the Bush administration made ChoicePoint a de facto data-warehousing arm of the federal government.

This company also maintained a strategic alliance with Department of Defense contractor, Science Applications International Corporation (SAIC).[7] SAIC was the architect of the main brain of TIA, the Information Awareness Prototype System.[8] SAIC also had a commercially available product called the Automated Data Analysis and Mining (ADAM) information management suite, which was designed to retrieve and analyze data pulled from ChoicePoint's data warehouses. Thus, according to SAIC's 2006 Web site,

> ADAM is a service bureau, employing a suite of information management tools developed by SAIC to maximize the utility and value of data pulled from the electronic data-warehouses of ChoicePoint Incorporated. Our customers require rapid results from their queries of ChoicePoint's data stores, and our tools allow the fastest and most reliable return of the data possible. ADAM provides the specific analyses required by our clients to turn data into useful knowledge. In short, ADAM provides clients with the ability to obtain and analyze enormous amounts of data to create explicit profiles of target groups and collect critical data on each of the individual members of that group.[9]

According to the *National Journal*, the Defense Department paid Choice-Point for access to its vast databases, which contained "billions of personal records about nearly every person—citizens and noncitizens alike—in the United States." Moreover, according to this report, federal documents obtained by the *National Journal* and *Government Executive*, ChoicePoint provided the FBI and Department of Defense access to a "previously undisclosed, and vaguely described 'exclusive' data-searching system." According to said documents, in early 2003, the agencies also ordered Internet-based services from ChoicePoint, which "effectively put the power of the company's databases at government agents' fingertips on their desktop computers."[10] The government also purchased access services from ChoicePoint such as AutoTrackXP, which can "provide Internet access to more than 17 billion current and historical records on individuals and businesses, and allow users to browse through those records instantly" and with as little information as a name or Social Security number to cross-reference public and proprietary records.[11] ChoicePoint also developed Consolidated Lead Evaluation and Reporting (CLEAR), a second-generation AutoTrackXP product designed especially for use by government and law enforcement.[12]

ChoicePoint thus provided the federal government data warehousing capabilities to harvest its massive data reservoir. Further, given the alliances between CrossPoint, SAIC, and the Department of Defense, it is likely that the government also utilized SAIC data-mining technologies (perhaps a more sophisticated, customized version of ADAM) to perform actionable analyses.

It is worth emphasizing, however, that ChoicePoint warehouses are only one component of a massive, integrated TIA data reservoir, which also includes: all of the electronic messages and internet searches collected by the National Security Agency (NSA) with the help of the telecom companies; the biometric data contained in the FBI's biometric database;[13] and video data obtained from surveillance cameras situated in major cities.[14] As will be discussed later, the data amassed in this colossal network of databases also spans continents.[15]

In 2008, Reed Elsevier, a major data-warehousing company and competitor of ChoicePoint reached an agreement with ChoicePoint to acquire the company, including its AutoTrackXP and CLEAR technologies and databases, for approximately US$4.1 billion. However, the Federal Trade Commission issued a complaint alleging that the merger would violate antitrust laws. Since Reed Elsevier owned Lexis Nexis, the competing data-warehousing product to ChoicePoint's product, the merger would allegedly have stifled competition in the data-warehousing market. The resolution of the complaint required Reed Elsevier and ChoicePoint to divest their assets related to AutoTrackXP and CLEAR electronic public records services to Thomson Reuters, another giant information company.

Thomson Reuters owns the Reuters Newswire service, one of the world's largest news services providing worldwide news to newspapers and mainstream media organizations. Having been known for its objectivity, unbiased reporting, and strict code of ethics, Reuters is now part of a conglomerate that sells databases containing the personal information of American citizens to the federal government.

Prior to its acquisition by Thomson in 2007, Reuters' first principle was that no single individual could own more than 15 percent of the company. According to its first principle, "Reuters shall at no time pass into the hands of any one interest, group or faction."[16] This requirement was intended to ensure that its reporting would remain free from bias and undue influence. Now that Thomson Reuters is also in the government surveillance business, there is all the more reason for concern that Reuters' coverage of news stories about government activities, especially surveillance and abridgement of civil liberties, will, like the rest of consolidated mainstream media, be tainted by conflict of interest.[17] This may be more disconcerting when it is learned that the Associated Press, Reuter's main competitor, has been accused of harboring bias favoring U.S. government positions.[18]

The Google/DoubleClick Merger

In a sense, companies such as ChoicePoint and Thomson Reuters are less formidable violators of privacy than companies such as Google. This is because the former companies are quite candid about the fact that their primary business is to amass personal information. Not so with companies like Google.

For millions of Internet users, entering search terms into Google's search engine is seen as a way of acquiring information. In fact, from the perspective of Google, Internet users are not primarily consumers of information. They are themselves *sources* of incredibly personal information.

When a user enters a search term, it reveals his or her interests. A person's interests—anything from health issues to sexual desires—is very personal. However, Google saves the search under the user's Internet Protocol (IP) address, thereby establishing a record of these interests. The user's IP address is a person's computer address, which uniquely defines his or her Internet identity in terms of the data that is collected under it.

While Google provides information about its "privacy policy," the information is not directly accessible or prominently placed on the homepage. Instead a user must click on two links before reaching a statement on how information is collected and used. According to this statement,

> When you visit Google, we send one or more cookies—a small file containing a string of characters—to your computer or other device that uniquely identifies your browser. We use cookies to improve the quality of

our service, including for storing user preferences, improving search results and ad selection, and tracking user trends, such as how people search. Google also uses cookies in its advertising services to help advertisers and publishers serve and manage ads across the web. We may set one or more cookies in your browser when you visit a website, including Google sites that use our advertising cookies, and view or click on an ad supported by Google's advertising services.[19]

This collection and retention of personal user information is performed by Google without providing an opt-out option for users who do not want cookies implanted in their computers and their personal search information stored.

In fact, Google's main reason for "tracking user trends" is to amass behavioral information for purposes of targeted online advertising, its main source of revenue. In 2007, for this purpose, Google merged with DoubleClick, a major provider of digital marketing technologies and services.

DoubleClick's primary business is helping advertisers to find targets for their ads by tracking and collecting Internet user information. It uses a form of technology known as Dynamic Advertising, Reporting, and Targeting (DART), which stores tracking cookies in users' computers. This technology permits advertisers to serve their ads to prospective customers by gathering information about them including the Web sites they visit and their shopping-cart behavior. Hence, the merger between Google and DoubleClick has enabled the team to combine user information collected by DoubleClick technologies with search histories gathered by Google to create a massive database of consumer information. This in turn leaves Internet users vulnerable to having their *Internet identities or profiles* accessed by the federal government and linked to the other personal data it has amassed.

In 2006, Google refused to comply with a subpoena from the federal government asking it to turn over its search information allegedly for purposes of looking into the threat posed by online pornography to children.[20] This is in contrast to Microsoft, AOL, and Yahoo, who cooperated with their subpoenas. However, the increasingly close business ties that Google now enjoys with federal agencies makes it likely that the information giant will cooperate with government demands for information in the future. For example, more recently, Google has partnered with the NSA, CIA, and FBI to create an intelligence database that lets these agencies share information with each other.[21] Such close-knit relationships with these federal agencies along with the lucrative defense contracts it stands to gain (or lose) makes cooperation a probable option for a giant corporation like Google with an immense appetite for profit.

Facebook's Ties to DARPA

A central feature that makes the Internet distinct from information services, such as cable and broadcast media is its potential for interactivity. The net offers users a forum for the exchange of ideas between large numbers of people. While broadcast and cable networks also reach millions of people, the exchange is unidirectional, that is, information travels down a one-way street from the few to the many. In contrast, the Internet permits information to travel down a two-way street from the many to the many. It is this potential for interaction that makes the Internet a democratic medium of exchange.

The social media is a marked example of a media with such potential for democratization. According to Wikipedia,

> **Social media** is media designed to be disseminated through social interaction, created using highly accessible and scalable publishing techniques. Social media uses Internet and web-based technologies to transform broadcast media monologues (one to many) into social media dialogues (many to many). It supports the democratization of knowledge and information, transforming people from content consumers into content producers.[22]

One might, therefore, conclude that the rise of social media such as Twitter and Facebook marks a trend toward a culture of autonomy and away from a culture of control. Unfortunately, there are reasons to think that at least some social media have in fact been created for the opposite purpose; that is, to leverage state control over interpersonal communication. At least, so it seems in the case of Facebook.

Facebook, which was started in February 2004 by 21-year-old Harvard student Mark Zuckerberg, is presently the world's largest social media network with over 350 million users. Its fast-growing popularity among college students attracted the attention of entrepreneurs with high-level connections in the federal government. It received its first financial backing in late 2004 by Peter Thiel in the amount of US$500,000.

Thiel, who is on the board of Facebook, was founder and CEO of Paypal and a former board member of Vanguard.org, a conservative activist organization. According to Vanguard's Web site,

> The Vanguard Project is an effort to build a state-of-the-art technological platform, plus the organizational infrastructure behind it, to enable a level of conservative activism—both online and offline—previously achieved only by MoveOn.org and Obama for America.[23]

Many of Vanguard's advisors and members are also members of the Counsel for National Policy, an organization of conservative political leaders, financiers, and far-right activists, which, according to Mark Crispin Miller, is a "highly secretive theocratic organization" that seeks "religious rule."[24]

In 2009, Thiel was an invited guest at the annual conference of the Bilderberg Group, another highly secretive organization of powerful and influential conservative powerbrokers. This international group, which aims at economic globalization collectively owns a substantial part of the world's wealth, appears to have exerted influence on world policy, and has ties to the NSA.[25]

So, was Facebook slated to be a technological political weapon used to advance a right-wing agenda? This possibility is difficult to dismiss once its ties with the Department of Defense have been brought to light.

In 2005, Facebook received US$12.7 million from Accel Partners, a venture capital firm. One of Accel's partners is Jim Bryer, who now serves on the Facebook board along with Thiel. Bryer also served on the board of directors of BBN Technologies—the company contracted in 1969 by DARPA to build the Arpanet, which was the forerunner of the Internet.[26]

Serving on the board of directors of BBN, at the same time as Bryer, was Anita Jones, who had previously, from 1993 to 1997, served as the director of DARPA, which was the Defense Department agency that (in 2002) established the "Information Awareness Office" (IAO) to direct the TIA project.[27]

A former chair of the National Venture Capital Association (NVCA), Bryer also served on the NVCA board with Gilman Louie, who was the first CEO of In-Q-Tel, a venture capital company started by the Central Intelligence Agency (CIA).[28] Anita Jones also presently serves on the board of In-Q-Tel.

Formed in 1999, In-Q-Tel sought out technology companies that could serve CIA surveillance interests. Louie remarked, "There's a new urgency within the CIA to find technology that makes sense of all the unstructured data floating around on the Internet and elsewhere. The agency can't train analysts quickly enough."[29] Accordingly, in 2001, under Louie's direction, In-Q-Tel financed a small startup company, Attensity Corp, which produced text-analyzing software that mapped sentences and extracted common threads in documents, thereby attempting to help analysts detect patterns. This was the beginning of development of pattern-recognition software that would provide an important component of the TIA project. The Facebook Web site appears to have been a further advance by the DARPA in this direction.

Recall from Chapter 2 that one of the original TIA technologies was "Scalable Social Network Analysis" technology, which looks for behavioral patterns of terrorist groups by comparing them to the behavioral patterns of masses of innocent people. These technologies must, therefore, place these innocent masses under surveillance in order to acquire information about their behavioral patterns. Facebook obviously provides en masse the needed "social networking" data for this component of the TIA project; and given the ties of Facebook to DARPA, it is reasonable to suspect that Facebook is DARPA's tool for collecting data on the masses in order to construct algorithms to distinguish anomalous, terrorist cases from usual ones.

If so, then 350 million users of Facebook are being used as experimental subjects by the government without their informed consent. Such mass spying contravenes respect for privacy. In fact, while Facebook has settings to restrict access to information that is posted, most people who subscribe to Facebook speak openly even about the most intimate details of their personal lives, do not bother with making privacy adjustments, and simply assume that their safety and privacy are protected.[30]

But careful reading of Facebook's privacy statement suggests otherwise:

> To respond to legal requests and prevent harm. We may disclose information pursuant to subpoenas, court orders, or other requests (including criminal and civil matters) if we have a good faith belief that the response is required by law. . . . *We may also share information when we have a good faith belief it is necessary to prevent fraud or other illegal activity, to prevent imminent bodily harm, or to protect ourselves and you from people violating our Statement of Rights and Responsibilities. This may include sharing information with other companies, lawyers, courts or other government entities.*

Facebook's abovementioned policy is broad enough to permit wholesale disclosure of millions of users' personal information to federal agencies such as DARPA and the NSA or certain private companies under contract with these agencies, such as the SAIC. For example, the abovementioned privacy policy could arguably permit such disclosure insofar as Facebook's board of directors, including politically motivated members like Thiel and Breyer, could claim to have a "good faith belief" that it was necessary in order to fight and win "the war on terror."

In fact, in December, 2009, the Electronic Frontier Foundation, a non-profit, electronic civil rights organization, filed a complaint against the Department of Defense, the CIA, the Office of the Director of National Intelligence, and three other federal departments under the Freedom of Information Act, seeking release of records concerning the use of social networking Web sites "as investigative, surveillance, and data collection tools."[31] But, even in the absence of such records, it is evident that government agencies are using social networking sites—in particular, Facebook, Twitter, and MySpace—to collect evidence for various investigations.[32]

As users of social networking sites become increasingly complacent about disclosing personal information without unequivocal assurances of privacy protection, it will become easier for government and its corporate accomplices to whittle away at this civil right until the idea becomes an empty relic. Such evisceration of privacy is an earmark of a totalitarian state; for, in such a state, the government will have access to even the most intimate details of the lives of its citizens while the latter will know little or nothing about the former. This unidirectional quality of information flow from the people to the state authority without reciprocity is the final death note of any democratic culture in transition toward a culture of control. Whether or not this component of the totalitarian equation is fulfilled will depend largely on the ability of mass media, including the Internet, to keep the people informed. The next three chapters of this book will examine this major challenge to the survival of democracy in America.

Ignorance is Strength: Complicity of the Corporate Media Behemoths

The degree to which the mass media are independent of government provides a useful index for gauging just how controlled or autonomous a culture really is. The less people know, the easier it is to manipulate and control them; the more informed they are, the more capable they are of making rational decisions and the harder it is to manipulate them through lies and deception.

In dictatorships where civil liberties are virtually nonexistent, the media are mouthpieces of government, and what the governed are permitted to see and hear is largely political propaganda. For example, in Syria, the media are largely state owned and operated through the Ministry of Information of the Ba'ath party. In this controlled environment, it is illegal to criticize the ruling party and the military; and any independent media must be licensed by the Ministry of Information, which monitors all media to ensure that it toes the party line. Internet sites are also passed through government filters to ensure that anything politically averse to it is not accessible to Syrian citizens. Here one need not appeal to Orwell's novel, *1984*, to find a clearer case of "Big Brother is Watching You."

Between such oppressive regimes and ones that are democratic and free, there are many shades of gray. Relative to the state of media in a nation, such as Syria, even the mainstream (corporate) media in the United States may appear to be "free" and "democratic." Still, this may be more a matter of degree than of kind. Moreover, the state of mainstream media in America is always capable of moving incrementally closer to that of more oppressive cultures by imperceptible changes. Thus, a central question is not so much whether the American mainstream media is controlled, but instead whether it is moving incrementally toward greater levels of control. Unfortunately, the answer to this question is not an optimistic one.

Consolidation as a Major Factor in Mainstream Media's Complicity with Government

One main reason for this lack of optimism is the rising tide of media consolidation in the American mainstream media. Currently, broadcast TV is dominated by five major corporations: Fox/News Corp, CBS/Viacom, NBC/General Electric,[1] Tribune Company, and ABC/Disney. Radio is largely controlled by Clear Channel and Infinity/Viacom. Cable/Satellite TV giants include Comcast, DirecTV/News Corp, and Time Warner. These conglomorates form an intricate web of joint ventures, which spills over into other media, including the Internet. For example, NBC/General Electric, Fox/News Corp, and ABC/Disney jointly run a Web site called Hulu, which streams TV shows and movies; and Time Warner and CBS/Viacom have a joint venture with Comcast, which allows cable subscribers to access TV through the web, using Comcast's "On Demand Online" system. Thus, despite the number of apparent choices, most of what Americans see and hear is filtered through just a handful of interconnected monolithic media and telecom companies.

These relatively few giant corporations are motivated primarily by maximizing profit and providing dividends to stockholders. At the same time, these companies' continued existence and ability to expand their profitable horizons is in the hands of government. This is because the Federal Communications Commission (FCC) and Congress can place regulatory strangleholds on media and telecom companies if they fail to cooperate with the current administration's policies and goals. In this way, government can literally regulate a corporation out of existence. Alternatively, government can reward cooperation with deregulation or just not passing certain regulations. It could raise or lower taxes; award or withdraw lucrative defense contracts; provide special incentives for investing in potentially profitable industries, and provide other government perks—all of which depend on the company's willingness to cooperate with government.

True, keeping consumers of news (the American public) informed about questionable government practices counts in corporate cost-benefit analyses about what, and how, to report. A news company cannot afford to alienate its audience as this leads to lost advertising revenue. The company must also look for breaking news that will increase ratings. Still, failure to break stories that expose government breaches of public trust or other questionable government practices does not necessarily turn away customers and decrease company revenues, especially if the public never even finds out the (whole) truth anyway. So, in trading off between keeping the public informed and cooperating with government, the corporate mainstream media may incline toward the latter.

For example, General Electric, presently the mother company to NBC, builds the engines and other supportive components for the unmanned "drones" armed with hellfire missiles that have been used by the Bush administration and now by the Obama administration to attack suspected al Qaeda officials in Pakistan and Afghanistan.[2] However, news coverage of drone attacks by MSNBC has tended to stress the efficacy of such technology in killing alleged al Qaeda targets, and has been less open about its drawbacks. For example, in the 60 known drone attacks in Pakistan between January 2006 and April 2009, 14 al Qaeda leaders were killed but also 607 civilians.[3] Yet, according to NBC national security analyst Dana Priest, "Drones can't be built fast enough for the demand,"[4] a comment that reads like a promotional ad for GE. In its present form, such technology is aided by human judgment; however, now in its infancy it is the next generation of autonomous, unmanned aircraft, which will have the purported ability to distinguish civilians from combatants. As General Electric in cooperation with other military contractors, such as Lockheed Martin, takes these flying robotic killers to market, it will be edifying to see how closely the mainstream media will track "collateral damage." Unfortunately, without an autonomous newsroom, free from manipulation by politico-corporate pressures, such facts are likely to be buried along with the dead bodies of innocent civilians.

The Rise of Corporate Media Consolidation in America

This consolidated corporate media landscape has been facilitated by easing of federal restrictions on how large a corporation can become. A landmark legal reform of this nature, enacted during the Clinton administration, is the 1996 Telecommunications Act. As prescribed by this act, the FCC raised the national audience-reach limitation of broadcast TV companies from 25 percent to 35 percent.

In June 2003, with the support of the Bush administration, the FCC raised the national media cap to 45 percent, thereby permitting broadcast networks such as Fox and ABC to own local TV stations that reached 45 percent of the national market, a 10 percent increase from that permitted by the 1996 Telecommunications Act. The FCC also let a single company own up to three TV stations in the largest markets; and, in all except the smallest markets, it permitted a company to have "cross-ownership" of both a newspaper and a radio or television station in the same market.

In August 2003, these new media-ownership rules came under fire by a media activist organization known as the Media Access Project (MAP), a team of civil rights lawyers, which represented in federal court, the Prometheus Radio Project, an activist organization for advancing low-frequency FM community radio. The MAP/Prometheus Radio Project challenged the new FCC rules in the U.S. Court of Appeals for the Third Circuit in Philadelphia, and was able to get the court to issue a stay on the new rules.

In November 2003, another activist organization, The Free Press, organized a campaign aimed at stopping the new FCC rules from taking effect. The campaign encouraged millions of Americans who were dissatisfied with the new FCC rules to write letters to their congresspersons. Responding to the public outcry, the Whitehouse slipped a rider into the Consolidated Appropriations Act as a compromise with Congress, which rolled back the national broadcast cap from 45 percent to 39 percent, still 4 percent higher than the 1996 Act's 35 percent cap.

On June 24, 2004, the U.S. Court of Appeals for the Third Circuit in Philadelphia decided to send the FCC's new media-ownership rules back to the FCC until it could justify its claim that the rules would not adversely affect competition. The court ruled, "The commission has not sufficiently justified its particular chosen numerical limits for local television ownership, local radio ownership, and cross-ownership of media within local markets." While several media companies appealed the case to the Supreme Court, the Court refused to hear the case. As a result, the newspaper/broadcast cross-ownership rule and the local TV multiple-ownership rule, which were in effect prior to June 2003 were reinstated. As before, a media company could not own both a newspaper and a radio or TV station in the same market; nor could it own more than one TV station in the largest markets.

The efforts expended by the MAP/Prometheus Radio Project and the Free Press in helping to slow the rise of corporate media consolidation are instructive in that they show how grassroots movements can effect positive change. Still, Congress' rollback of the national broadcasting cap to 39 percent was largely symbolic, because it was set at a percentage that still permitted Viacom (CBS) and News Corp (Fox) to keep their current holdings. Both companies had already been operating above the earlier 35 percent cap, just under the new 39 percent. Other major media corporations operating substantially below the 39 percent cap, such as General Electric (NBC) and Disney (ABC), were also now permitted to increase their holdings without violating the law. So, the legislative change still afforded giant media corporations the opportunity to continue their mergers and acquisitions.

Further, the 39 percent national cap on ownership of local TV stations could in some cases actually be as much as 90 percent when the 50 percent UHF discount was figured. This discount, which had originally been provided as an incentive for media companies to broadcast on frequencies on the UHF dial (stations 14–83), counted only half of a company's UHF market reach for purposes of assessing ownership caps. In 2009, when conversion to digital occurred, companies, such as Fox and CBS had their UHF stations grandfathered in.

Further, the staying of the cross-ownership rule banning the ownership of a newspaper and a TV or radio station in the same market was only temporary. In 2007, in response to the 2004 Prometheus decision, the FCC relaxed the newspaper/broadcast cross-ownership rule, thereby allowing a media company to own a daily newspaper and a radio station in a top-20 designated market area (DMA), or a daily newspaper and a television station in a top-20 DMA. However, the FCC retained the other media-ownership rules that were in effect; and it did not revisit the 39 percent national TV media-ownership cap enacted by Congress in 2003.

Cable companies have also been successful in extending their market reach. In August 2009, Comcast succeeded in getting a U.S. appeals court to strike down a Federal Communications Commission's rule that disallowed a cable operator from serving more than 30 percent of U.S. households. Accordingly, companies such as Comcast and Time Warner Cable received the green light to continue national expansion making likely further consolidation in the provision of cable services.

From this brief survey, it should be evident that the already-gigantic corporate media companies continue to find the means to grow even larger. Such expansion in the form of increased market reach means less competition in a given market, and, therefore, less independent alternative information channels open to consumers. Given the vital role that mainstream media and cable companies play in keeping Americans informed, the trend toward ever-increasing control of the content and flow of information by a few behemoth companies portends serious consequences for a democratic and free state.

If these giant corporations had an internal moral compass and automatically acted in good faith in keeping the public adequately informed about issues of importance, especially matters of state, then we might not see the danger of the trend toward consolidation. Unfortunately, this would only be wishful thinking out of gear with the reality of how giant media corporations operate.

The Replacement of Investigative Reporting with Government Spokespersons

Corporate media consolidation has also played a role in the downsizing of independent, investigative-reporting divisions of the giant media corporations. The single-minded drive of corporate media to reduce costs and increase profits has led to reliance on government spokespersons as sources of news about government activities in lieu of more costly, independent, investigative reporting. Thus, cable news networks, such as CNN and Fox fill their 24-7 news holes largely with the statements of government spokespersons, kept at close range to provide a continuous news feed. The obvious problem with such a system is that government cannot be relied on to objectively assess the veracity of claims against itself. This would not be unlike placing a crime suspect on trial and settling the matter by asking the accused if he or she is guilty of the charges, and then acquitting the suspect based on the defendant's denial.

Corporate media's drive to eliminate the costs of original investigative reporting has also set the stage for an even more insidious form of reliance on government spokespersons. On April 20, 2008, the *New York Times* disclosed that the Bush administration had been systematically recruiting lobbyists, senior executives, board members, and consultants for military contractors to serve as "military analysts" to give seemingly objective analyses of war policy. According to the *Times*, the Bush administration sought to "transform the analysts into a kind of media Trojan horse—an instrument intended to shape terrorism coverage from inside the major TV and radio networks."[5] To effect this transformation the Bush administration contracted with the Rendon Group, a public relations firm in Washington, D. C. headed by John Rendon.[6] As discussed below, this company had been hired by the Bush administration to "manage" public perception and to conduct "information warfare," including the use of Total Information Awareness (TIA) technologies as a defensive weapon of mass deception against emerging news reports that were adverse to Bush administration policies.

According to a study conducted by a media watchdog group Media Matters, between January 1, 2002, and May 15, 2008, the "military analysts" named in the *Times* article collectively appeared or were quoted by mainstream media more than 4,500 times as authorities on the Iraq war and other national security or government policy issues. These media organizations included ABC, ABC News Now, CBS, CBS Radio Network, NBC, CNN, CNN Headline News, Fox News, MSNBC, CNBC, and NPR.[7]

For example, Robert S. Bevelacqua, a retired Green Beret and former Fox News analyst told the *Times*, "It was them saying, 'We need to stick our hands up your back and move your mouth for you.'" Nevertheless, Bevelacqua toed the Bush administration line in the early years of the Iraq war by claiming that "Our current success in Iraq is testimony to the fact that we have adequate force structure,"[8] and "Capturing Saddam would 'go a long way toward a lasting democracy in Iraq.'"[9] Unfortunately, the American people were not informed by the mainstream media that the "experts" being quoted and interviewed were cogs in a government propaganda machine to manipulate public perception.

Injection of Prepackaged News into the Mainstream Media

Another manner in which the mainstream media news has been manipulated by government is the injection of prepackaged news. On March 13, 2005, the *New York Times* also disclosed that, under the Bush administration, the federal government had used public relations firms to create prepackaged news feeds favorable to its policies and had it programmed into network news local affiliates throughout the United States. "An examination of government-produced news reports," stated the *Times*, "offers a look inside a world where the traditional lines between public relations and journalism have become tangled, where local anchors introduce prepackaged segments with 'suggested' lead-ins written by public relations experts. It is a world where government-produced reports disappear into a maze of satellite transmissions, Web portals, syndicated news programs and network feeds, only to emerge cleansed on the other side as 'independent' journalism."[10]

The American public was not informed that these news feeds were the products of public relations firms working for the federal government. Instead, the corporate media were willing to relinquish their role as a watchdog of government in order to save the expense of finding original material.

The Government Accountability Office subsequently determined that a federal agency cannot publish prepackaged news reports "that conceal or do not clearly identify for the television-viewing audience that the agency was the source of those materials."

However, an indirect channel for injecting propaganda into the American mainstream media still remained. As a charge of the Office of Disinformation, the Bush administration sought to plant phony news favorable to its war policy into the news coming out of foreign presses throughout the world. In the current digital age, if a story is planted in the foreign media, it can "blow back," and, therefore, find its way into the American media.

On November 30, 2005, the *Los Angeles Times* broke a story that the Bush administration had been injecting American propaganda into the Iraqi press in an attempt to stem anti-American resistance among Iraqis. Thus, ironically, while the United States had allegedly invaded Iraq to liberate it from oppression, it was systematically interfering with the fundamental right to freedom of the press.

According to the *LA Times*, the Pentagon had hired the Lincoln Group, a small Washington, D.C. public relations firm for this purpose. Lincoln's

Iraqi staff, or its subcontractors, had sometimes posed as freelance reporters or advertising executives when they delivered the stories to Baghdad media organizations. "The arrangement with Lincoln Group," said the *LA Times*, "is evidence of how far the Pentagon has moved to blur the traditional boundaries between military public affairs—the dissemination of factual information to the media—and psychological and information operations, which use propaganda and sometimes misleading information to advance the objectives of a military campaign."[11] This is not to mention the blowback that can result from such foreign media deception.

Embedded Reporters as Purveyors of Government Propaganda

The Pentagon has also been injecting propaganda into mainstream media through its embedded reporters program. Since the inception of the Iraq war, reporters on the ground have not been permitted to function autonomously but instead must be "embedded" in military units. Such reporters are required to pass all information through their military unit commanders before the information can be released and turned into "news." As a result, embedded reporters become mouthpieces of government war propaganda. As one forthright commander confessed, "Frankly, our job is to win the war. Part of that is information warfare. So we are going to attempt to dominate the information environment. Embedding journalists honorably served that end."[12] John Rendon has also been quite clear about the purpose of embedding reporters within army units, which he says is to control the media.[13]

Judith Miller, a former reporter and embed for *The Times*, is an instructive example of an embedded reporter who became a mouthpiece for the Pentagon. "During the Iraq war, the Pentagon had given me clearance to see secret information as part of my assignment 'embedded' with a special military unit hunting for unconventional Weapons," she said. "I was not permitted to discuss with editors some of the more sensitive information about Iraq." Miller's admission that she was not permitted to discuss "the more sensitive information about Iraq" was, of course, an admission that the government censored and controlled her stories.

Miller not only acquiesced in such government censorship; she also helped the Bush administration to forge a war in Iraq on the basis of false information. On December 20, 2001, Miller wrote an article for the *New York Times* titled "An Iraqi Defector Tells of Work on At Least 20 Hidden Weapons Sites," in which she reported the false account by Saeed al-Haideri about Hussein's WMD program. "The interview with Mr. Saeed," she said, "was arranged by the Iraqi National Congress, the main Iraqi opposition group, which seeks the overthrow of Mr. Hussein. If verified, Mr. Saeed's allegations would provide ammunition to officials within the Bush administration who have been arguing that Mr. Hussein should be driven from power partly because of his unwillingness to stop making weapons of mass destruction, despite his pledges to do so." Miller reported that al-Haideri had personally worked on secret facilities for biological, chemical, and nuclear weapons and added, "The experts said his information seemed reliable and significant."[14]

Unfortunately, what Miller did not report was that U.S. intelligence had previously subjected al-Haideri to a polygraph test, which he flunked. Instead, Miller reported the anti-Hussein propaganda of the Iraqi National Congress (INC), an Iraqi opposition group organized, even named, by the Rendon Group for purposes of instigating a national uprising against Saddam Hussein. As was discussed in Chapter 2, the Rendon Group was hired by the George W. Bush administration to aid the Office of Strategic Information ("Office of Disinformation") to conduct a campaign of government propaganda and disinformation.[15]

It is, therefore, ironic that, in 2009, in full light of its past history, the Rendon Group should have been contracted for US$1.5 million by the Obama administration to screen prospective embedded journalists before embedding them with military units.[16] According to the military newspaper, Stars and Stripes, U.S. public affairs officials in Afghanistan acknowledged that "any reporter seeking to embed with U.S. forces is subject to a background profile by The Rendon Group"[17] According to Stars and Stripes, the Rendon group had been hired to vet potential embeds to determine if their recent reporting has been positive, negative, or neutral toward the U.S. military. And, despite the denial by military public relations, it appears that this vetting was for purposes of weeding out journalists who had been critical of the U.S. military. Thus, Stars and Stripes reported that, two months earlier, U.S. Army officials in Iraq engaged in a similar vetting practice when they refused to allow a Stars and Stripes reporter to embed with a unit of the 1st Cavalry Division because "the reporter 'refused to highlight' good news that military commanders wanted to emphasize."[18] Further, according to a public affairs officer with the 101st Airborne Division, "when his unit was in Afghanistan and in charge of the Rendon contract, he had used the conclusions contained in Rendon profiles in part to reject at least two journalists' applications for embeds."[19]

Amid protest from journalism groups who called the arrangement "alarming," one week after Stars and Stripes disclosed that the government had contracted with the Rendon Group to screen prospective embeds, the Pentagon announced that it was canceling the contract. "The decision to terminate the Rendon contract was mine and mine alone," said Rear Admiral Gregory J. Smith. "As the senior U.S. communicator in Afghanistan, it was clear that the issue of Rendon's support to US forces in Afghanistan had become a distraction from our main mission."[20] Nevertheless, it would be naïve not to question the veracity of a Pentagon steeped in a campaign of misinformation and deception, and which had deceptively announced earlier that it was closing the door to its Office of Disinformation.

Information Warfare: Deployment of TIA Technologies to Control Public Perception

John Rendon has described himself as an "information warrior" and a "perception manager." According to Rendon, "Because the lines are divergent, this difference between perception and reality is one of the greatest strategic communications challenges of war." Accordingly, Rendon sees the goal of information warfare as bringing reality into line with the desired perception, that is, the perception that he is paid by the government to create.

Rendon's perception management has several related tentacles. One aspect consists of recruiting and training a team of "information warriors to launch a worldwide propaganda campaign in developing and delivering specific messages to the local population, combatants, front-line states, the media and the international community." Another aspect consists in online "military deception" such as participation in chat rooms and creation of news Web sites for the purpose of spreading false information and prowar propaganda. Another aspect consists in coaching White House staff in shaping the daily information that comes out of the White House.[21]

Still another aspect of Rendon's perception management involves accessing negative news feeds before they are published, and then tactically attempting to neutralize them with media propaganda. When the Office of Strategic Influence was allegedly shut down in 2002 by the Bush administration, many of its operations were assumed by the Information Operations Task Force (IOTF), a clandestine Pentagon operation charged with manipulating news and information. The Rendon Group apparently played a central role in managing these operations. According to Pentagon documents, its charge was to construct an "Information War Room" to monitor international news reports using high-tech computer technology having the capacity to read and respond instantaneously with counterpropaganda. This included a "proprietary state-of-the-art news-wire collection system called 'Livewire,' which takes real-time newswire reports, as they are filed, before they are on the Internet, before CNN can read them on the air, and twenty-four hours before they appear in the morning newspapers, and sorts them by keyword. The system provides the most current real-time access to news and information available to private or public organizations."[22]

The idea of government knowing the headlines before they are published is paradigmatic of a culture of control. Ideally, "information warfare" here equates to "Total Information Awareness," which includes the ability to neutralize any unfavorable information that might seep through the cracks of a wall of censorship. Presumably, such an awesome power to read the news before it goes online, airs, and hits the newsstands suggests that Rendon had high-level NSA clearance to spy on journalists and access to state-of-the-art TIA technologies, such as those discussed in Chapter 2. This would include equipment capable of intercepting electronic communications before they reach their intended recipients and copying and transmitting this information to government databases for keyword searches and analyses.

Rendon's "Live Wire" could not accomplish this formidable object alone. The system is promoted on its Web site as "Early Warning Radar" and is modestly described there as having the capability to "typically beat television news and, in the case of print media, often drive the next day's newspaper coverage."

While Rendon appears to be marketing "Live Wire" services to nongovernmental organizations, its program of information warfare pursued on behalf of the government has been far more aggressive. According to Pentagon documents, the Rendon Group has been authorized "to research and analyze information classified up to Top Secret/SCI/SI/TK/G/HCS."[23]

"SCI" refers to "Sensitive Compartmented Information," which has a classification status that exceeds "Top Secret," while "SI" refers to "Special Intelligence," *which signifies communications intercepted by the NSA*; "TK" refers to "Talent/Keyhole," code for reconnaissance aircraft and spy satellite images; "G" refers to "Gamma," information intercepted from sensitive sources; and finally, "HCS" refers to "Humint Control System," information from sensitive human sources. Therefore, Rendon had access to NSA eavesdropping, imaging satellites, and human spies.[24]

As was discussed in Chapter 2, Russell Tice, a former NSA officer, claimed that NSA had been expressly targeting U.S. journalists and news organizations as late as 2005. In this same time period, between 2001 and 2005, the Rendon Group's information warfare services were being used by the Pentagon; Rendon was conducting its "Live Wire" early warning operations; and also had access to electronic communications intercepted by the NSA. Given these facts and the veracity of Tice's claim, it is likely that the Rendon Group was directly involved in the unlawful surveillance of journalists and journalistic organizations as claimed by Tice. More exactly, it is likely that it assisted in intercepting and analyzing electronic (e-mail, Internet, and phone) communications of journalists and news organizations in order to counter potentially damaging news stories with propaganda and misinformation.

Given the clandestine nature of such operations, it is difficult to gauge whether Rendon's black op still operates under the Obama administration.

However, consider the past history of this company, which included the tactical use of media manipulation, deception, and misinformation (including creating the phony intelligence used to defend the Iraq war), and (probably) the eavesdropping on journalists' private electronic communications; nevertheless, the Obama administration was willing to contract with Rendon for the purpose of censoring journalists in the field. Such willingness on the part of the Obama administration cannot put the possibility of Rendon's current involvement in such black ops past reasonable doubt. Moreover, as was discussed in Chapter 3, the oversight role of the FIS Courts has been seriously diminished by the passage of the 2008 FISA Amendments Act, which increases the chances that such clandestine, illegal NSA practices could continue to be carried out beneath the radar of the courts.

The Web of Military-Industrial Inbreeding behind the TIA Project

As mentioned above, Rendon had been instrumental in organizing the INC, which was part of a public relations campaign to create a worldwide unsavory image of Saddam Hussein as a hated dictator. In fact, in May 1991, President George H. W. Bush directed the Central Intelligence Agency (CIA) to "create the conditions" for Hussein's overthrow. In response, the CIA contracted with the Rendon Group to accomplish the said conditions. Robert Gates, the current Secretary of Defense, was then Assistant to the President and Deputy National Security Advisor and became Director of the CIA in November 1991; he served in this position until January 1993. During these years, in his capacity as CIA director, Gates worked with the Rendon Group to try to bring about the overthrow of Hussein.

It is, therefore, not surprising that Gates, in his capacity as Secretary of Defense in 2009 under President Obama would not have been reticent to once again work with the Rendon Group. In fact, Gates' own past history had been flavored with involvement with the Iran-Contra scandal in his capacity as Deputy Director of the CIA under President Ronald Reagan; he had also been accused of falsifying evidence to make the Soviet threat appear greater than it actually was. Accordingly, it is possible that Gates' own penchant for "perception management" may have informed his judgment in hiring Rendon.

In 1993, Gates was also on the board of directors of another major Department of Defense contractor, Science Applications International Corporation (SAIC). Also trading in information warfare, SAIC is a behemoth Fortune 500 company, which serves the Pentagon with experts in areas as diverse as Islamic studies, artificial intelligence, military intelligence, and psychological warfare. In fact, Hicks & Associates, a fully owned subsidiary of SAIC founded in 1986, was awarded a contract for US$19 million in

2002 to build the main brain of TIA, the Information Awareness Prototype System.[25] Hicks also built Genoa II (later renamed "Topsail" when it was moved to ARDA).[26]

Gates' relationship with SAIC/Hicks continued beyond his board membership. In 2005, Hicks' Senior Vice President, Michael Donley, became the Director of Administration and Management for the Department of Defense and served as Secretary of Defense Gates' Chief Information Officer in charge of information technology, which presumably included management of the TIA Project. In 2003, Gates also served as an advisor to VoteHere, an electronic voting machine technology company, which had ties to SAIC. In fact, the Chairman of the Board of VoteHere at the time Gates was an advisor to this company was W.A. Owen, who was also a former Vice Chairman of the SAIC Board.

Accordingly, an intimate military-industrial web of information warfare has been assembled, which spins out deception, government propaganda, and misinformation. This inbred environment, where the line between Defense Department officers at the highest echelons and board members of private defense contractors, has been breached, coupled with a systematized culture of government-media quid pro quo and censorship has placed American citizens in the challenging circumstance of having to distinguish truth from a manufactured version of reality.

7

Web of Deceit: The Tenuous Future of Net Neutrality

According to a December 2008 Pew Research Survey, the Internet has surpassed all other media except television as an outlet via which people receive national and international news. According to the study, 40 percent of people receive most of their national and international news from the Internet, as compared to 24 percent in September 2007. In this study, only 35 percent of people surveyed cite newspapers as their main source of news, whereas 70 percent still cite television as their main source.[1]

These statistics underscore the importance of keeping the free, open architecture of the Internet alive as we move further into the twenty-first century. Indeed, as digital technology continues to evolve, and to become omnipresent (we already have it on our cell phones), it is likely that the net will overtake television—or television, now digitized, will itself be an indistinguishable part of it. Already, as was discussed in the Chapter 6, the giant media corporations have Web sites that stream movies and television shows over the Internet.

There is also an expanding presence of major media corporations on the Internet. So, the Pew Study may be less impressive if one learns that most people get their Internet news from a mainstream corporate media Web site like *Fox.com* or *MSNBC.com*. What this suggests is that the absorption of TV into an expanding cyberspace may also mean greater and greater corporate control over of the Internet, and less and less Internet freedom and democracy. Unfortunately, this is just what appears to be going on.

Now unfolding is a legal-political-corporate current moving closer to turning a vibrant, democratic Internet into a global extension of the corporate mainstream media, which would portend a web of manipulation, censorship, and control over information. The signs exist, but the stakeholders (the federal government and a small group of interconnected, powerful telecom and mainstream media monopolies) have kept them from public awareness.

The days may now be numbered for surfing an uncensored, open-access Internet, using your favorite search engine to search a bottomless cyber-sea of information in the grandest democratic forum ever conceived by humankind. Instead, you can look forward to "Googling" or "Binging" about on a walled-off, carefully selected corpus of government propaganda and sanitized information "safe" for public consumption. Indoctrinated and sealed off from the outer world, you will inhabit a matrix where every ounce of creative, independent thinking that challenges government policies and values will be quietly squelched.

This is not groundless speculation about what may become of the Internet. Behind the scenes, invisible to the public eye, governmental and corporate forces have been placed in motion that, unless stopped, will turn the Internet nightmare just described into reality. The corporate mainstream media have been quiet about the telecom lobbies in Washington, and the filing of suits in state and federal courts to halt production of community Internet, all aimed at monopolizing and controlling the net. From Fox News to CNN, there has been scarce mainstream media coverage as the free open architecture of the net; so-called "net neutrality," is being challenged by the giant telecoms. One such challenge came in the form of a Supreme Court decision that has changed the legal landscape of the Internet to lean toward increased corporate control. Not surprisingly, neither this monumental decision nor its implications for the survival of net neutrality have, to date, been seriously broached by the mainstream media.

The *Brand X* Case: How the Telecoms Took Control of the Internet Pipes While the Mainstream Media Censored the Story[2]

On June 27, 2005, in a 6 to 3 decision in *National Cable & Telecommunications Association vs. Brand X Internet Services,*[3] the United States Supreme Court ruled that giant cable companies like Comcast and Verizon are not required to share their cables with other Internet service providers (ISPs). The Court opinion, written by Justice Clarence Thomas, was fashioned to serve corporate interests. Instead of taking up the question of whether corporate monopolies would destroy the open-access architecture of the Internet, it used sophistry and legally suspect arguments to obscure its constitutional duty to protect media diversity, free speech, and the public interest.

The Court accepted the FCC's conclusion, reached in 2002, that cable companies do not "offer" telecommunication services according to the meaning of the 1996 Telecommunication Act, which defines telecommunication purely in terms of transmission of information among or between users.

According to the FCC, cable modem service is not a telecommunications offering because consumers always use high-speed wire transmission as a necessary part of other services like browsing the web and sending and receiving e-mail messages. The FCC maintained that these offerings are information services, which manipulate and transform data instead of merely transmitting them. Since the act only requires companies offering telecommunication services to share their lines with other ISPs (the so-called "common carriage" requirement), the FCC concluded that cable companies are exempt from this requirement.

However, the FCC's conceptual basis for classifying cable modem services as informational was groundless. Not even the FCC could deny that people use their cable modems to transmit information from one point to another over a wire, regardless of whatever else they use them for. The FCC's classification could not possibly have provided a reasonable interpretation of the 1996 Telecommunication Act since it was inconsistent with it. Section 706 (C) (1) of this act defines "advanced telecommunications capability," without regard to any transmission media or technology, as high-speed, switched, broadband telecommunications capability that enables users to originate and receive high-quality voice, data, graphics, and video telecommunications using any technology.

Broadband cable Internet offers "advanced telecommunications capability" since it clearly fits this legal definition. Therefore, cable modem service must legally be regarded as telecommunications service.

To classify it as an information service is instead to treat high-speed broadband Internet as though it were similar to cable services such as Fox News and CNN. These networks send information down a one-way pipe unlike Internet transmissions, which, in contrast, are interactive, two-way exchanges resembling telephone conversations. The 9th Circuit Court of Appeals made this quite clear in its decision in *AT&T v. Portland*.

Accessing Web pages, navigating the Web's hypertext links, corresponding via e-mail, and participating in live chat groups involve two-way communication and information exchange unmatched by the act of electing to receive a one-way transmission of cable or pay-per-view television programming. And unlike transmission of a cable television signal, communication with a Web site involves a series of connections involving two-way information exchange and storage, even when a user views seemingly static content. Thus, the communication concepts are distinct in both a practical and a technical sense. Surfing cable channels is one thing; surfing the Internet over a cable broadband connection is quite another.

The Supreme Court had to strain to find some alleged legal basis to defer to the FCC's classification of high-speed Internet as an information service; so it put the entire weight of its argument on the FCC's claim that cable companies do not "offer" the telecommunication aspects of their services to consumers. Instead, they "offers end users information-service capabilities inextricably intertwined with data transport." Justice Scalia, writing the minority opinion in *Brand X*, analogized, you might as well say that a pizza service doesn't deliver pizzas because it also bakes them! Countering with its own analogy, the majority rationalized that you might as well say that a car dealership "offers" engines to consumers because it offers them cars. According to the majority's perspective, since the finished product is the car and not the engine, it makes more sense to say they offer consumers cars rather than engines. Similarly, it argued, the finished product that cable modem customers seek is Internet services, such as being able to surf the net, not simply a transmission over a wire.

The Court's claim is makeshift and oversimplified. It obscures the scope of consumer motivation by assuming that consumers have just one, broad perspective that defines what a company "offers" them. Realistically, consumers are also interested in the quality of the engines they get when they purchase cars (whether it is a V-8, V-6, 3.8 liter, 2.0 liter, etc). From *this* consumer perspective, the car dealer is indeed "offering" engines to consumers (and bucket seats, antilock brakes, dual air bags, and all other components that determine the car's drivability, safety, comfort, design, durability, speed, and so forth). Similarly, from the perspective of average cable Internet consumers who care about how reliable and fast the cable connection they purchase is, the cable company can, in a very practical sense, be said to be "offering" a telecommunication service. The FCC's distinction that cable modem data-transmission service is inextricably bound up with information services—just as an engine is inextricably bound up with a car—is, in this instance, a distinction without a difference.

In the end, the Court retreated to the claim that the Telecommunication Act was ambiguous. So why did it side with the FCC's interpretation even though there was clear, prior legal precedent for classifying cable modem services as telecommunication offerings?[4]

Citing its own decision in *Chevron U.S.A. Inc v. Natural Resources Defense Council*, the Court maintained that "if a statute is ambiguous, and if the implementing agency's construction is reasonable, . . . a federal court [is required] to accept the agency's construction of the statute, even if the agency's reading differs from what the court believes is the best statutory interpretation."[5] Therefore, it argued, since the FCC's construction is reasonable, it should determine what counts as "offering" telecommunication services.

In the first place, the Court provided no legitimate legal, moral, or conceptual basis to think the FCC's construction was reasonable. If it really cared about what consumers wanted, it would have determined what was reasonable *for purposes of regulating competition of an Internet that was designed to provide free, unfettered access to information in a democratic society*. Instead, the Court rested its substantive case on a specious argument advanced by the FCC:

> The Commission concluded that ... broadband services should exist in a minimal regulatory environment that promotes investment and innovation in a competitive market. ... This, the Commission reasoned, warranted treating cable companies unlike the facilities-based enhanced-service providers of the past. ... We find nothing arbitrary about the Commission's providing a fresh analysis of the problem as applied to the cable industry, which it has never subjected to these rules. This is adequate rational justification for the Commission's conclusions.[6]

What "rational justification" was the Court talking about? The FCC made an unsupported claim that giving cable companies monopolies on broadband Internet cable service, thereby doing away with open access, will spawn more competition. Where was the empirical evidence that would justify the claim? In reality, such deregulation portends less competition, not more, from independent service providers.

Even if giving giant cable corporations monopolies on cable modem service could encourage more investment in relevant technologies, not all "innovations" are worth having and some may be grotesquely antidemocratic, for example, using innovative filtering technologies to build a wall around the Internet, and increasing the speed and efficiency by which government propaganda reaches consumers. The Court's decision simply covered up the fact that there was in fact *no* justified defense given by the FCC for its construction. The more *plausible* explanation (not at all a justification) is this: by giving big cable business what it wants (namely, big money), big government will get what it wants in return, which is control over what people are permitted to know.

By deferring to the FCC instead of exercising its own judicial discretion in determining what really was reasonable, the Court defeated the point of having an independent, ultimate court of appeals in the first place. This is to provide checks and balances on the activities of the other two branches of government, and to settle controversial, politically significant cases with far-reaching social consequences. Instead, it abandoned its constitutional charge to protect the First Amendment right of all Americans to freedom of speech in cyberspace from encroachment by big businesses acting in tandem with federal government.

In the second place, the Court's appeal to *Chevron* may not have been lawful by its own admission. The Court stated:

> A court's prior judicial construction of a statute trumps an agency construction otherwise entitled to Chevron deference only if the prior court decision holds that its construction follows from the unambiguous terms of the statute and thus leaves no room for agency discretion. This principle follows from Chevron itself.[7]

In 1999, before the FCC rendered its construction in 2002, the U.S. 9th Circuit Court of Appeals, in *AT&T v. Portland*, held that its construction of the 1996 Telecommunication Act followed from the unambiguous terms of the statute:

> Under the Communications Act, this principle of telecommunications common carriage governs cable broadband as it does other means of Internet transmission such as telephone service and DSL, "regardless of the facilities used" 47 U.S.C. S 153(46). The Internet's protocols themselves manifest a related principle called "end-to-end": control lies at the ends of the network where the users are, leaving a simple network that is neutral with respect to the data it transmits, like any common carrier. On this rule of the Internet, the codes of the legislator and the programmer agree.[8]

Here, the 9th Circuit Court was quite clear that there was no ambiguity about whether cable broadband must be regarded as a telecommunications service and, hence, subject to common carriage. It stated that "the codes of the legislator and the programmer agree." The only one who claimed any ambiguity was the Court.

According to *Chevron*, agencies' constructions are "given controlling weight unless they are arbitrary, capricious, or manifestly contrary to the statute." As you can see, the FCC's construction was all of these things. As a result, giant cable companies can now enjoy a monopoly on high-speed, cable Internet. As discussed below, not only are these monoliths poised to noncompetitively control the price of their services, thereby preventing poorer citizens from broadband access, they are now able to monitor and control the content of information that can be accessed by millions of American through these pipes.

The main alternative to high-speed Internet (broadband) via cable is modem connectivity via Digital Subscriber Line (DSL) service over telephone lines. Telephone companies have traditionally been required by government to share their lines with other ISPs, thereby assuring greater competition and diversity in content. But in *Brand X*, the Court gave the FCC the right to abandon this common carriage requirement to render it consistent with the broadband cable industry. As a result, just three weeks after the decision was handed down, the FCC seized the opportunity to grant this right, effectively ushering in the beginning of the end of free-access Internet.

The Telecom's "Pay for Play" Plan: The Next Step toward the Demise of Net Neutrality

Brand X set the legal stage for a further maneuver in challenging the free Internet. As a consequence of the *Brand X* decision, the giant telecom and telephone companies like Comcast, Verizon, and AT&T had overcome a major hurdle in gaining control of Internet content, namely control over the conduit of transmission. Now these behemoth companies want to exploit this right by setting up tollbooths on the Internet.

According to this "pay for play" plan, only content providers with deep pockets, such as Time Warner, News Corp, Viacom, and Disney would be allowed optimum Internet connectivity (bandwidth). This would mean that Americans logging on to the Internet would be able to connect quickly and securely to the Web sites of these rich and powerful companies, while leaving the rest of the Internet community spinning out in cyberspace, unable to get their messages heard. The net result would be the demise of Internet neutrality. No longer would all of us, including most independent media Web sites, have an equal voice within a free and democratic forum. The news Americans would receive online would instead resemble that of the corporate news networks that presently monopolize the cable, radio, and broadcast news.[9] As such, online news would be filtered through a politico-corporate web of censorship, government propaganda, and deception.

Powerful telecom lobbies in Congress with the potential to make campaign contributions to politicians who are willing to do their bidding give the telecoms a formidable voice in the political arena; not to mention the power of the vast telecom-media empire to give congresspersons who play the game favorable airtime. On the other side of the equation is the awesome government power to grant corporate mergers, relax national media caps, give tax breaks, offer lucrative government contracts (especially for national defense), as well as "punish" an uncooperative company (Qwest is one example) by taking away some of these perks—or perhaps regulating the corporation out of existence altogether. Caught in this bilateral trajectory of quid pro quo, it is not hard to see how the public's right to a free net can receive the short end of the stick.

Under the Obama administration, there have been some efforts to protect net neutrality against these opposing politico-corporate forces. In September 2009, FCC Chair Julius Genachowski proposed strengthening of the principles that guide the FCC in enforcing communications laws.[10] The previous principles adopted by the Kevin Martin chaired FCC in 2005 enjoined that network operators not prevent users from accessing lawful content, applications, and services, and that they not prohibit users from attaching safe devices to the network. Genachowski proposed adding a principle of nondiscrimination, holding that "broadband providers cannot discriminate against particular Internet content or applications"; and a principle of transparency according to which, "providers of broadband Internet access must be transparent about their network management practices."

The transparency principle comes after a ruling by the FCC in 2008 against Comcast, which had made a practice of controlling Internet traffic by selectively blocking or slowing the transfer of large files that use certain types of file-sharing software. While the FCC had instructed Comcast not to block files, it still failed to assess a fine, and Comcast has continued to argue that its management of bandwidth is legal.[11]

Comcast's practice of controlling Internet traffic was brought to the attention of the FCC only because an Internet user figured out that his attempts at sharing public domain recordings of old barbershop recordings were being stifled. It was only because of this person making it known to others in the Internet community that the FCC was able to learn about Comcast's file-blocking activities. The proposed principle of transparency aims at improving providers' public accountability by increasing their openness about their management policies.

Nevertheless, in the absence of any clear legislation that prevents such violations of net neutrality, it is likely that the giant Internet service providers will continue to become more emboldened in their efforts to determine what content we can access through the net. For example, in 2005, AT&T was gearing up to create a "pay for play" system, according to which they would charge their premium web companies more for preferential treatment of their traffic. In late 2006, AT&T agreed to put its plan on hold as a condition of the FCC's granting its merger with BellSouth.[12]

The Congressional Battle over Net Neutrality

At the time of this writing, Congress has yet to pass legislation that clearly protects net neutrality. In 2009, the Internet Freedom Preservation Act was introduced in the House amending the Communications Act of 1934 to "protect the right of consumers to access lawful content, run lawful applications, and use lawful services of their choice on the Internet."[13] And President Obama had verbalized the importance of net neutrality. However, there was ongoing, strong opposition in Congress, especially from Republicans, such as Kay Bailey Hutchison (S.R., Texas), who had taken the standard telecom line that any such attempt to regulate the Internet would stifle competition and decrease incentive to invest in the Internet.[14] There have also been resolutions, such as House Resolution 30, "Expressing the sense of the House of Representatives that in order to continue aggressive growth in our Nation's telecommunications and technology industries, the United States Government should 'Get Out of the Way and Stay Out of the Way.'"[15]

It is not clear how regulations of telecom and phone companies aimed at preserving net neutrality could have untoward consequences on competition and investment. True, regulations aimed at preserving net neutrality would decrease *unfair* competition by preventing giant corporations who control the pipes from blocking and interfering with the content of their competitors. Also true, such regulations could stem incentives to invest in questionable Internet practices, such as in technology that unlawfully tracks, censors, or blocks content.

Those who oppose regulating the Internet because they think that restricting "free enterprise" is somehow undemocratic confuse distinct concepts. It is a fallacy to suppose that profit maximization equates to democracy. To the contrary, in the present corporate context, it equates to the marginalization of any perspectives that are not cost-effective. Preserving freedom and democracy on the net may not be cost-effective for the giant telecoms.

The Internet owes its growth and present-day prosperity to its free, interactive, and democratic spirit, not to an insatiable corporate appetite for maximizing profit. It is, therefore, not surprising that, under the influence of the latter, in concert with self-interested government having leverage over these corporations' bottom line, the Internet should undergo an identity crisis. In fact, this change in identity has already begun. Witness the ever-increasing, corporate presence of the likes of Fox and NBC on the net.

As there does not appear to be an end in sight to such corporatization, the Internet is presently in grave danger of becoming an extension of the corporate media, owned and operated by a few giant corporations that control the information Americans receive. This trend toward media consolidation and oligopoly threatens to infect the Internet just as it has radio, broadcast, and cable TV. In the case of these traditional media, the transition has not been politically benign. As was discussed in chapter 6, big money has teamed with politics to usher in an age in which quid pro quo between mainstream media corporations and government largely defines what Americans see and hear. Sadly, this is the same dysfunctional relationship that now threatens to undermine net neutrality.

But this does not mean that government cannot bear a functional, regulatory relationship with giant corporations, such as mainstream media and telecom companies. For example, net neutrality and democracy can be preserved by regulations that require ISPs to be more transparent about their operating policies; or that prevent ISPs from discriminating against the small Web site operator; or that prevent ISPs from selectively filtering out Web sites on the basis of a political bias. In such cases, insisting that government should "Get Out of the Way and Stay Out of the Way" is both oversimplified and dangerous. The past decade has provided a lesson about the need to regulate financial institutions. The lesson learned may be equally as edifying with respect to the Internet. However, once Internet freedom has been destroyed, it may be far more difficult to resurrect it than it has been to affect an economic recovery. The history of oppressive regimes has shown it easier to lose freedom than to regain it.

Nor is the value of freedom and democracy purely quantifiable in monetary terms. This value is about the quality of the lives of Americans, not about how much money is produced, even if this money "trickles down" from big business to the average American. A very oppressive government is still consistent with making economic provisions for those subject to it. An America in which the Internet becomes a weapon of government to control and manipulate its citizens is a danger to democratic and free living, even if (and this is a stretch) it proved to be sound economic policy. Unfortunately, politicians who are currently walking lockstep with the telecoms in favoring "getting out of the way and staying out of the way" have little vision of what America would be losing if the free and democratic nature of the net were usurped.

Searching for Truth in a Web of Deceit

It is not likely that we will wake up one day and discover that the Internet is no longer free and democratic. The chilling truth is that we may never find out. Like Alice in Wonderland, a false "reality" can be constructed that is internally consistent even if it bears little resemblance to truth. Thus, few Americans saw through it when the Bush administration fabricated foreign intelligence to justify a war in Iraq, sent an army of "military analysts" into the mainstream media to confirm these "facts," and "edited" the reports of embedded journalists to fit the war policy.

Relatively few Americans were able to realize that they were caught in a web of deception. But those Americans who did realize it were kept informed largely through news sources on the net, including alternative media and news from foreign Web sites. For example, the American mainstream media censored the Downing Street memo story, which had been leaked by the *London Times*. The Downing Street memo contained the minutes of a July 22, 2002, meeting of British officials discussing the Bush administration's attempt to fabricate a justification for going to war in Iraq—"the intelligence and facts," it said, "were being fixed around the policy." Were it not for the Internet, which enabled access to the British press and independent media sites that picked up the story and ran it, even fewer, if any, Americans would have even known about it.

But what if the search engines did not search for independent media and foreign Web sites? While the Internet comprises a vast sea of information, a search engine is usually necessary to find what one is looking for. Consider how much less resourceful the net would be if one could only access sites for which one knew the URL. So, what if the behemoth corporation Google and its more recent Microsoft rival, Bing, did not permit Americans to readily access foreign and independent news sites? What if Google.com were like Google.cn?

The latter is the version of the Google search engine that, since 2005, had served the People's Republic of China. Built in compliance with the block list of the Chinese government, when searches for keywords prohibited by the Chinese government are conducted, it displays the message, "In accordance with local laws, regulations and policies, part of the search result is not shown"; and in some cases, the search results are blocked entirely.

In June 2009, the Chinese government ordered Google to suspend foreign Web site searches entirely on the basis of a report by a Chinese government-backed Internet watchdog, which claimed that Google was "disseminating pornography and vulgar information" from abroad. Unfortunately, Google capitulated.[16]

In December 2009, Google became the target of a sophisticated cyber attack aimed at accessing the gmail accounts of Chinese human rights activists. While Google did not officially accuse the Chinese government of sponsoring these attacks, the Chinese government denounced Google for insinuating as much. On the other hand, the popular alternative Chinese search engine, Baidu, enjoyed the support of the Chinese government, making it difficult for Google to compete. Moreover, Baidu continued to show large growth, nearly 40 percent in 2009, and by February 2010 had captured 60.9 percent of the Chinese market share compared to Google's 31.8 percent.[17] In fact, Google characterized its own revenues from the Chinese market as "insignificant."[18] Thus it was not surprising that, in March, 2010, Google shut down its search engine in mainland China.

Citing its discomfort with the Chinese government's censorship requirement as its official reason for discontinuing its mainland service, Google took its operation to Hong Kong where it could operate outside Chinese law, including the Chinese government's censorship requirement. Google then redirected all Google.cn traffic within mainland China to Google.com.hk in Hong Kong. So, all Google searches launched from inside the Chinese mainland must now pass through the "Great Firewall" operated by the Chinese government. That is, all traffic redirected from Google.cn to its unfiltered search engine, Google.com.hk, is now filtered by the Chinese government.

It remains to be seen how Google will respond in the future to the changing tide of the Chinese market. However, Google's past history of complying with the Chinese government in building and maintaining a government-censored search engine is a disturbing reminder of how corporate power can yield to the authority holding the purse strings. Google was willing to censor Web sites according to the demands of one of the world's most notorious transgressors of human rights. So, what reason could there be to think that, as the world's largest Internet search engine provider, it would not also be willing, for profit, to build a "Great Firewall," around the rest of the world?

Clearly, how supportive of Internet freedom Google will be depends largely on its cost-benefit analysis. Thus, while Google has defended net neutrality over a tiered system, this could be predicted based on its narrow, self-interested profit incentive. If a tiered system were implemented, Google would have to pay ISP's like Comcast for play; and since Google is a major player, its operating costs would significantly cut into its profit. On the other hand, if Google were to find out that it could attain a special exemption due to its essential role as a search engine operator, it is predictable that Google would capitulate to a "pay for play system." Accordingly, profitability is an extremely fragile basis upon which to ground net neutrality. Without government regulations, it is unreasonable to expect behemoth corporations like Google (or Microsoft/Bing) to choose not to "be evil."

Meanwhile, while corporate giants like Google and Comcast vie for profit, the plot thickens as the Pentagon intercedes with its own plan for amassing power and control over the world's information network.

8

The Global Firewall:
Internet as a Military Weapon
of Mass Deception and World
Domination

The idea of reinventing the free architecture of the Internet to a form etched in state-control has historical antecedents. As was mentioned in Chapter 1, in 1997, a neoconservative think tank emerged called The Project for the New American Century (PNAC). Its main mission was to promote corporate globalization and the increase in U.S. military dominance throughout the world. This included defeating all regimes opposed to U.S. corporate interests. In its blueprint of what would be required for the transition, it stressed the necessity of government control of the Internet. In one of its documents entitled "Rebuilding America's Defenses" (2000), the PNAC stated,

> An America incapable of protecting its interests or that of its allies in space or the "infosphere" will find it difficult to exert global political leadership.... [A]s with space, access to and use of cyberspace and the Internet are emerging elements in global commerce, politics and power. Any nation wishing to assert itself globally must take account of this other new "global commons."[1]

Speaking of "cyber-war" it stated:

> Although ... the role of the Defense Department in establishing "control," or even what "security" on the Internet means, requires a consideration of a host of legal, moral and political issues, there nonetheless will remain an imperative to be able to deny America and its allies' enemies the ability to

Table 8.1 Successive stages toward a state-controlled Internet

Stages	Description
1 Corporatize	Give telecoms the legal authority and means to control the flow of information across the Internet pipes and to establish the dominance of mainstream corporate media on the Net.
2 Sanitize/Propagandize	Censor information that is critical of government policies. Inject false or deceptive information favorable to government policy into Internet news.
3 Militarize	Bring total net content under government control through use of filtering technologies with algorithms and definitions preprogrammed by government.
4 Globalize	Enclose as much of the "free" world as possible inside one "Global Firewall"

disrupt or paralyze either the military's or the commercial sector's computer networks. Conversely, an offensive capability could offer America's military and political leaders an invaluable tool in disabling an adversary in a decisive manner.[2]

It is disconcerting to think what the terms "control" and "security" might portend for a militaristic government bent on defeating its "enemies." Indeed, we have already witnessed the erosion of privacy through the passage of FISA protections that effectively allow warrantless spying of millions of Americans. The Total Information Awareness (TIA) technologies are already being harnessed to police the Internet and e-mail activities of American citizens. It is not much of a stretch from here to suppose that government is (or soon will be) blocking and constraining content it deems an affront to "national security." At the present juncture, in light of the aforementioned legal, political, and corporate realities, it is also not difficult to envision the progressive stages the net might undergo in being transformed into a vehicle of world domination:

Stage 1: Corporatizing the Net

As was discussed in the Chapter 7, the *Brand X* Supreme Court decision has already "corporatized" the Internet by giving telecom and phone companies like Comcast and AT&T the authority to control the Internet pipes; and these companies are now aggressively attempting to establish a tiered system in which only Web site operators who have the financial means to pay for fast bandwidth will have a decisive voice on the net. This would include a handful of consolidated mainstream media corporations such as Fox/News Corp, CBS/Viacom, Clear Channel, and the *New York Times.*

Stage 2: Sanitizing/Propagandizing the Net

As was discussed in Chapter 6, the conventional mainstream news venues (broadcast television, cable, radio, newspapers) have already been substantially "sanitized" and "propagandized." The government has aggressively enlisted the help of public relations firms, such as the Rendon Group to engage in "information warfare" and "perception management." Such firms have screened embedded journalists on the basis of how supportive they have been of government war policy; injected government propaganda into foreign presses; placed phony news into local network affiliate coverage; recruited "military analysts" to use as "Trojan Horses" for injecting government propaganda into network and cable television news programming; used top secret National Security Agency (NSA) clearance to spy on journalists using powerful TIA surveillance equipment; and, thereby, anticipated unfavorable news reports so that responses could be speedily generated, even before these unfavorable news stories break.

Insofar as mainstream media already has a strong presence on the Internet, such sanitized and propagandized "news" is already a fact of the worldwide web. If the corporate control of the Internet moves to the next level of a tiered system of "pay for play," it is predictable that this presence will become dominant, and that independent news media will be largely phased out. Web sites permitted on this now private roadway will be required to comply with the demands of the net's corporate owners, who in turn will take marching orders from the government.

Stage 3: Militarizing the Net

Stage 2 paints a rather bleak picture of the future of the Internet; but it can get even worse by moving to the next stage of being "militarized." Stage 3 is the transformative level envisioned by the PNAC. It would involve harnessing e-mail and web-filtering technologies not merely to intercept and disable service attacks, viruses, and other attempts to shut down the Internet. It would also involve deployment of content-filtering technologies using sophisticated algorithms to block e-mail and web transmissions of whatever is deemed harmful to "national security." "Harmful" in this context might mean different things for different government administrations. At the hands of an excessively paranoid and militant administration, it could involve the virtual annihilation of freedom of speech. Indeed, saying that "American is no longer free" could be viewed as subversive. Further, since such "subversive" speech would not only be blocked but could also end up in quarantine for inspection by the "Internet police," the potential for abuse of human rights at this stage should not be underestimated.

In Stage 2 (Sanitizing/Propagandizing the Net) the NSA copies and screens all electronic transmissions, including all domestic and overseas e-mails, web searches, phone calls (voice-over IP and telephone modem transmissions). Although the content of web pages and e-mail transmissions is being "read" by the state, it is still not systematically being blocked through the use of web and e-mail filtering technologies. However, these technologies exist and the Department of Defense has had a long-standing interest in them.

By the mid 1990's, content-filtering technologies had in fact become a major interest of the Department of Defense. Security software companies, such as Secure Computing (now part of McAfee), which developed software under national defense contracts to protect military and diplomatic information, began to install content-filtering capabilities onto their firewall security systems. For example Secure's Sidewinder product incorporated "news filtering" capabilities:

> News Filtering—If so selected by the System Administrator, the Sidewinder will block posting to embargoed news groups.... [T]he screening algorithms can also be used to filter incoming and outgoing news on the basis of content similarity to postings deemed to be in violation of the site's policy. Outgoing news which has been blocked by the filter is forwarded to the System Administrator for disposition. Incoming news which has been blocked by the filter is discarded.[3]

If used by the DOD to enforce government policies and protect "national security," such "news filtering" technologies could render the First Amendment right to freedom of the press null and void. Moreover, such a capacity to notify a system administrator "for disposition" portends a police state. As was mentioned in Chapter 6, the NSA appears to have already conducted surveillance of journalists and news organizations. However, the stories generated by these journalists and news organizations critical of government policy have not to date been systematically blocked by the state. Nor have the purveyors of such news been subjected to the Orwellian equivalent of serving time in the "Ministry of Love."

However, server-side filtering technologies have been routinely used in the private, corporate sector to block employee's outgoing e-mail messages, and then to alert system administrators or quarantine blocked messages for review by corporate officers. In fact, according to one recent study, 41 percent of the largest companies surveyed (ones having 20,000 or more employees) reported that they hire staff for the sole purpose of reading or analyzing the content of employees' outgoing e-mail messages. According to the same study, 26 percent of companies surveyed terminated an employee for violating a company e-mail policy in the last 12 months.[4] Such data is remarkable insofar as it signals the willingness of the private sector, in particular giant corporations, to police employees.

The main purpose companies have for engaging in such policing of outgoing e-mail is not to block forbidden news subscriptions, but rather to prevent release of sensitive or confidential information, or otherwise inappropriate content. Still, these concerns are largely or entirely bottom-line driven. Thus, a company that felt its bottom line would be threatened by not attempting to screen for news content would also be motivated to do so. Since the state has the authority and power to tighten the reigns on large companies that fail to conform to government demands, the disposition of large companies (not just telecoms and phone companies) to violate the privacy of their employees sets the stage for state control.

In the militarized Internet stage, "national security" always trumps privacy. Moreover, the state defines what is in the interest of national security, which includes what conforms to the political interests of the powers that be. In other words, the state determines what information we can know, and it places us all under surveillance to ensure that the forbidden information remains out of public reach. This is what we can expect if the current progression away from net neutrality continues down the slippery slope generated by each progressive stage.

Stage 4: Globalizing the Net

This last stage in the progression toward state control of the Net involves encapsulating the world, or as much of it as possible, behind a "Global Firewall" managed by government with the cooperation of the telecommunication giants. As conceived by PNAC, this stage would use corporate globalization as a mechanism to attain U.S. military dominance throughout the world. According to this vision, the Internet would figure as a key element "in global commerce, politics and power"; for whoever controls the Internet (and cyberspace) has a decisive advantage in attaining global control.

Indeed, it remains to be seen *who* will, in fact, control the Internet in the future. As discussed in Chapter 11, there are presently antinationalistic currents moving the world toward world government. With the rise of transnational corporations, the breakdown of trade barriers, and digital technologies that connect the far corners of the earth, there has been movement toward the breakdown of national boundaries and the restructuring of the world into more globalized units—for instance, the European Union and the significant possibility of a North American Union in the not-so-distant future. Thus, while it is reasonable to suppose that the United States would play a major role in such a "new world order," the PNAC's nationalistic concept of world domination may itself be transformed as the world becomes more consolidated.

In any case, it is clear that the giant telecoms and phone companies, such as Comcast and AT&T are poised to play a decisive role in helping the United States or some other politico-corporate world organization attain global, cyber-dominance. Now deferent to the United States government, these companies already assist in monitoring all electronic communications that pass through American switches. Down the slippery slope, they are also prepared to control the content of the Internet through a "pay for play" system likely to be dominated by mainstream corporate media like Fox, NBC, CBS, ABC, and CNN. These corporate media foot soldiers of the U.S. government would accordingly present sanitized and propagandized versions of reality that reflect the ideals and principles of the administration in power. Once militarized, NSA surveillance would progress to a system of Total Information Control through content filtering, blocking, quarantining, analysis, and enforcement of self-serving, politically motivated, government policies.

Israeli wiretapping firms already appear to be assisting telecom and phone companies, such as Verizon and AT&T in conducting the NSA's warrantless spying program,[5] so it is not unreasonable to suppose that Israel will work cooperatively with the United States or other world authority in helping it to expand the global outreach of its fire wall. Encapsulating "liberated" nations, such as Iraq is also reasonable insofar as the United States has already made inroads in injecting American propaganda into Iraqi news (see chapter 6).

Echelon: The Global Total Information Awareness Network

In fact, progress has already been made toward encapsulating the world inside a global, transnational TIA network. Since the 1970s, during the cold war with the Soviet Union, the U. S. government has spearheaded a partnership with the United Kingdom, Canada, Australia, and New Zealand to expand its surveillance capabilities globally. This involved deployment of "Echelon," the code name for a massive global surveillance network for data capture, exchange, and analysis. A 2001 European parliamentary investigative report described the system as follows:

> Within Europe, all email, telephone and fax communications are routinely intercepted by the United States National Security Agency, transferring all target information from the European mainland ... to [The headquarter of NSA] ... a global surveillance system that stretches around the world to form a targeting system on all of the key Intelsat satellites used to convey most of the world's satellite phone calls, internet, email, faxes and telexes. ... [u]nlike many of the electronic spy systems developed during the cold war, ECHELON is designed for primarily non-military targets: governments, organisations and businesses in virtually every country.... Five nations share the results with the US as the senior partner.... Britain, Canada, New Zealand and Australia are very much acting as subordinate information servicers [6]

Each member state of this so-called UKUSA alliance was purportedly responsible for monitoring different regions of the globe. Thus, in 2000, the United States was reported to have used its vast array of spy satellites and listening posts to monitor most of Latin America, Asia, Asiatic Russia, and northern China. Great Britain monitored Europe and Russia west of the Urals, and Africa; Australia monitored Indochina, Indonesia, and southern China; New Zealand monitored the western Pacific; and post-cold war Canada monitored Central and South America.[7]

Information extracted by global outposts was then sent to the main hub of Echelon at Fort Mead, Maryland, where it was analyzed by the NSA. Such analyses of raw data were seldom shared with the other UKUSA members. As technology shifted from transmission of information via microwaves and radio waves to light traveling through fiber-optic cables, Echelon's space satellite technologies became outdated. Thousands of miles of fiber-optic cables were laid deep beneath the surface of the ocean, making it challenging to get at the cables. It also appeared that these cables could not be effectively tapped. However, such methods as fiber-optic splitting proved effective for data extraction and the obstacle of getting at the cables beneath the sea was circumvented by developing submarines specially equipped for purposes of installing taps. Accordingly, Echelon's technologies were updated and overhauled to address this changing climate of electronic transmission.

Further, TIA technologies were supposed to have been integrated with the global taps set up by the Echelon project. As such, the edifice may now exist on which to build a global firewall. Thus, instead of having optic splitters that copy but permit information to flow to the intended recipient, intercepted electronic communications, including e-mail and web traffic could be blocked when it fails to conform to U.S. government standards, thus globalizing American dominance in cyberspace. This gives chilling substance to PNAC's assertion that "access to and use of cyberspace and the Internet are emerging elements in global commerce, politics and power"; and that, "Any nation wishing to assert itself globally must take account of this other new 'global commons.'"

Unfortunately, unless the present trend toward politico-corporate control of media is contained, the possibility that such a global firewall will become a reality should be taken seriously. A significant key to halting or slowing this incremental, degenerative decline of Internet freedom must be to resist the attempt by the telecoms to implement a tiered system of Internet use and access. Once such a system is implemented, there will eventually be little to distinguish the content of the Internet from the present state of broadcast and cable network news and information. In fact, given the move to digital media, the Internet will become the primary if not exclusive host to these traditional media platforms.

It is important to emphasize that this process will not be sudden but will instead be subtle and gradual over time. Most Americans today do not even realize that there is such a progressive degeneration at hand, largely because the mainstream corporate media has downplayed or covered it up. And, while the increasing presence of the giant media companies on the net may be apparent to most Internet surfers, this is simply accepted as a benign fact about the Net. We simply think that, since cyberspace is unbounded, there will always be room enough for both behemoths and small, independent web operators. We do not take seriously the real danger that the former has the capacity (and the will) to crowd out and eviscerate its competition. In fact, most people do not even know about the legal and political forces now in motion, which aim at such crowding out of competition.

Even a cursory study of the history of mainstream media will demonstrate how media consolidation has provided the initial foray into the stifling of competition and, ultimately, the narrowing of diverse, independent voices speaking to us. It does not take rocket science to figure out that the same thing can and is happening to the Internet.

However, there should be even more concern about this trend when it comes to the Internet. This is because the Internet is a two-way, interactive information highway rather than a one-way information delivery system. It is a forum for free and independent discussion and back-and-forth between countless Internet users in a global community. Thus, people living clear across the world have the capacity to participate in an Internet forum and to have their voices heard. The traditional media platforms were never capable, nor were they ever conceived to create such a magnificently democratic forum. So the destruction of net neutrality and, ultimately, the commandeering (and hijacking) of the Net by the state is an even more serious and devastating assault on democracy than that which has taken place elsewhere in the mass media. This is not to discount the seriousness of the damage already done to the mainstream media. As discussed in Chapter 5, the extent to which Americans have been manipulated and kept in the dark by a vast military, industrial, corporate media web should set off Orwellian alarms. Still, it can get so much worse if this media metastasis is also permitted to devour the Internet.

9

War is Peace: The War on Terror

In Orwell's *1984,* the true meaning of the Party's slogan, "War is Peace," is revealed in the revolutionary book, *The Theory and Practice of Oligarchical Collectivism,* presumed to have been written by the enemy of state, Emmanual Goldstein. As conveyed, the key idea is that, by embroiling a nation in perpetual war, the ruling party is able to keep the masses ignorant, poor, and dependent on government. This is because war economies direct production to military arsenals instead of education, health services, and other social goods that could otherwise have improved the lives of the masses. "War is a way of shattering to pieces, or pouring into the stratosphere, or sinking in the depths of the sea, materials which might otherwise be used to make the masses too comfortable, and hence, in the long run, too intelligent."[1]

Included in this Orwellian idea is that war is not fought to be won. In the case of Oceana, war was unwinnable because there were two other super-powers that were equally matched to itself in power:

> The very word 'war,' therefore, has become misleading. It would probably be accurate to say that by becoming continuous war has ceased to exist. . . . The effect would be much the same if the three super-states, instead of fighting one another, should agree to live in perpetual peace, each inviolate within its own boundaries. For in that case each would still be a self-contained universe, freed for ever from the sobering influence of external danger. A peace that was truly permanent would be the same as a permanent war. This . . . is the inner meaning of the Party slogan: War is Peace.[2]

America's Orwellian War on Terror

Ironically, depicted in this fictional account of war are some salient features of waging a "war on terror" in twenty-first-century America:

1. Like Oceana's war, such a "war" is, in principle, incapable of ever being won, because it is impossible to ever completely eradicate terrorism. A war on terror is therefore, in principle, *endless.*

2. Like the enemy of Oceana, the enemy in a war on terror is obscure and subject to change. Oceana had been allied with Eurasia and at war with Eastasia, when all records were suddenly changed by the Ministry of Truth to reflect the opposite. Similarly, in a global war on terror, virtually anyone and everyone can be branded a "terrorist" or "unlawful enemy combatant," including, for example, an antiwar protester. Because these terms are vague, they can conveniently be pinned on virtually anyone who opposes the government's war policy or who provides an excuse for going to war. Accordingly, Saddam Hussein provided such an excuse for the Bush administration to invade Iraq.

3. In twenty-first-century America, as in Oceana, the idea of a war that cannot be won finds it protractors in those who wield money and power. Thus, for the corporate CEO, the gains of war are largely aimed at feeding the corporate appetite for profit. For example, the goal of a military contractor, such as Lockheed Martin is not to win a war but rather to profit off of it. Therefore, the longer the war lasts, the more profitable it becomes. In this manner, a war on terror, which is perpetual war, is a corporate bonanza.

4. However, the present war on terror has helped the corporate sector to expand its bottom line at the expense of the masses. On October 2009, President Obama signed the largest military budget in world history, US$680 billion for the Pentagon, which included US$130 billion to fight wars in Iraq and Afghanistan. For top contractors, such as Lockheed Martin, Northrop Grumman, and General Dynamics, this meant lucrative wartime government contracts.

   On the other hand, such enormous military budgets portend reduction in funding for social services, education, and other non-military employment opportunities. Thus, for 2010, the health and human services budget was US$76.8 billion and, for education, only US$46.7 billion.[3] This compares with prewar totals for fiscal year 1997, under President William Jefferson Clinton, of US$270 billion for national defense; US$124 billion for health; and US$53 billion for education.[4]

   Further, while corporate wealth may be presumed to "trickle down" to the people through the creation of corporate jobs, more realistically, the drive for profit that propels giant corporations today has led to outsourcing of cheap (including slave) labor and unsatisfactory employee benefits and salaries for the working class. Accordingly, the tendency of a twenty-first-century war economy aimed at fighting a perennial war on terror is to support big business, especially military contractors, while failing to substantially offset the skewed distribution of wealth by adding jobs for the American people.

5. In this climate of perpetual war on terror, war ceases to exist and becomes a state of peace wherein we, as Americans, live in a self-contained universe, "freed for ever from the sobering influence of external danger." However, this "freedom" must be purchased at the price of relinquishing our civil liberties, especially privacy. Not only is a war on terror perpetual, it is also *without boundaries*, having no geographical limits. It can be fought globally—in some far off corner of the universe; but it can also be fought in the living room of an American suspected of being a terrorist.

6. Mass, warrantless surveillance is, therefore, a necessary corollary of a war on terror. In order to hunt down and capture terrorists, who may be hiding anywhere and everywhere, it is necessary that government have the technological means of mass search and seizure. It is in this manner that the current war on terror has provided the pretext for the systematic invasion of privacy of millions of Americans (indeed billions of human beings throughout the world) through mass, warrantless surveillance. This is because such an Orwellian climate of state control becomes indispensible to rooting out terrorists where they hide—so the argument goes.

7. The current war on terror, like the perennial war waged in Oceana, is based on mass manipulation and deception. It has been sold to the American public on the basis of wholesale fabrication of the rationale for going to war in the first place. The true basis for this pretext has not been to protect the borders of America against future terrorist attacks; relatively few dollars have actually been spent on securing these boards. If this rationale has entered into the calculus, it has never been a primary reason for going to war in Iraq and Afghanistan. The primary reason has instead always been the amassing of geopolitical power and world dominance. Unfortunately, this is not groundless speculation. It can be documented.

The War on Terror as Pretext for Preemptive War

In a speech delivered on October 7, 2002, prior to taking the United States to war in Iraq, George W. Bush declared,

> America must not ignore the threat gathering against us. Facing clear evidence of peril, *we cannot wait for the final proof*—the smoking gun—that could come in the form of a mushroom cloud. ... Saddam Hussein must

disarm himself—or, for the sake of peace, we will lead a coalition to disarm him.[5] (italics added)

In September 2002, the month prior to the delivery of these famous lines, the Bush administration advanced its "National Security Strategy" for the United States, which, it claimed, was necessary for dealing with the rising threat posed by international terrorism. This document stated,

> The gravest danger our Nation faces lies at the crossroads of radicalism and technology. Our enemies have openly declared that they are seeking weapons of mass destruction, and evidence indicates that they are doing so with determination. . . . And, as a matter of common sense and self-defense, America will act against such emerging threats *before they are fully formed*. . . . History will judge harshly those who saw this coming danger but failed to act. In the new world we have entered, the only path to peace and security is the path of action.[6]

Here was a new war strategy that contradicted international law and the United Nations Charter, which prohibits the use of international force that is not in self-defense after an armed attack or undertaken with the approval of the United Nations.[7] The offical purpose of this new doctrine of justified warfare was to protect the U.S. homeland against "regimes that harbor, support, and use terrorism to achieve their political goals" by preemptively attacking them, even if these "regimes" happened to be sovereign nations. It claimed a right to invade sovereign nations preemptively, just as long as they were *thought* to be a threat to "national security." In fact, this new policy of preemptive war for fighting a "war on terror" was largely a pretext for setting in motion a plan that would have been ill-received by most had it been honestly stated.

Consider this telling advice of Hermann Goering, the Reich Marshal of Adolph Hitler:

> Why of course the people don't want war. But, after all, it is the leaders of the country who determine the policy and it is always a simple matter to drag the people along, whether it is a democracy, or a fascist dictatorship, or a parliament, or a communist dictatorship. Voice or no voice, the people can always be brought to the bidding of the leaders. That is easy. All you have to do is tell them they are being attacked, and denounce the peacemakers for lack of patriotism and exposing the country to danger. It works the same in any country.[8]

As was discussed in Chapter 6, the U.S. government had systematically engaged in "information warfare" and "information management" aimed at convincing the American public of the justness of the war in Iraq. In the years following the September 11, 2001, attacks on the U.S. homeland leading up to the launching of the Iraq war in March 2003, the Bush administration, using the mainstream media as its mouthpiece, had kept the image of the twin towers falling asunder emblazed in the minds of millions of Americans, and had artfully linked Saddam Hussein's Iraqi regime to this image, albeit groundlessly. In this environment of heightened terror alerts and the repeated reminder of "evil doers" who "hate our freedom," it was patriotic to wave the American flag and "support the troops." This was what was expected of "loyal" and "patriotic" Americans, while to demonstrate against the war or to advocate bringing the troops home was "anti-American," "unpatriotic," and even "treasonous."

In fact, the Bush administration had sought to associate the peace movement with those who advocated appeasement of Adolph Hitler (in particular, with Neville Chamberlain's appeasement policies in dealing with the Nazis). "In the 20th century," said George W. Bush, "some chose to appease murderous dictators, whose threats were allowed to grow into genocide and global war. In this century, when evil men plot chemical, biological and nuclear terror, a policy of appeasement could bring destruction of a kind never before seen on this earth." The politics of fear was, thus, used to frighten and intimidate American citizens into submissively supporting the new American concept of just war in terms of preemption.

The "preemptive" war in Iraq and now the intensified "preemptive" war in Afghanistan had been set in motion by forces having little or nothing to do with fighting terrorism. In fact, these forces had been set in motion well before the September 11, 2001 attacks, and well before the Bush administration had come to power.

Preemptive War as a Pretext for Seeking Global Dominance

In 1992, under Dick Cheney's Defense Department, in the final months of the George H. W. Bush administration, White House staffers Paul Wolfowitz, I. Lewis Libby, and Zalmay Khalizad, drafted the Defense Planning Guidance (DPG). This document (which became known as the "Wolfowitz Doctrine") was an unofficial, internal document that advocated massive increases in defense spending for purposes of strategic proliferation and buildup of military defenses.

The Soviet Union had collapsed in 1991, opening up the opportunity for the United States to claim the title of preeminent world superpower. The purpose of the DPG was, thus, to fortify and maintain this status. To this purpose, the document advocated attacks with nuclear, chemical, or biological weapons on "regimes" that threatened its geopolitical interests; and it boldly proclaimed that, "the U.S. must show the leadership necessary to establish and protect a new order that holds the promise of convincing potential competitors that they need not aspire to a greater role or pursue a more aggressive posture to protect their legitimate interests." The DPG was also abundantly clear about what should be the United States's main objective in the Middle East, especially Iraq and Iran, which was to "remain the predominant outside power in the region and preserve U.S. and Western access to the region's oil."[9]

However, to the dissatisfaction of Cheney and company, the DPG was leaked to the *New York Times* and the *Washington Post,* who published excerpts from it.[10] Amid a public outcry, President George H. W. Bush retracted the document and it was substantially revised.

The original mission of the DPG was not lost, only postponed, however. In 1994, Senator John McCain presided as President of the New Citizenship Project, the main mission of which was to secure funding for the Project for the New American Century (PNAC). The point of the PNAC was, in turn, to advocate for the militant, geopolitical tenets of the DPG. In 1997, under the direction of William Kristol and Robert Kagan, who shared the "neo-conservative" ideals of the DPG, the PNAC was finally implemented.

As was discussed in Chapter 8, in 2000, the PNAC published a report entitled, "Rebuilding America's Defense" (RAD). This document was intended as a blueprint for the incoming George W. Bush administration to follow in affecting a transformation of the geopolitical military and national defense strategies for the twenty-first century. In fact, in 1999, even before this report surfaced, and before George W. Bush became president, the seeds were set for the new strategy. In a little discussed speech presented on September 23, 1999, to the Citadel, Bush declared, "Even if I am elected, I will not command the new military we create. That will be left to a president who comes after me. The results of our effort will not be seen for many years."[11]

It remains to be seen whether Barack Obama will emerge as the president to "command the new military" or whether this awesome task will be bequeathed to a subsequent American president, some other form of global power, or if nearly two decades of strategizing will never be fully actualized. Nevertheless, the Obama administration was bequeathed a war machine already set in motion by the Bush administration. This included the war in Afghanistan as well as Iraq; billions of dollars already paid out to a powerful military industrial complex; ongoing contracts with these behemoth corporations; and thousands of American lives already spent. Like Orwell's nation of Oceana, America was geared up and steeped in a culture of perpetual war.

10

Obama's War on Terror: Not Change We Can Believe In

On January 22, 2009, speaking at the State Department, Obama stated, "We are confronted by extraordinary, complex and interconnected global challenges: war on terror, sectarian division and the spread of deadly technology. We did not ask for the burden that history has asked us to bear, but Americans will bear it. We must bear it."[1] Here, at this early stage of his administration, Obama made clear what he expected all Americans to do, namely accept the "global" challenge of a "war on terror." And, on May 21, 2009, in his Guantanamo speech, in provocative terms reminiscent of George W. Bush, he drove his point home:

> In the midst of all these challenges, however, my single most important responsibility as President is to keep the American people safe.... This responsibility is only magnified in an era when an extremist ideology threatens our people, and technology gives a handful of terrorists the potential to do us great harm. We are less than eight years removed from the deadliest attack on American soil in our history. We know that al Qaeda is actively planning to attack us again. We know that this threat will be with us for a long time, and that we must use all elements of our power to defeat it.[2]

Here, Obama evoked the chilling image of the "deadliest attack on American soil in history," which he could have reasonably calculated would arouse fear of another 9/11 in the hearts of Americans; and he admonished that this threat would be with us "for a long time." Still, he told Americans that they must "defeat" it.

Obama's presidential campaign promise of "change you can believe in" has accordingly been muted by his demand that Americans accept the challenge of a "war on terror." While he has somewhat softened the rhetoric of war to include references to specific groups, such as war against al Qaeda,[3] this has been largely a cosmetic change dressed up to look like genuine change. The chilling imagery of the "deadliest attack on American soil in history" and a "war" waged against the militant religious extremists who were responsible for it is still being emblazoned in the hearts and minds of Americans; and all the while playing in the background is the somber tune of mounting casualties in two ongoing "preemptive" invasions of sovereign states, allegedly in order to "root out" the terrorists and "win the war." This is not change with any substance; nor is it something that one can (rationally) believe in.

Ever since the attacks of September 11, 2001, the American culture has revolved around such a "war." On a daily basis Americans have been inundated with movies, television shows, music, and mainstream media that carry the theme of terrorism and its "defeat." From counterterrorism shows such as NBC's "The Wanted" to the fear-mongering rants of Fox's Glenn Beck,[4] America has been transformed into a culture fixated on averting the next terrorist attack. Unfortunately, while it is distracted by this hobgoblin and its politico-corporate ambassadors, the veridical threat of withering civil liberties amid a burgeoning Orwellian culture, monitored and censored, festers beneath the radar of public consciousness.

Meanwhile, surveys poll Americans about whether we are "winning" this so-called "war" and Americans respond with increasing optimism.[5] But while the question is raised, there is rarely if ever raised the more sobering, and logically prior, question about whether there really is, or should be, such a war. This assumption is not typically questioned, because Americans have already been convinced that this so-called "war" is not only a real war, but also one that is vital to national security.

The War on Terror: Not Really War

In fact, the war on terror is a product and fabrication of an aggressive media blitz and public relations initiative launched by the Bush administration in the aftermath of the 9/11 attacks, which exploited these attacks for purposes of frightening, intimidating, and indoctrinating Americans into surrendering their civil liberties and rallying around the flag.[6]

Speaking of a "war on terror" can only be understood in a metaphorical sense not unlike speaking of a "war on drugs." Fighting drugs in some respects resembles a war, because it involves trying to remedy an evil that "threatens" the well-being of a nation and its people. But such a "war"— even one against a particular terrorist organization, such as al Qaeda—is not a military matter; it relates to organized crime and is, as such, a matter of law enforcement under the auspices of the criminal justice system.

In a nonmetaphorical sense, wars are (conceptually and historically) always temporally finite. They have a beginning and an end. They are also waged against an "enemy" of a recognized state, and this enemy typically wears the uniform of that state. Moreover, while we have experienced two "world wars," these wars have been geographically limited to the battlefield, and the personal living quarters of civilians have been off limits, at least in legitimate warfare.

As Michael Walzer explains, "The war convention rests first on a certain view of combatants, which stipulates their battlefield equality. But it rests more deeply on a certain view of noncombatants, which hold that they are men and women with rights and that they cannot be used for some military purpose, even if it is a legitimate purpose."[7] Indeed, it is terrorism itself—our purported "enemy"—that fails to meet the war convention on account of its failure to distinguish between civilian and military targets. And, ironically, a program of warrantless, mass surveillance of American civilians as an alleged strategy for fighting a war on terror fails to satisfy this convention, because it fails to respect the right of millions of civilians not to be spied on, and hence not to be used for some military purpose, "even if it is a legitimate one."

Thus, the war on terror is not really a legitimate war; nor is it even correctly called "war" in any but a metaphorical sense. It has neither beginning nor end; it is not waged against a recognized state, and, therefore, its enemy does not wear a recognized state uniform; it is not limited to the battlefield; and it does not obey the war convention of respecting the right of civilians not to be used for a military purpose.

Nevertheless, Americans have been successfully indoctrinated *to believe* that they are immersed in the fighting of a legitimate, real war, and that, as President Obama admonished, "we must bear it." Thus, in a May 2006 *Washington Post* poll, when asked if, *for purposes of detecting terrorist activities,* they would allow the National Security Agency (NSA) to keep track of every phone call (both domestic and foreign) they made and received, about two-thirds of Americans polled said it would be all right. They were willing to accept such an invasion of privacy, notwithstanding that it was illegal, for the sake of preventing another terrorist attack.

Unfortunately, in this climate of unblinking acceptance of a pseudo-war on terror, it is likely that the Total Information Awareness (TIA) project will gradually continue to escalate. That is, unless Americans begin to thinking critically about what they are being asked to bear, they will continue to accept more and more intrusions into their privacy—always for "their own protection"—as government with cooperation from corporate accomplices finds newer and more innovative means to control and manipulate the channels of public information.

If this Orwellian trend is to be reversed, then the war on terror must be unmasked for what it truly is, namely a clever and well-orchestrated use of corporate media and public relations firms to transform America into a militant culture of control aimed at world domination.

Unmasking the War on Terror

As was discussed in Chapter 9, a key mechanism of this global initiative is the doctrine of preemptive war. Indeed, seen in the light of its historical and ideological roots, "preemptive" here is largely euphemistic for wars fought to advance the economic and political interests of America in the maintenance of its preeminence as the world's sole superpower.

In its report on Rebuilding America's Defenses (RAD), The Project for the New American Century (PNAC) clearly laid out some of the main objectives under girding the preemptive war strategy. Unfortunately, these objectives, which were initiated during the Bush administration, have to a significant extent been embraced by the Obama administration.

Fighting and Winning Multiple, Simultaneous Major Wars

While winning the so-called "war on terror" is impossible, it does not follow that winning decisive victories in the process of fighting this perennial war is itself impossible. Among the core missions detailed in the RAD report was the rebuilding of America's defenses sufficient to "fight and decisively win multiple, simultaneous major theater wars."[8] And it explicitly advocated sending troops into Iraq regardless of whether Saddam Hussein was in power. According to RAD, "While the unresolved conflict with Iraq provides the immediate justification, the need for a substantial American force presence in the Gulf transcends the issue of the regime of Saddam Hussein."[9]

The RAD report also admonished, "Iran may well prove as large a threat to U.S. interests in the Gulf as Iraq has. And even should U.S.-Iranian relations improve retaining forward-based forces in the region would still be an essential element in U.S. security strategy given the longstanding American interests in the region."[10] Therefore, it had both Iraq and Iran in its sight as zones of multiple, simultaneous major wars for purposes of advancing "longstanding American interests in the region"—in particular, its oil.

The Obama administration has not disclaimed the possibility of unilaterally invading a sovereign nation to protect our "vital interests." In fact, in his "American Moment" speech of April 23, 2007, in language subject to interpretation, Obama admonished, "No President should ever hesitate to use force—unilaterally if necessary—to protect ourselves and *our vital interests* when we are attacked *or imminently threatened*" (emphasis added).[11] In August 2007, Obama warned Pakistani President Pervez Musharraf, that as president he would be prepared to send U.S. troops into Pakistan unilaterally if it failed to take action against Islamic extremists. In no uncertain terms, he stated, "The first step must be to get off the wrong battlefield in Iraq and take the fight to the terrorists in Afghanistan and Pakistan."[12] Further, he asserted that "There will be times when we must again play the role of the world's reluctant sheriff. This will not change—nor should it."[13]

Accordingly, Obama has expanded Bush's preemptive war on terror. In 2009, Obama increased missile strikes on anti-Pakistani government militants, which were carried out by unmanned drones inside Pakistan. He has also escalated deployment of U.S. troops in Afghanistan to fight the Taliban, and to fight al Qaeda along the Pakistani border.

Like the war in Iraq, the motivation for fighting a war in Afghanistan appears to have been largely motivated from the start by corporate interests. In 1998, Unocal, a major oil company had given up on its attempt to build an oil pipeline through Afghanistan that could have allowed the Central Asian republics to export energy to Western markets without using Russian routes. However, plans for the pipeline were thwarted by the Taliban, which refused to permit U.S. troops on the ground to guard the pipeline against attacks by hostiles.

It was clear that the pipeline was a pipedream unless a government was formed in Afghanistan that supported its construction; Hamid Karzai was such a leader. "Elected" in December 2004, Karzai had firm ties to the U.S. Defense Department and had allegedly also been a consultant for Unocal. In addition, Zalmay Khalilzed, a former Unocal lobbyist and consultant, became the U.S. Ambassador to Afghanistan in 2003.

Curiously, Condoleezza Rice, Secretary of State under George W. Bush, was a former CEO of Chevron Oil, which in 2005 purchased Unocal, and therewith its interest in the Trans-Afghan pipeline. In 2008, plans were again made to build the pipeline through Afghanistan. Work was to begin in 2010, and completion of the project was anticipated by 2014. It is, therefore, not surprising that in December 2009 Obama announced the deployment of an additional 30,000 troops to Afghanistan in the coming months.

Obama's penchant for the defense strategies of the Bush administration is also reflected by his having retained Robert Gates, the Secretary of Defense under the Bush administration, as his own Secretary of Defense.[14] This was one way to preserve continuity with the previous administration in war policies and planning. A break with the old guard might have signaled a change in the direction of U.S. war policy. Unfortunately, no such change appears imminent at the present juncture in time.

Designing and Deploying Global Missile Defense Systems

RAD also emphasized, as an additional core value, the need to "transform U.S. forces to exploit the 'revolution in military affairs.'" This included the design and deployment of a global ballistic missile defense system consisting of land-, sea-, air- and space-based components said to be capable of shielding the United States and its allies from "limited strikes" in the future by "rogue" nations, such as Iraq, North Korea, and Iran.

Consistent with advancing the geopolitical interests of the U.S., the RAD conceived such defense systems in the broader context of the promotion of world domination:

> Projecting conventional military forces or simply asserting political influence abroad, particularly in times of crisis, will be far more complex and constrained when the American homeland or the territory of our allies is subject to attack by otherwise weak rogue regimes capable of cobbling together a miniscule ballistic missile force. Building an effective, robust, layered, global system of missile defenses is a prerequisite for maintaining American preeminence.[15]

Here, the interest in such missile defenses was not that of shielding the homeland from an unprovoked missile attack but rather from one arising in the course of "projecting conventional military forces or simply asserting political influence abroad." In other words, the interest in such defenses was to allow the United States to carry out "preemptive" wars and other aggressive military and political actions aimed at world domination while protecting the U.S. homeland and that of its allies from retaliation.

So far, Obama has remained committed to going forward with continued development of such antiballistic systems. In September 2009, he decided not to locate a long-range, antiballistic missile system in Poland and the Czech Republic. However, he has remained resolute about the need for such missile systems for purposes of protecting against "rogue" nations, in particular Iran and North Korea.

About Iran, Obama stated, "President Bush was right that Iran's ballistic missile program poses a significant threat. And that's why I'm committed to deploying strong missile defense systems which are adaptable to the threats of the 21st century."[16] Since Obama judged that a shorter-range system would be more effective against the Iranian threat, he opted for concentrating on building a mobile, sea-based system that could be deployed closer to Iran. His concern was, therefore, with utilizing the most expedient manner of deploying an antiballistic missile system, not with whether or not to build such a system. Therefore, given Obama's use of preemptive warfare to fight a perpetual war on terror, it is no stretch of the imagination that, in line with the PNAC mission, he might make use of an antiballistic missile system (such as a short- or medium-range, sea-based system) in the course of "projecting conventional military forces or simply asserting political influence abroad."

The Use of Genocidal Biological Warfare for Political Expediency

Not only did RAD advocate the design and deployment of defensive weaponry, it also stressed the updating of conventional offensive weapons, including cruise missiles along with stealthy strike aircraft and longer-range Air Force strike aircraft. But it went further in its offensive posture by envisioning and supporting the use of genotype-specific biological warfare. According to RAD, "advanced forms of biological warfare that can 'target' specific genotypes may transform biological warfare from the realm of terror to a politically useful tool."[17] In this chilling statement, a double standard is evident. In the hands of al Qaida, such genocidal weapons would belong to "the realm of terror," but in those of the United States, they would be "politically useful tools." It is not clear how far down this treacherous road our nation may have already traveled during eight years of the Bush administration.

Since 1943, under President Franklin Roosevelt, the United States has been actively involved in developing biological and chemical weapons. However, while international law—such as the 1925 Geneva Protocol and the 1972 Biological and Toxin Weapons Convention—and U.S. federal law—such as the 1989 Biological Weapons Anti-Terrorism Act—ban such weapons, there is evidence that the United States has still continued to develop them. For example, it is known that the United States conducted experiments with anthrax in the early 2000s under the George W. Bush administration. Moreover, shrouded in secrecy, it is uncertain that the United States' current biodefense program does not also include research into *offensive* uses of lethal or dangerous biological and chemical agents.[18] Hence, the future of programs aimed at development of biological and chemical weapons cannot simply be assumed to be laid to rest under the Obama administration.

Rejection of the United Nations

PNAC also rejected the idea of a cooperative, neutral effort among the nations of the world to address world problems, including the problem of Iraq. "Nor can the United States assume a UN-like stance of neutrality," states the RAD report. "The preponderance of American power is so great and its global interests so wide that it cannot pretend to be indifferent to the political outcome in the Balkans, the Persian Gulf or even when it deploys forces in Africa. Finally, these missions demand forces basically configured for combat."[19]

It is significant that the Obama administration has not ruled out unilateralism. In fact, Obama stated, "I would also argue that we have the right to take unilateral military action to eliminate an imminent threat to our security—so long as an imminent threat is understood to be a nation, group or individual that is actively preparing to strike U.S targets."[20] Notwithstanding that such unilateral action as Obama described would be against a force "actively preparing to strike U.S. targets," it is still contrary to Article 39 of the United Nations Charter, which states, "The Security Council shall determine the existence of any threat to the peace, breach of the peace, or act of aggression and shall make recommendations, or decide what measures shall be taken in accordance with Articles 41 and 42, to maintain or restore international peace and security." And, according to Article 51, the right to unilateral military action of which Obama speaks exists in response to an armed attacked that has already occurred, not one for which a force is "actively preparing." Thus: "Nothing in the present Charter shall impair the inherent right of individual or collective self-defense *if an armed attack occurs* against a Member of the United Nations, until the Security Council has taken measures necessary to maintain international peace and security" (emphasis added). It, therefore, appears that Obama's view of national defense goes further toward unilateral action than that permitted by the international law set by the United Nations Charter.

Nevertheless, as will be discussed in Chapter 11, Obama's view of the role of the United Nations as a world authority appears to depart substantially from RAD's nationalistic dismissal of this organization. It may be that Obama's preemptive war stance is in lieu of a UN that has political capital and the power to enforce its mandates. But, as will become evident in Chapter 11, Obama's global vision is consistent with giving the UN a more decisive role to play in setting national and international policy.

Control of Space and Cyberspace

PNAC's quest for global domination transcends any literal meaning of the *geo*political, and extends also to the control, rather than the sharing, of outer space. Moreover, as was discussed in Chapter 7, it also has serious implications for cyber freedom. Thus, RAD also states, "Much as control of the high seas—and the protection of international commerce—defined global powers in the past, so will control of the new 'international commons' be a key to world power in the future."[21]

However, there is a difference between protecting the Internet from a cyber attack and controlling it for purposes of amassing "world power." The former is defensive while the latter is offensive. Under the Obama administration, there appear to have been substantial strides taken to defend cyberspace from attacks. For example, in June 2009, Defense Secretary Robert Gates established a subcommand focused on cyber security, based in Forte Mead Maryland, which reports to U.S. Strategic Command.[22] Further, in October 2009, the Obama administration established the National Cybersecurity and Communications Integration Center (NCCIC), which has been described as "a 24-hour, DHS-led coordinated watch and warning center that will improve national efforts to address threats and incidents affecting the nation's critical information technology and cyber infrastructure."[23]

In fact, the NSA will be involved in operation of the NCCIC, whose principle role will be "to monitor and assure the security and safety of civilian-government computer networks and to provide early warning to private businesses about cyber-attack threats."[24] Clearly, the NSA's role in monitoring private civilian computer networks as well as military ones represents a dangerous concession to state control of cyberspace. While the threat to the economic infrastructure of the U.S. is a legitimate concern of the federal government, its policing of "private property" in cyberspace may be no less defensible in a presumed democratic and free nation than is the policing of private real estate.

Moreover, given the NSA's direct involvement with the TIA project, it is not unreasonable to believe that the stated electronic monitoring will interface with the NSA's computerized data base and extraction and link technologies discussed in Chapter 2. This appears likely insofar as the interfacing of these technologies would help to identify potential threats to cybersecurity. Further, it is possible that the NCCIC has been slated to be the new central command and control facility (or at least a major hub) for operation of the TIA project. This also suggests the possibility that the Echelon system,[25] which globally extracts, monitors, and analyzes electronic data, may be keyed into the NCCIC/NSA command and control.

Ending the War on Terror

Without the camouflage of fighting a war on terror, the TIA project will be defused; for the official reason for conducting a warrantless, dragnet of *everybody's* personal electronic communications is the hunt everywhere and anywhere for terrorists. Without a "war on terror," covert operations to locate international criminals can be conducted as it had been pursuant to the 1978 Foreign Intelligence Surveillance Act, namely by search warrants approved by a FIS Court. Thus, the claimed need for FISA reform in the first place has been largely misrepresented.

Unfortunately, the Obama administration has not surrendered the idea of fighting a war on terror, and it has shown no signs of dismantling the TIA system or of taking a lead in reforming the current FISA laws. In fact, as discussed above, it appears to have substantially incorporated many of the aforementioned components of the PNAC plan into its own policies. Accordingly, there is now another version of PNAC taking root in America. This one speaks in terms of world unity instead of in nationalistic terms. But it is still a culture of control, albeit a global one.

World Government, Incorporated: The Bilderberg Plan

In a speech before the General Assembly of the United Nations on September 23, 2009, President Obama said, "[T]he time has come for the world to move in a new direction. We must embrace a new era of engagement based on mutual interest and mutual respect, and our work must begin now."[1]

After eight years under a government administration that worked hard at alienating most of the world, the prospect of "a new era of engagement based on mutual interest and respect" would have seemed a welcome change to any rational person. However, underlying such rhetoric of world solidarity is another strategy for world domination that has taken root and is feeding off the steady growth of giant multinational corporations. For decades now, the corporate sector of America has enjoyed relative freedom to merge, consolidate, and amass incredible profits and political capital.

In 1994, President Clinton signed the North America Free Trade Agreement (NAFTA), which united North America by dissolving economic borders between the United States, Mexico, and Canada. However, the price paid for such a "unified" North America was not the engagement of "mutual interest and mutual respect" but rather a bonanza for giant corporations who seized the opportunity to exploit poor laborers in Mexico while taking jobs away from Americans.

The Bush administration followed suit in supporting NAFTA and, by creating a war economy, spurred the growth of the military-industrial complex. From Blackwater mercenaries to Halliburton's no-bid government contracts to restore Iraq's oil infrastructure, the Bush administration helped to foster a form of globalization that lived off invading sovereign nations.

The recent Supreme Court decision in *Citizens United v. Federal Election Commission,* giving corporations the unrestricted ability to pour a bottomless pit of money into campaign advertisements for candidates who support their special interests, will predictably further increase the political clout of these companies.[2] Moreover, such unrestricted access to campaigns at both state and local levels also has the potential of further breaking down national boundaries by permitting foreign corporations to make campaign advertising contributions.

Giant multinational corporations are now the glue that binds nations together, and it is not likely these companies, which have insatiable appetites for profit, will care about anyone else's interests except their stockholders or show respect for anything other than what will produce dividends for them.

The Bilderberg Plan

Obama's penchant for a unified world order should, therefore, be viewed in this context of giant corporations, which wield great political power and influence. In fact, the Obama administration appears to have ties to the Bilderberg group, an organization consisting of international bankers, media moguls, oil barons, officers of the military-industrial complex, politicians, influential academicians, and other major power brokers. The group, which got its name from the Dutch hotel where it held it first meeting in 1954, meets yearly under a veil of secrecy and confidentiality to discuss world affairs. There are typically between 100 and 150 members and special invitees from North America and Western Europe.

Bilderberg's primary ideology is the creation of a world government. "The supranational sovereignty of an intellectual elite and world bankers is surely preferable to the national auto-determination practiced in past centuries," said David Rockefeller, codirector of Bilderberg and founder of its sister organization, the Trilateral Commission. And Rockefeller is quite direct about his own role in attempting to bring about world government:

> Some even believe we are part of a secret cabal working against the best interests of the United States, characterizing my family and me as "internationalists" and of conspiring with others around the world to build a more integrated global political and economic structure—one world, if you will. If that's the charge, I stand guilty, and I am proud of it.[3]

While the cloak of secrecy behind Bilderberg's meetings makes it difficult to draw conclusions, some have claimed that the group has exerted profound influence on world affairs. The European Union was allegedly a brainchild of Bilderberg. Daniel Estrulin, a journalist who has tracked Bilderberg agendas for decades has maintained that such events as the collapse of Lehmann Brothers, the downturn of the stock market, and the rising price of oil were the results of decisions made by Bilderberg members. It is also alleged that Bilderberg member James A. Johnson was responsible for selecting presidential running mates, including John Edwards for Kerry and Joseph Biden for Obama.[4]

Whether or not Bilderberg exerted such political influence, it is fact that many movers and shakers in the Obama administration also appear on the Bilderberg membership list. These include Robert Gates, Secretary of Defense; Hillary Clinton, Secretary of State; James Steinberg, Deputy Secretary of State; Kathleen Sebelius, Health Secretary,[5] Timothy Geithner, Secretary of the United States Treasury; Paul Volcker, Chair Economic Recovery Advisory Board; Ben Bernanke, Chair of the United States Federal Reserve; Richard Holbrooke, special envoy to Afghanistan and Pakistan; George Mitchell, special envoy to the Middle East; James Jones, National Security Advisor; Lawrence Summers, Director of the White House's National Economic Council; and Lt. Gen. Keith Alexander, National Security Agency (NSA) Director.[6]

While this intersection of the Obama administration with Bilderberg has received scant if any coverage by the American mainstream media, it has not escaped the notice of some independent, online news sources. According to Judi McCleod, editor of Canada Free Press,

> Bilderbergers pull the puppet strings of contemporary politicians. While the media tends to present Bilderberger luminaries as bigwigs in pinstripe suits attending endless secret meetings, they're the global elitists pushing the envelope on one-world government. . . . Barack Obama may look like the Messiah For Change when in reality he's just another Bilderberg Boy.[7]

Bilderberg's influence is also evident in the global arena. For example, reading like a book of who's who in Bilderberg, all presidents of the World Bank have belonged to this group since its inception in 1954 with the one exception of Alden W. Clausen, who served between July 1981 and June 1986. These Bilderberg members and World Bank presidents are Eugene R. Black, Sr. (1949–1963), George D. Woods (January 1963–March 1968), Robert McNamara (April 1968–June 1981), Barber Conable (July 1986–August 1991), Lewis T. Preston (September 1991–May 1995), James Wolfensohn (May 1995–June 2005), Paul Wolfowitz (June 2005–June 2007), and Robert Zoellick (July 2007–Present).

The current president, Robert Zoellick, was also a member of the Project for the New American Century (PNAC) along with Paul Wolfowitz.

Recently, Zoellick made clear his desire to give the World Bank, among other international organizations, power over national policies. "If leaders are serious about creating new global responsibilities or governance," stated Zoellick, "let them start by modernizing multilateralism to empower the WTO (World Trade Organization), the IMF (International Monetary Fund), and the World Bank Group *to monitor national policies*."[8]

The Council on Foreign Relations' Global Governance Initiative

Bilderberg is also allied with the Council on Foreign Relations (CFR). In fact, David Rockefeller has maintained a lifelong connection with the CFR. Beginning his relationship in 1946, he became its director in 1949, maintained its chairmanship from 1970 to 1985, and is currently its honorary chairman. There is also a substantial intersection between CFR and Bilderberg members.[9] Several Bilderberg members who are in the Obama administration are also CFR members, including George Mitchell (a former CFR director[10]), James Steinberg, Timothy Geithner, Richard Holbrooke, James Jones, and Lawrence Summers.

While CFR claims on its Web site to take "no institutional positions on matters of policy," its history suggests otherwise. In particular, in May 2005, the CFR published a task force report, which provided a blueprint for a North American Union merging the United States, Canada, and Mexico. The CFR stated,

> Task Force proposes the creation by 2010 of a North American community to enhance security, prosperity, and opportunity. We propose a community based on the principle affirmed in the March 2005 Joint Statement of the three leaders that "our security and prosperity are mutually dependent and complementary." Its boundaries will be defined by a common external tariff and an outer security perimeter within which the movement of people, products, and capital will be legal, orderly, and safe. Its goal will be to guarantee a free, secure, just, and prosperous North America.[11]

The CFR called for building a common security border around North America by 2010; free movement of people, commerce, and capital within North America; and a North American Border Pass that would replace a U.S. passport. It also called for a central North American government consisting of a court, interparliamentary group, executive commission, military defense command, customs office, and a development bank.[12]

The CFR report was prepared in tandem with the George W. Bush administration's Security and Prosperity Partnership (SPP) agreement signed in Waco, Texas, on March 23, 2005, by President Bush, Mexican

President Vicente Fox, and then Canadian Prime Minister Paul Martin. According to a WorldNetDaily report, the Bush administration had set up 20 working groups under a special SPP office to implement the agreement without congressional approval or oversight.[13] As of August 2009, the SPP initiative has allegedly been deactivated,[14] and the SPP Web site has been updated to say, "This website is an archive for SPP documents and will not be updated."[15] However, the precedent has now been set to establish a North American Union, and the thrust toward world government is still in gear.

On May 1, 2008, the CFR announced the launching of a new five-year CFR program called the, "International Institutions and Global Governance Program: World Order in the 21st Century." According to the CFR, the purpose of this initiative is "creation of new frameworks for global governance," which it said, "will be a defining challenge for the twenty-first century, and the attitude of the United States will be among the most important factors in determining the shape and stability of the world order that results from these efforts." The CFR pointed to a host of issues that require a new global agenda "from terrorism to climate change to the proliferation of weapons of mass destruction—that no single country, no matter how powerful, can address on its own."[16]

"Among the most important factors determining the future of global governance," said the CFR, "will be the attitude of the United States, likely to remain the world's most prominent actor at least until 2050." The reasons for what it perceives to be the United States' "ambivalent and selective posture toward multilateral cooperation," are "America's overwhelming power, its unique political culture, and its constitutional traditions." More succinctly, Americans fear losing their sovereignty, their constitutional rights, and their standing in the world. This "instinctual skepticism toward multilateral cooperation," said the CFR, was "particularly pronounced" during the first term of the George W. Bush administration, and the CFR admits that it is "unlikely to disappear."[17]

So the CFR's "pragmatic and flexible" solution to this "attitude" problem is to draft "blueprints for new structures of international cooperation that are … consistent with long-term U.S. national interests, and sensitive to historic U.S. concerns about domestic sovereignty and international freedom of action."[18] But, what is to be regarded as "long-term U.S. national interests" and being "sensitive to historic U.S. concerns about domestic sovereignty and international freedom of action"?

This may be a matter of widely varying interpretation. Thus, the Nazis believed that it was in Germany's "long-term national interest" to exterminate Jewish people. Once the move is made to refashion domestic sovereignty along with the U.S. Constitution to accommodate a new world order, protections against encroachment of basic rights presumed to be guaranteed to all Americans will no longer have legal effect.

As emphasized in this book, there have already been serious breaches in constitutional protections. In particular, the Fourth Amendment has been eviscerated as a result of passage of the U.S. Patriot Act and the 2008 FISA Amendments Act. Unfortunately, as the United States is transitioned into a new world order, it is likely that such programs as mass, warrantless surveillance will become permanent fixtures. This is because the earlier privacy protections, such as were built into the 1978 FISA Act, assumed domestic sovereignty in the first place. According to this earlier act, electronic surveillance could not target *American* persons without a court warrant, which already assumes national sovereignty. Americans must be distinguished from citizens of other nations in order for such a rule to be applied.

Americans would be justified if they frowned upon the CFR initiative. They would also be justified if they demonstrated en masse against it. But most Americans do not know about such an initiative in the first place, because the mainstream media does not cover the story. Hence, it is curious that CFR points to the "attitude" of Americans as its major hurdle and claims that Americans were especially "instinctually skeptical" of multilateralism during the first term of the Bush administration. Perhaps it has anticipated (and inferred) that such resistance will present an obstacle from the display of nationalism that ensued in the aftermath of the September 11, 2001, attacks.

Yet there is something to be said for publicity. Subjecting a view to public scrutiny can be a constructive way of determining if it is ethical. If the public is skeptical of a view after it is given to careful public discussion, then there is probably a serious ethical objection to it.[19] Unfortunately, the CFR and its government associates have launched their initiatives without public knowledge, and there is therefore not likely to be any public discussion. Instead, there may be gradual, incremental policy shifts away from domestic sovereignty and toward world government. Perhaps one such change will be the creation of a world tax that is assessed and collected by a world authority.

Global Taxation without Representation

According to James Tucker, a Bilderberg tracker who claims to rely on inside informants, Bilderberg has for many years sought to use its influence to establish a world tax to be collected by the United Nations. Such a tax, paid to the United Nations could serve to give it standing as a world government. According to Tucker, while such a tax is likely to be ill-received by the public, over time the public will come to accept it. "Bilderberg," he predicted, "will dictate stories to the U.S. media about how 'a fraction of a penny' paid at the gas pump will feed the starving Third-World like Christ's magical 'loaves and fishes' fed the multitude 2,000 years ago."[20]

In fact, there have been some attempts made at establishing such a tax. In July 2004, *Inter Presse* news service reported that a United Nations study was being prepared that outlined several alternative global tax proposals to be considered by the General Assembly at its September meeting. The proposals outlined included global taxes on e-mails and Internet, a global gas tax, and levies on airline travel. According to the news report, such a tax would have committed American taxpayers to paying hundreds of billions of dollars each year to the United Nations.[21]

In February 2008, Accuracy in Media, a media watchdog organization, reported that a bill called the "Global Poverty Act" (S.2433) sponsored by then Senator Barack Obama, was to be voted on by the Senate. This bill, which never became law, would have imposed a global tax on the United States and would have given the United Nations control over a certain percentage of U.S. foreign-aid spending.[22]

NAFTA and the Trend toward World Unification

According to Tucker, Bilderberg also seeks to use its political influence to promote expansion of NAFTA to help solidify an "American Union" consisting of all nations in North, Central, and South America.[23] Such progressive breakdown of trade borders is allegedly Bilderberg's strategy for attainment of a one-world order. In 1993, when campaigning for the passage of NAFTA, former Secretary of State and early Bilderberg member Henry Kissinger (since 1957), put the point bluntly: "NAFTA is a major stepping stone to the New World Order."

In fact, there has recently been movement in this direction with Congress's passage of the Free Trade Agreement between the United States and Peru in 2007 and its implementation in 2009. While the FTA was predicted to improve economic and social conditions in Peru, in the one year since passage, according to a report released by Public Citizen in February 2010, there has been rapid deterioration of economic and labor conditions in Peru.[24] Again, as the trend toward corporate globalization moves forward, the world continues to be "unified" at the expense of mass exploitation.

A main goal of Bilderberg's sister organization, the Trilateral Commission, is currently stated as fostering "closer cooperation" among the core democratic industrialized areas of the world"—Japan, Europe (European Union countries), and North America (United States and Canada)—"with shared leadership responsibilities in the wider international system."[25] According to Trilateral Commission cofounder, Zbigniew Brzezinski (former national security advisor to Jimmy Carter), "This regionalization is in keeping with the Tri-Lateral Plan which calls for a gradual convergence of East and West, ultimately leading toward the goal of one world government. National sovereignty is no longer a viable concept."[26]

Apparently, Brzezinski perceives Barrack Obama as being aligned with such a new world order. Obama, he said, "recognizes that the challenge is a new face, a new sense of direction, a new definition of America's role in the world."[27] Brzezinski has also been a foreign policy advisor to Obama.[28]

The dissolution of national borders should be evident to anyone who attempts to purchase fruits or vegetables, clothing, an automobile, or other products. It should also be evident in the obvious outsourcing of service jobs. A phone call or e-mail message to the tech support department of a major technology corporation can predictably be expected to reach a service provider in India or other nation where labor can be cheaply purchased. The world is shrinking at a voluminous speed with the advent of new and faster communication technologies. "Cloud" computing has now largely replaced storage of data on one's own hard drive, making it possible to access this information from anywhere on the globe, thus making the concept of a geographical location of one's data largely irrelevant for practical purposes.

From PNAC to Bilderberg: The Emerging One-world Ideology

In this age of advancing digital technologies and corporate globalization, it is not astounding that the ideological thrust of a group such as Bilderberg would take hold and supersede the nationalism embedded in the PNAC.[29] While the latter ideology drove the Bush administration in its first term, PNAC officially closed its doors at the end of 2006. Curiously, however, the founding members and major representatives of PNAC are also Bilderberg members. This includes Paul Wolfowitz, William Kristol, Robert Kagan, Richard Perle, Robert Zoellick, and Donald Rumsfeld.[30]

Despite their fundamental disagreement over domestic sovereignty, between these two diametrically opposed ideologies is unsettling common ground. At the core of each are corporate globalism and the blending of big business and government in the attempt to control economic and political outcomes. The PNAC ideology sought the fighting of simultaneous wars, feeding the bottom-line appetites of military contractors with robust defense-spending budgets, and exploiting tragedies such as the 9/11 attacks as a pretext for invading a sovereign Iraq to gain control of its oil resources.

Bilderberg's ideology is also one that mixes political with corporate wealth and power. Thus, as was discussed in Chapter 10, the Afghanistan

War was in the vested interest of giant oil companies, notably Chevron, which sought to build a Trans Afghan pipeline for the transport of energy across this region. As mentioned, the former CEO of this company was Condelezza Rice, who was also a member of Bilderberg.

Both Bilderberg and PNAC ideologies are versions of real politik.[31] Their main proponents such as PNAC cofounder William Kristol and Bilderberg codirector David Rockefeller subscribe to the use of power, manipulation, and deception to attain their ends. "We are on the verge of a global transformation," said David Rockefeller on September 23, 1994. "All we need is the right major crisis and the nations will accept the New World Order."[32] Such a willingness to turn a national crisis to political advantage is reminiscent of the Bush administrations use of the 9/11 attacks as a pretext for invading Iraq. It is also markedly akin to the PNAC's chillingly prophetic statement, made one year prior to the 9/11 attacks, that "the process of transformation, even if it brings revolutionary change, is likely to be a long one, absent some catastrophic and catalyzing event—like a new Pearl Harbor."[33]

Philosophically, the replacement of PNAC with Bilderberg as the ruling ideology of the time may representative a Hegelian synthesis between a thesis (PNAC) and antithesis (Bilderberg). Unfortunately, this synthesis may be moving from a nationalistic culture of control to one of global proportions.

Bilderberg and Mass Media Censorship

As stressed in this book, a culture of control seeks unilateral control of information, that is, information that flows in only one direction. The government of such a culture seeks total information while at the same time keeping citizens in the dark. It appears that this is also the temperament of Bilderberg's management, for the secrecy that permeates the group's meetings suggests an almost obsessive drive to hide information while at the same time acquiring it. Thus, David Rockefeller had no compunction in crediting mainstream media for keeping its secrets. Stated Rockefeller,

> We are grateful to the Washington Post, The New York Times, Time Magazine and other great publications whose directors have attended our meetings and respected their promises of discretion for almost forty years. It would have been impossible for us to develop our plan for the world if we had been subjected to the lights of publicity during those years.[34]

Such a clandestine environment of media censorship would not be necessary if this organization were merely a forum for the free expression of ideas. It would make more sense in the context of an organization actively seeking to implement its "plan" in action and did not wish to have outside interference.

In fact, there are a sizeable number of mainstream media moguls who are listed on the Bilderberg membership list. These include, among others, Paul Gigot, Editor, Editorials, Wall Street Journal; Donald Graham, Board Chair, The Washington Post; George Will, columnist, Washington Post; Katharine Graham, former Publisher and Chairman of the *Washington Post*; Rupert Murdoch, Chair, News Corp; George Stephanopoulos, Chief Washington Correspondent, ABC News; Andrea Mitchell, reporter/anchor, NBC News; Lesley Stahl, 60 Minutes, CBS News; Thomas L. Friedman, columnist, *New York Times*; Phillip Crawley, *Globe* and *Mail* Publisher (Canada); Osborn Elliott, former Editor-in-Chief, *Newsweek*; Paul Finney, former Managing Editor, *Business Week*; Henry Grunwald, former Managing Editor, *Time Magazine*; Arthur Taylor (1977), former President, CBS; and Will Hutton, former Editor-In-Chief, *The Observer* (London).[35]

With the exception of a few independent reporters such as James Tucker, Daniel Estrulin, and Alex Jones, Bilderberg has been remarkably successful in keeping the media from disclosing its proceedings. In any other case, inasmuch as, each year, the mainstream media is aware of 150 or so major movers and shakers from the highest levels of political and corporate walks of life assembling in one space, one would expect it to be covering it with great detail. Consider the fact that the mainstream press is all over it when even one celebrity comes to town. So why is media so compliant?

Members of Bilderberg, such as Rupert Murdoch, CEO of News Corporation, are obviously interested in making money. The presumption here is, therefore, that it is more profitable to keep mum than to get the story out. Unfortunately, given the mainstream media blackout, this raises many unanswered questions. This makes Bilderberg a breeding ground for speculation.

This also makes those few independent journalists who are attempting to investigate the group liable to being called "conspiracy theorists." The effect of this label is to destroy the credibility of any information they report. In this way, Bilderberg can remain insulated from being taken seriously as a politically influential organization.

Nevertheless, a rational investigation should not be short-circuited by intimidation through the use of emotively pejorative labels. There are bewildering facts in need of explaining (such as mainstream media's substantial representation in the group and its acquiescence in a media blackout); and, therefore, it is rational to raise questions and to formulate preliminary hypotheses.

Bilderberg and the TIA Project

In particular, how much influence, if any, has Bilderberg wielded over the development and deployment of the TIA network? Given that the director of the National Security Agency (NSA) under Obama (Lt. Gen. Keith Alexander) is also a Bilderberg member, there is at least a reasonable suspicion that Bilderberg bears some connection to warrantless, mass surveillance.

According to Tucker (who claims to have received his information from unnamed inside sources), during the 2008 Bilderberg conference in Chantilly, Virginia, a session was held on the possibility of mass, subcutaneous implanting of computer chips in human beings in order to track them under the pretext of fighting the war on terror. Such a program would permit "the 'good guys' ... to travel freely from airports so long as their microchip could be scanned and the information stored in a database."

According to Tucker, the session participants suggested that such a program of mass-chipping could be sold to the public on the grounds that al Qaeda has been recruiting individuals who do not "look like terrorists"—blonde, blue-eyed westerners. Tucker also said participants discussed the utility of such chipping to gain fast access to patient information in hospitals in emergency situations. As will be discussed in Chapter 14, such computer chips are already being implanted in certain select human populations. Bilderberg's alleged suggestion to implant surveillance chips into *all* human beings is, therefore, not far-fetched.

Given Bilderberg's global interests we would expect that Bilderberg surveillance would indeed also be globalized and would therefore track not just Americans but citizens of all other nations too. As was discussed in Chapter 8, the infrastructure already appears to be in place to engage global surveillance. This would portend a culture that transcends nationalistic or state control, one wherein the world is monitored and policed by a single governing authority.

While the pretext for devising such a system has been to track terrorists, the U.S. Patriot Act has already blurred the boundaries between foreign intelligence gathering and criminal investigations in the U.S. Pursuant to this Act, law enforcement can now use information acquired through terrorism searches in criminal prosecutions that are unrelated to the terrorism investigation. This means, in effect, that probable cause does not have to be established in order to conduct an electronic criminal investigation of an American person. This in turn means that warrantless mass surveillance can in principle be used as a means of criminal law enforcement. This raises the chilling image of Big Brother trolling for law offenders in order to "bring them to justice."

The New World Order of Law Enforcement

Electronic surveillance law enforcement is already a fact of life in nations, such as the United States and Great Britain, albeit with regard to enforcement of traffic laws. Consider that a commonplace manner of being served with a traffic violation is now through being contacted by mail after a surveillance camera catches a traffic infraction. However, the legal floodgates are now open to extend this model of electronic law enforcement to more serious offenses. Further, with the increasing ubiquity of video surveillance cameras, RFID tracking chips, and other new and emerging surveillance technologies,[36] we can expect facility for expansion of electronic criminal law enforcement.

Insofar as this manner of law enforcement becomes a model for the world, localized forms of law enforcement may gradually give way to more centralized, electronically managed varieties. Virtual courtrooms located in cyberspace may replace the current system of state and federal courts. With gradual disintegration of geographical state and national borders, the need for a world criminal court and a central authority to preside over it will become increasingly more evident. At least, this appears to be what Bilderberg anticipates.

In 2002, the United Nations established the International Criminal Court (ICC), which is intended to have jurisdiction over all nations in the prosecution of individuals for such crimes as genocide, crimes against humanity, war crimes, and crimes of aggression. More than one hundred nations are presently members of this court.[37] While the United Nations is not presently one of these nations, there is evidence that Obama supports the United States' membership. In response to a 2004 questionnaire conducted by Citizens for Global Solutions, (then) Senator Barrack Obama indicated that he supported U.S. ratification of the ICC Treaty, which would bring the United States under ICC jurisdiction.[38]

According to Tucker, Bilderberg expects Obama to ratify the UN's ICC Treaty in the near future. "Bilderberg owns President Obama, who sees himself as a 'citizen of the world,'" said Tucker. "He will be sweet-talking Senate supporters who are afraid to back the treaty. He will be hoping for an even more left-wing Senate after the 2010 election. His goal, as dictated by Bilderberg, is to persuade the new Senate (to be seated in January 2010), to ratify the ICC treaty late on a Saturday night, too late for the Sunday papers or to make changes in the Sunday TV talkies."[39] At the time of this writing, it remains to be seen whether the United States will indeed sign on to the ICC under Obama. But, if it does, this will represent a further move toward world government and away from national sovereignty.

World Government: No Panacea for Liberals

The genuine possibility of a new world order in which there is a single governing worldwide authority may sound attractive to the liberal-minded. For, like the Marxist ideology of communism, it may seem to suggest a world united as one community of humanity and which human rights might be preserved. However, as the experiment in communism has shown, pure theory may lose something on its way to being practiced.

Under careful inspection, the Bilderberg ideology portends such a material lose in its application. It's reliance on corporate entities to set social and political priorities has already shown its dangerous potential in terms of exploitation of labor and the despoiling of the environment. Moreover, the Bilderberg credo appears to be one that shuns transparency, operating in private and seeing mass media as a tool to be manipulated for its own ends. This is likely to be a Machiavellian world regime bent on the amassing of power and the unilateral acquisition of knowledge, keeping an electronic worldwide eye on all of us, and crushing any opposition to its own rule. This is the Orwellian Big Brother on stilts.[40]

12

The American Death Squads

It was always at night—the arrests invariably happened at night. The sudden jerk out of sleep, the rough hand shaking your shoulder, the lights glaring in your eyes, the ring of hard faces round the bed. In the vast majority of cases there was no trial, no report of the arrest. People simply disappeared, always during the night. Your name was removed from the registers, every record of everything you had ever done was wiped out, your one-time existence was denied and then forgotten. You were abolished, annihilated: *vapourized* was the usual word.[1]

These are the words that George Orwell used to describe the "Thought Police." This was the arm of government, a group of assassins, whose job it was to kill any citizen who challenged the authority of Big Brother.

Every authoritarian regime has such a death squad. These assassins, which operate in secret, report directly to the executive branch of government and are not subject to oversight by any other branch of government. The United States may now also have its own death squad.

In July 2009, the *New York Times* reported that a Central Intelligence Agency (CIA) assassination program linked to former Vice President Dick Cheney and concealed from Congress had been terminated by CIA director Leon Panetta on June 23, 2009.[2] However, another fully operational assassination program, operated by the U.S. Defense Department's Joint Special Operations Command (JSOC), may still exist. While the Obama administration's top national security officer, Dennis Blair, has contended that the CIA program was not illegal, this contention is highly questionable, and, unless rebutted, could obstruct a thorough and comprehensive congressional investigation and leave the Cheney death squad intact.

In March 2009, *New Yorker Magazine's* Seymour Hersh went on MSNBC's Countdown with Keith Olbermann and stated that the JSOC, answering directly to Dick Cheney, has been "going into countries, not talking to the ambassador or the CIA station chief, and finding people on a list and executing them and leaving. That's been going on, well, in the name of all of us." Hersh's allegation came out of research he had been doing for a new book, which he said might take a year or two before it was published. There are two salient differences between the program reported by the *Times* and that reported by Hersh. First, while the former program had been operated by the CIA, the latter has allegedly been operated by the JSOC, a military wing of the intelligence community separate from the CIA; and second, the purported JSOC program was fully operational while, according to *Times* sources, the CIA program was not. Given these two fundamental distinctions between the programs in question, they could not possibly refer to the same program.

In fact, in 2008, Hersh had reported that the Bush administration believed that covert CIA operations were harder for the President to keep from congressional oversight than clandestine military activities. So, it classified anything secret as military rather than as CIA. This provides a possible rationale for why the Bush administration may have had a military intelligence program that operated independently of the CIA.

Assuming the accuracy of both Hersh's and the *Times'* sources, the logical conclusion to draw is that there might have been, and still may be, a fully operational assassination program under the Obama administration, notwithstanding the fact that the CIA program has now been ended. If this is true, it represents a chilling aspect of a burgeoning culture of control in America.

As discussed in Chapter 3, on July 31, 2008, President Bush issued an amended version of Executive Order 12333, which placed the National Director of Intelligence (NDI) in charge of the entire intelligence community, answerable directly to the President, and requiring the heads of each agency, including the Defense Department, to "provide the Director access to all information and intelligence relevant to the national security or that otherwise is required for the performance of the Director's duties." Therefore, if the JSOC program presently exists, then the current NDI, Dennis Blair, is probably aware of its existence; in which case, Blair may have reason to fear a thorough investigation of the CIA program inasmuch as it may lead to exposure of the JSOC program. As such, it is possible that the termination of the CIA program may serve as a red herring, deflecting further attention from the existence of an assassination ring currently in operation by the Pentagon.

There are two reasons why such a program would be illegal. The first is that political assasinations were outlawed under the Gerald Ford administration. In 1976, Gerald Ford issued Executive Order 11905, which stated, "No employee of the United States Government shall engage in, or conspire to engage in, political assassination" (5(g) Prohibition on Assassinations).

Second, according to Title V—"Accountability for Intelligence Activities"—of the amended 1947 National Security Act, consistent with procedures established by the DNI to protect unauthorized disclosure of classified information,

> The President shall ensure that the congressional intelligence committees are kept fully and currently informed of the intelligence activities of the United States, including any significant anticipated intelligence activity as required by this title.[3]

Still, DNI Dennis Blair denied that the CIA program breached the National Security Act. While he agreed with Panetta that the CIA program should be closed down, this was not because it was illegal. Rather, according to Blair, the program raised serious questions among intelligence officials about its "effectiveness, maturity and the level of control." According to Blair, the law did not require notification of congressional intelligence committees but was instead "a judgment call."[4]

A "judgment call?" The basis of Blair's claim appears to derive from a dubious interpretation of the National Security Act. According to the *Times*, while the amended Act requires the president to make sure the intelligence committees "are kept fully and currently informed of the intelligence activities of the United States, including any significant anticipated intelligence activity," the Act also

> leaves some leeway for judgment, saying such briefings should be done "to the extent consistent with due regard for the protection from unauthorized disclosure of classified information relating to sensitive intelligence sources and methods or other exceptionally sensitive matters."[5]

However, this interpretation of the Act is misleading at best because the proviso that briefings be done consistent with "due regard for protection from unauthorized disclosure" is addressed in Section 1102 of the Act, which requires that the DNI establish "programs and procedures by which sensitive classified information relating to human intelligence is safeguarded against unauthorized disclosure" by all employees of the intelligence community.[6] This means that disclosure to congressional intelligence committees must be made in accordance with programs and procedures established by the DNI to guard against unauthorized disclosure. This is far from saying that the DNI or any other member of the intelligence committee has discretionary power as to whether or not to disclose actual or anticipated covert intelligence activities to congressional intelligence committees.

Such an interpretation of the law, especially with regard to a program of political assassination (which is already illegal), would fly in the face of the point of the disclosure provision of the Act. This point is to guarantee that there is adequate congressional oversight of the intelligence community. Inasmuch as the DNI reports directly to the president and has authority over all other elements of the intelligence community, a discretionary law would be tantamount to giving the president unitary executive authority over intelligence. While this is consistent with dictatorship, it is not consistent with the system of checks and balances conceived by the Founding Fathers.

Accordingly, the National Security Act was violated insofar as the congressional intelligence committees were not informed of actual or anticipated activities of the CIA or JSOC assassination programs. Indeed, if such a law applies anywhere, it applies in the case of systematic programs aimed at conducting political assassinations.

Given the legal requirement that the president keep congressional intelligence committees informed of such activities, it is clear that President Obama is legally required to ensure that such disclosure is made. While this legal requirement appears to have been satisfied by the Obama administration regarding the CIA program, it remains to be seen whether it will be accomplished regarding the allegedly more robust JSOC program.

At least, there are now two sufficient reasons for thinking that the Bush administration violated the law by conducting its CIA assassination program, even if this program was not fully operational and only "anticipated" assassinating individuals on its list. Therefore, adequate closure of this issue demands a thorough congressional investigation. Should this investigation turn up the JSOC program that, according to Seymour Hersh, has been in full operation, then the Obama administration may also have to do some explaining.

A possible litmus test as to the involvement of the Obama administration in the continuation of the Bush death squads may be how cooperative it is in the launching of a thorough, impartial investigation. Unfortunately, Dennis Blair's denial that the CIA program was illegal already casts doubts on the Obama administration's willingness to cooperate in conducting such an investigation.

The Obama administration has persistently claimed allegiance to the rule of law; but to date, it has been reticent to conduct investigations into violations of the rule of law by the Bush administration. If America is to move beyond mere rhetoric in reestablishing itself as a moral leader, it should seize this opportunity to prove its forthrightness in practicing what it preaches. Unfortunately, the Obama administration's Justice Department has so far not conducted an investigation regarding the operation of such secret, unlawful programs of political assassination.

Nor has the mainstream media, including the *New York Times,* pursued the matter. This does not bode well for restoring America's moral authority and regard for the rule of law. To the contrary, it represents another case in which our system of checks and balances, those of both government and media, has failed to operate.

The death squad that existed under the Bush administration and the even more clandestine one that may exist now under the Obama administration do not literally read people's thoughts to check to see if they are guilty of crimes. However, as discussed throughout this book, government agencies, such as the NSA, CIA, FBI, and undoubtedly the JSOC have access to a vast system of Total Information Awareness (TIA) and warrantless mass surveillance. Inasmuch as this technology is imperfect and prone to false positives, it can misidentify and link innocent people to terrorist activities. Add to this, the existence of a secret assassination squad that operates beneath the radar of congressional oversight and the prospect of Orwell's Thought Police, who come in the dark of night to "vaporize" their suspects, is not farfetched. As if this were not enough to chill the air, the Defense Department is now at work on the technology that *literally* reads thoughts.[7]

13

Big Brother is (Literally) Watching You: The Manhattan Security Initiative

As has been emphasized in this book, America has become a culture fixated on fighting a bogus "war on terror." National fear and apprehension about the possibility of the next terrorist attack have made average Americans receptive to increasing levels of government interference with their civil liberties. Americans have now become desensitized to having their personal e-mail and phone messages searched by the National Security Agency (NSA). They have accepted the fact that any books that they purchase on a credit card or check out from the public library will be added to an NSA database along with credit card, healthcare, and financial information. Now, in major U.S. cities, such as Los Angeles, Chicago, and New York, Americans are facing another level of surveillance that will make the Orwellian mantra of "Big Brother is Watching You" a literal reality.

The Manhattan Security Initiative

In 2007, New York City began its "Lower Manhattan Security Initiative," which, when completed, will include a network of some 3000 television cameras "designed to help ensure public safety and security, and to detect, deter, and prevent potential terrorist activities."[1] As of 2009, this network spanned a 1.7-square-mile area, which included the New York Stock Exchange, Federal Reserve Bank, Brooklyn and Manhattan Bridges, World Financial Centers, World Trade Center memorial site, PATH train, and other major financial institutions; and approximately US$24 million in federal grants had been provided to expand the initiative to include Midtown Manhattan. The system also includes chemical, biological, and radiological sensors intended to detect potential terrorist threats; and it also includes license plate readers, which can zoom in on license plates of suspects.[2]

While video cameras have previously been used in public and private areas for crime prevention and monitoring, the new technology is significantly different. Conventional cameras have the capacity to capture and store moving video, but it must first be downloaded before it can be viewed and analyzed; and this might only be done when the need arises. In contrast, video captured by the new technology is sent directly to a central surveillance center (the so-called "Lower Manhattan Security Coordination Center") where it is monitored and analyzed by a team of counterterrorism specialists. According to the New York Police Department, this Center, which opened in October 2008, is staffed by police officers of the NYPD Counterterrorism Bureau, but also includes staff from the private sector.[3]

However, in addition to involving the local police, the new cameras can also transmit data in real time to federal agencies in Washington, including the Department of Homeland Security and the Federal Bureau of Investigation (FBI).[4] It appears, therefore, that the New York surveillance system is, or will be, a component of the Total Information Awareness (TIA) network, which can integrate the transmitted videos with all other federal databases including the FBI's biometrics database, which includes fingerprints, DNA samples, iris patterns, face-shape data, scars, tattoos, and unique mannerisms, such as the ways people walk and talk.[5] This also means that the data transmitted through the New York system can be filtered and linked to data in these other databases through use of the NSA's various TIA software technologies as was described in Chapter 2.

The New York Security system also integrates *private* security cameras as well as public ones. According to the NYPD, "When fully operational, it will include data from several thousand cameras, a significant portion of which are provided by private companies in the finance, banking, commerce, transportation, and telecommunications industries."[6] This means that surveillance is not limited to public areas such as streets, government buildings, and parks. Given this breakdown in boundaries between public and private zones, the chilling Orwellian image of telescreens in every room may be on the horizon.

The London Ring of Steel

In fact, the New York surveillance system is not novel and was based on the "Ring of Steel" system that surrounds London. The British government began developing this system in August 1993 after the bombing of Bishopsgate in London by the IRA. The system presently consists of a network of thousands of surveillance cameras that can read license plate numbers, and identify faces. According to the *Guardian,* a British newspaper, "It is understood the system also utilizes facial recognition software which automatically identifies suspects or known criminals who enter the eight-square-mile zone."[7] But, in order to have this capacity, the cameras must be keyed into a database, which contains biometric information used by facial recognition software to provide matches.

This indeed raises questions as to whether information being received through the London cameras is systematically being sent to British intelligence for analysis. Thus, according to Gareth Crossman, Director of the British human rights organization, Liberty, "We would be concerned that it would be just a 'fishing' exercise where large amounts of data are passed over to the police or the security services and they just sift through it." But, according to a source for the *Guardian,* "data would only be passed onto the intelligence and security services in the case of a genuine suspect or known criminal, in keeping with the law."[8]

Still, the use of facial recognition software to identify suspected terrorists suggests that the London surveillance system must already be interfaced with an intelligence's database containing terrorist suspects in order for it to find matches. According to the *Guardian,* "Images will be cross referenced to intelligence and police databases of suspects."[9] So it appears that the video cameras also routinely send digital images to British intelligence computers, which in turn use facial recognition software to look for matches between data stored in the government database and the transported digital images.

This plot thickens still because, as was discussed in Chapter 8, Britain is part of the UKUSA global surveillance alliance, which means that the London "Ring of Steel," through its interface with the British intelligence system, may ultimately also interface with Echelon, the global network based in the United States. So, what is caught on camera in London may be shared with the NSA in the United States through an intricate and massive surveillance web of network connections. In the least, it is quite clear that the infrastructure is in place to accommodate such an incredibly complex and throughgoing surveillance system. Hence, even if it is not currently fully operational, this may be only a matter of time.

Breaching the Divide between Public and Private Zones

There are two questions that cannot rationally be avoided. How effective is such a surveillance system likely to be in averting future terrorist attacks? And, is whatever protection that might be afforded by this system worth the sacrifice of privacy?

Systems such as the New York and London surveillance networks will have the capacity to learn the daily behavioral activities of average citizens, capturing them on camera—anything from someone going to the bathroom to a closet gay person having a "clandestine" rendezvous with his or her lover. Indeed, no matter how open a person may be about his or her personal life, everyone has secret, private things that he or she does not want monitored by state authorities. As Jim Harper, the Cato Institute Director of Information Planning, states, "When law abiding citizens go out in public and move around, they don't expect people to use new high-tech surveillance technology in order to track us and monitor us, extracting untold information in the process."[10]

When such mass, warrantless surveillance also occurs in private (non-public) zones, such as where one lives or works, the invasion of privacy is unequivocally unlawful; for while one cannot (legally) insist on privacy on a public thoroughfare, this is not the case when the invasion of privacy occurs in a private facility. And, while it may be contended that one tacitly consents to such surveillance when one uses this facility, even this lame argument unravels when surveillance cameras become ubiquitous and cannot reasonably be avoided. Unfortunately, once the boundaries between public and private domains have been breached, there are no constitutional constraints left to stop the invasive progression.

Shortcomings of Camera Network Technologies to Stop Terrorist Attacks

Given the inherent dangers of surveillance networks such as New York and London's, it is hard to see how these projects could be warranted even if it they had the potential to stop a future terrorist attack. However, there is no clear empirical evidence to suggest that a network of surveillance cameras like the ones in New York and London will be effective in stopping a further attack. Indeed, terrorists who are savvy enough to succeed at a terrorist attack will be aware of the existence of these cameras, know their vulnerabilities, and will find ways to work around them. For example, facial recognition software will be of little value if the suspect has undergone cosmetic surgery or has otherwise covered up or removed any identifiable markers on the basis of which the software could find a match.

Moreover, it appears that such cameras may be more effective in providing information after the fact than prior to a terrorist attack. For example, 500,000 cameras may have proved useful in figuring out what went wrong in the wake of the July 7, 2005, bombings in London when four terrorists set off bombs killing 50 and injuring 700. The terrorists in question were not on any government watch list and, therefore, facial recognition software could not have been of any use in the first place.

A more recent example is the May 1, 2010, attempt to explode a bomb that was left inside a car parked in Times Square. A surveillance camera captured footage of the suspect walking away from the car as he removed a layer of clothing; however this footage did nothing to prevent the attempt in the first place. Instead, a t-shirt vendor in the area noticed smoke coming from the car and contacted the police. Thus, the potential threat was already identified before the surveillance camera footage was even reviewed.[11]

Further, unless surveillance cameras are ubiquitous, terrorists can always target an area where there are no such cameras. But if the cameras are ubiquitous, then we will have won the battle at the expense of having lost the war; for then we will have transformed into a full-fledged police state.

Giving police and/or federal authorities the power to monitor law-abiding citizens in the course of their daily activities portends serious potential for abuse. In Chapter 6, it was seen how surveillance of electronic communications for the official purpose of searching out terrorists morphed into also monitoring journalists and media organizations; and how government's handling of the program of embedded reporters led to censorship, even to the point of using a public relations firm to screen out journalists who disagreed with the government's war policy. These and myriad other instances of government abuse suggest untoward potential for abuse in the case of systematic video camera monitoring of citizens.

For example, the system might be used to target antiwar demonstrators exercising their right to peaceful assembly, and perhaps follow around individual members. Technologies can also be attached to surveillance cameras that can capture citizens in private areas that would otherwise not be visible to other humans. For example, during the 2004 Republican National Convention in New York City, a police helicopter videotaped a nighttime demonstration, using a camera with special thermal-imaging equipment designed to fight terrorists. The camera was then turned on a couple having intimate moments on the terrace of a second avenue penthouse. "High above Second Avenue, they seemed to be shielded from view by a wall of shrubs and the nearly total darkness."[12] The video was eventually posted to the Internet.

Such incidents should underscore the fact that those who are watching behind the cameras are human beings, and human beings do not always play by the rules. If it is the job of an individual to sit behind a computer all day and watch citizens in the course of their daily activities, it is inevitable that at least some of these watchers will become bored and use their awesome spying power for things unrelated to looking for terrorists or criminals.

Add to this that new technologies have already been invented that can literally see through walls with use of computerized equipment that uses sound waves to capture three-dimensional images through a wall or door.[13] Military and law enforcement agencies already have designs on use of such computer technology and it may not be long before it shows up attached to mass surveillance systems like the ones in New York and London, thereby further eroding privacy, even behind closed doors.

Further, given the human propensity toward unfair discrimination (never mind police corruption), it would be naïve to suppose that at least some police officers would not be inclined to target an individual as "looking suspicious," say if this person looked to be Middle Eastern. Indeed, as was discussed in Chapter 3, the FBI's current surveillance rules already permit such discrimination. Now with networks of surveillance cameras, the state can not only target the electronic communications of persons who have Middle Eastern names; it can also target them based on how they look. Why not just program facial recognition software to confirm someone's Middle Eastern status by matching it up with a generic set of racial characteristics? A Pandora's box of unjust discrimination is opened when the hunt for terrorists by officers of a culture at "war" against terror is broadened to peering through incredibly powerful computerized lenses at the congested streets of cities like New York and London, searching for people who look "suspicious."

Further, surveillance cameras utilizing facial recognition software are inherently subject to error. In fact, according to studies sponsored by the Defense Department, such software is accurate only 54 percent of the time.[14] Its accuracy is also affected by such factors as glare on eyeglasses; wearing sunglasses; long hair obscuring the face; poor lighting that over or underexposes the face; or lack of resolution when the image is taken at a distance.[15] Insofar as facial recognition software has the potential to misidentify and confuse a law-abiding citizen with a suspected terrorist included in an FBI database, surveillance systems that utilize such software subject all of us to risk of being misidentified.

The Need for Technologies that Balance Security against Privacy

However, this does not mean that there are not any alternative technologies that may offer protection against terrorist attacks but are less likely to abridge civil liberties. For example, both New York and London surveillance systems include sensing technologies that can detect potential terrorist threats. While these sensors are incapable of detecting all types of chemical and biological threats, and false positives are a factor, they still are not likely to cause abridgments of privacy of the magnitude associated with mass surveillance using a network of cameras tracked to a main hub and keyed into the databases of federal agencies. Thus, a more sober approach to fighting crime—which is what fighting "terror" really is—might include deployment of such sensing technologies.

Such sensors might also be used in conjunction with security cameras while still not placing millions of people under surveillance. This would be true if such technology was interfaced with surveillance cameras that switched on *only if* the sensors were triggered by certain chemical, biological, or radioactive agents coming within range of the sensors; this would also mean that only the camera within the proximate vicinity of the agent in question need be activated. Such a system could accordingly offer added protection against terrorist attacks without using mass surveillance.

This is not necessarily to recommend such a system, because the infrastructure required to build it might still be used covertly to engage in mass spying. Other safety valves would need to be built into the technology. Unfortunately, in designing the infrastructure of the New York and London surveillance systems, federal and state authorities have apparently not made *any* such effort to balance the right to privacy of millions of Americans against whatever security these systems might provide.

The proposal to build failsafe systems that do not conduct mass surveillance is not likely to satisfy those who demand certainty in protecting against a future terrorist attack. However, it should be borne in mind that no technologies are perfect, and, as is true of any other type of crime prevention, it is unrealistic to demand certainty. But the same thing could also be said about mass surveillance through the use of a network of thousands of cameras equipped with facial recognition software and technology that could even see through walls, monitored by local police and federal agents.

Beyond *1984*: New Frontiers of Mass Surveillance

Surveillance cameras have finite ranges within which they can track a person. However, there are currently other technologies that can be used to track people in real time, which are not constrained by location.

Cell Phone Surveillance

One such technology is the common cell phone. Equipped with Global Positioning (GPS) capacity, if such a wireless phone is turned on, its location can be determined within 25 meters or less so that the individual carrying it can be tracked in real time.

In February 2010, following a lead from the Bush administration, the Obama Justice Department argued in favor of warrantless tracking of cell phones. Regarding a case before a U.S. appeals court, it held, "An individual has no Fourth Amendment-protected privacy interest in business records, such as cell-site usage information, that are kept, maintained and used by a cell phone company."[1] If so, then the government can follow anyone about, from place to place, without a warrant. Thus, not only can the content of our electronic messages and Internet activities be monitored, our physical location can also be tracked in real time.

In fact, the precedent for government to track our physical locations through our cell phones was set as early as 1994 with passage of the Communications Assistance for Law Enforcement Act under the Clinton administration. According to Section 103 ("Assistance Capability Requirements") of this Act, telecommunication carriers are required to ensure that their equipment, facilities, and services are capable of supporting government surveillance in the provision of "call-identifying information," such as the origin, direction, destination, and termination of each communication generated or received by a subscriber. And it required that telecommunication carriers ensure that they have the capability of "expeditiously isolating and enabling the government, pursuant to a court order or other lawful authorization, to intercept . . . all wire and electronic communications carried by the carrier within a service area to or from equipment, facilities, or services of a subscriber of such carrier."[2] Unfortunately, in contravention of the Fourth Amendment, the FBI has exploited such capability to conduct surveillance of individuals without warrant or probable cause.[3]

But cell phone surveillance is just the tip of a burgeoning technological iceberg. Cell phones can be left behind or turned off at will. However, there are new and emerging technologies that can be implanted *in* persons and therefore can track them wherever they go in real time without being disconnected. The twenty-first century will predictably make such 24/7 surveillance of millions of people a reality. The trend toward the development of miniaturized surveillance devices (so-called nanotechnology) is picking up momentum and these technologies are now beginning to be used.

Radio Frequency ID Technologies and Government Surveillance

One such technology is Radio Frequency Identification (RFID) microchips, which can be smaller than a grain of sand. These devices have the capacity to store data, which can be read at a distance by an RFID reader. Like our cell phones, the emerging technology also has GPS capacity and can thus be used to locate and track a person or object carrying the device.

A common use of RFID chips has been for inventory control. When embedded in a product, it can provide product information when scanned. In this respect, it functions like a bar code. However, unlike a bar code, which provides generic numbers for product lines, RFID chips assign a unique number to each particular item. Moreover, they can record the name of the purchaser of the product as well as credit card information if bought on credit. This means that the products with RFID chips in them have the potential to supply personal information to those who have the equipment to read them.

RFID chips have been embedded in animals such as livestock as well as in pets to keep track of them. They can be found in numerous other places, including driver licenses, passports, identification cards, automatic toll systems, credit cards, vehicle identification systems, airport baggage tags, and automatic gates.

Now RFID chips are also being implanted in human beings, not just human artifacts. In 2004, the Food and Drug Administration approved the use of RFID chips for subcutaneous implantation in patients in hospitals, which could be used by medical staff to access computerized patient information such as the patient' medical history.[4] The maker of this chip,

Verichip, has also lobbied the Department of Defense to embed RFID chips in soldiers to replace the standard "dog tags." Other human applications include implanting them in children, and even in prisoners.

No doubt, there are practical reasons for such applications to humans. Thus, this incredibly versatile, new technology can not only be used to identify a stolen vehicle but can now also be used to locate a missing child. In fact, Solusat, the Mexican distributor for Verichip, has marketed an RFID chip for this purpose under its VeriKid program.[5] RFID chips embedded in patients can provide quick access to patient information in emergency situations and help to avoid medical errors; embedding RFID chips in soldiers can hold more information and would be more difficult to remove than a dog tag;[6] and as a form of "inventory control," prisons can better keep track of prisoners by RFID-tagging them.

In fact, the London justice department has begun to explore the idea of using a hypodermic needle to inject such devices into the back of the arms of certain inmates, such as sex offenders, then releasing them from prison, thereby freeing up space in overcrowded British prisons. The prisoners would be tracked by satellite and barred from entering certain "safe" zones such as schools, playgrounds, and former victims' homes.[7]

An Emerging Internet of Humans

One wave of research concerns the creation of "an internet of things" whereby RFID interfaces are constructed between cyberspace and physical objects, thereby permitting two-way exchanges between online software technologies and databases, on the one end, and objects in the material world, on the other end. Thereby, these objects can be identified, tracked, traced, monitored, and controlled.

The "internet of things" project began as a research project by Massachusetts Institute of Technology's Auto-ID Labs to help the Department of Defense precisely track and control billions of dollars of military inventory; but there is already concern by prominent technology watchdog organizations, such as the Electronic Frontier Foundation, that the government may also have designs on using such systems for purposes of monitoring and collecting information on peoples' interests, habits, and activities through the things that they purchase.[8]

While giant retail corporations, such as Wal-Mart—a major proponent of the use of RFID chips—would probably be motivated to use the acquired information to tailor advertising campaigns to the purchasing inclinations of potential customers, the government would still be able to acquire this personal information from the commercial sector for surveillance purposes. Further, since RFID chips have already begun to be embedded in human beings, the progressive development of such a project may come to embrace human beings along with physical objects. Thus, with the advance of an "internet of things," human beings, like physical inventory, might be "tagged" with an RFID chip and systematically tracked, traced, monitored, and controlled.

Indeed, once the infrastructure is set for putting human beings online using RFID technologies, it will be possible for government to take the war on terror to new heights by keeping track of all persons residing or entering the United States, requiring that they have online tracking status. This would be the logical conclusion of a "war" policy that subordinates privacy to "winning" the war on terror. It would take to its logical conclusion the technological imperative that says to use whatever surveillance technology works best to stop terrorism.[9]

In fact, for purposes of fighting the war on terror, the 9/11 Commission Report Implementation Act of 2004 was passed, which directs that the U.S. plan for "a comprehensive integrated screening system" and a requirement for "biometric passports and other secure identification for all travel into the United States by U.S. citizens and individuals for whom immigration and nationality documentation requirements have previously been waived." These provisions have been taken to provide the authority to develop a *national identification card.* Such cards would utilize "biometric technologies" and would "link to relevant databases and data systems," presumably including the FBI's biometric database.[10] For these purposes, biometric "identifiers" might include anything from fingerprints to an individual's genome.

While such a card would not be embedded beneath our skin, we would all be required to carry one at all times. Eventually, however, issues of expedience, such as eliminating problems of loss, damage to RFID chips, and greater efficiency in hunting down terrorists, could be used as rationales to embed these chips in one's body, perhaps at birth.

As the "internet of things" evolves and becomes more mainstream, the need to establish checkpoints at which our cards (or our bodies) are scanned by an RFID reader may become obsolete. The next logical step in fighting the war on terror would then be to require that all citizens be wirelessly connected to government central command and control at all times, thereby assuring that we will each be constantly monitored in real or near-real time.

Are such possibilities speculative? Yes, but the potential of RFID technologies to become an incredibly oppressive kind of surveillance is not speculative. As was discussed in the preceding chapters, there is now a trend for government to override privacy for the sake of "winning the war on terror." Viewed in this light, it would be presumptuous to think that such technology would not be so used—at least if government does not depart from its current tendency to abridge the right to privacy in the name of national security.

RFID Surveillance Cameras in the City

RFID technologies are also currently being combined with surveillance camera technology. For example, the Tokyo-based, high-tech corporation, NEC, has created such a hybrid system that can provide continuous tracking of people and vehicles. When one of the system's cameras recognizes a moving object with an RFID tag, an RFID reader reads the tag. The system can also track the position of the object using its RFID reader, even if the object is not detected by the surveillance camera.[11] Such technology may well find its way into such surveillance systems as the New York and London systems discussed in Chapter 13.

DARPA's Persistent Stare Exploitation and Analysis System

As if such ground-based surveillance camera systems were not enough, the Defense Advanced Research Projects Agency (DARPA) has also solicited proposals for research into development of a "Persistent Stare Exploitation and Analysis System" (PerSEAS),[12] a software program "for automatically and interactively discovering actionable intelligence from wide area motion imagery (WAMI) of complex urban, suburban, and rural environments."[13]

This form of information system would use aerial surveillance cameras and sensors to look for relationships and anomalies in WAMI data that indicate "suspicious behavior, match previously learned threat activity, or match user defined threat activity." To carry out these functions, PerSEAS would also receive and send information from and to other intelligence databases, and would, therefore, appear to be another anticipated component of the existing Total Information Awareness (TIA) network of databases and link and analysis technology. In this interactive, supercomputing environment, PerSEAS would be able to issue near-real time alerts intended to interdict developing threat activities.[14]

We might, therefore, expect to see PerSEAS being deployed to avert terrorist threats in major U.S. cities. In this case, we might look forward to a time in the not-so-distant future when unmanned drones will fly over the rooftops of our homes, businesses, and schools carrying airborne surveillance technology; collecting data on our daily activities; and sending it to an NSA supercomputer for analysis.

The DARPA/IBM Global Brain Surveillance Initiative

Going beyond monitoring such aspects of human life as behavior, electronic messaging, and geographical location is the direct monitoring of people's mental aspects, such as their thoughts, perceptions, and emotions. In December 2008, IBM and collaborators from several major universities were awarded US$4.9 million from DARPA to launch the first phase of its "Systems of Neuromorphic Adaptive Plastic Scalable Electronics (SyNAPSE) initiative." Under this grant, IBM has launched its "cognitive computing initiative" to develop a (literal) "global brain."[15] According to Dharmendra Modra, IBM researcher and manager of the initiative,

> So the quest is cognitive computing, which is about engineering aspects of mind such as emotion, perception, sensation, cognition, emotion [sic], action, interaction by reverse engineering the brain and then to deploy this technology by connecting it to vast array of sensors, billions, trillions of sensors, such as sight, hearing, taste, touch, and smell; but even going further, to non-biological sensors: sensors monitoring the forest; sensors monitoring the oceans; sensors monitoring people, animals, organizations, homes, cars; and to stream this vast amount of data in real time or near real time to [a] global brain that can extract patterns, large scale invariant patterns, from the sensory overload and to act and respond to this data.[16]

The enormity of this project is glaring. Nonetheless, its intentions seem clear, and they include, among other things, the global monitoring of *human beings'* most intimate and personal space: what is going on inside their minds; and then what is going on inside their organizations, their homes, and even their cars.

A brain that literally contained *everyone's* cognitions might be the ideal of such a system of control, but even a less ambitious project of this nature would be chilling. DARPA's other research may provide a clue as to what direction this project might take regarding the monitoring of human subjects.

DARPA's interest in brain machine interfaces has been ongoing at least since 2000. It has succeeded in "reading" the brain of a monkey using electrodes implanted into its cerebral cortex. In 2004, DARPA funded a US$19 million program led by a Duke University neurobiologist, Miguel Nicolelis, in which a monkey was able to control a remote robotic arm hundreds of miles away, through a two-way wireless interaction between the monkey's cerebral cortex and the robotic arm.[17] DARPA's military goals for this project included giving combat soldiers the power to remotely control military equipment and weapons at a distance through such brain machine interfaces (BMI). As was mentioned in Chapter 1, another goal of DARPA is to remotely control the soldiers *themselves* through the use of peripheral devices wirelessly interfacing with their brains, including remotely controlling natural emotions, such as fear, and feelings, such as that of fatigue, in combat situations.

According to DARPA, an objective in connection with building such remotely controlled BMI interfaces is,

> Extraction of neural and force dynamic codes related to patterns of motor or sensory activity required for executing simple to complex motor or sensory activity (e.g., reaching, grasping, manipulating, running, walking, kicking, digging, hearing, seeing, tactile). Accessing sensory activity directly could result in the ability to monitor or transmit communications by the brain (visual, auditory, or other). This will require the exploitation of new interfaces and algorithms for providing useful nonlinear transformation, pattern extraction techniques, and the ability to test these in appropriate models or systems.[18]

Here, there are profound implications for DARPA/IBM's cognitive computing initiative to build a "global brain." If sensors that monitor and control soldiers' motor and sensory brain activities were "plugged into" a global brain through BMI interfaces, the possibility would emerge of remotely controlling and coordinating an entire army of soldiers by networking their individual brains with TIA link and analysis software, and all databases of the remote, main brain. The stored data and supercomputing capabilities could then take account of exact coordinates of enemy lines, military targets, geographical conditions, such as weather, terrain, and climate, and a host of other relevant data input that could give an army a marked, logistical advantage over a nonnetworked opponent.

Of course, this advantage would be purchased at the expense of turning human soldiers into military robots plugged into a literal network of remotely controlled fighting machines. There would be little left that would make them distinctively human. Their brains would serve as biological peripheral devices of a main "motherboard" that would contain the primary hard drive, to which all sensory and motor input would be uploaded, and from which all pertinent information and commands pertaining to real time or near-real time military operations would be downloaded.

DARPA has already succeeded in learning how to remote control insects such as the giant flower beetle using BMI interfaces:

> The beetle's payload consists of an off-the-shelf microprocessor, a radio receiver, and a battery attached to a custom-printed circuit board, along with six electrodes implanted into the animals' optic lobes and flight muscles. Flight commands are wirelessly sent to the beetle via a radio-frequency

transmitter that's controlled by a nearby laptop. Oscillating electrical pulses delivered to the beetle's optic lobes trigger takeoff, while a single short pulse ceases flight. Signals sent to the left or right basilar flight muscles make the animal turn right or left, respectively.[19]

While it may be possible to create nonbiological, robotic beetles, it appears to have made more sense to DARPA to utilize the innate, natural flight control capacities of the insect, integrating sensory feedback from its own sensory systems, instead of attempting to replicate these systems robotically. Analogously, DARPA's goal of using BMI technologies to control biological soldiers, rather than robotically replicating humans' natural navigational capacities, may have seemed to it the most expedient approach.

It is possible that, with the aid of a tiny surveillance camera attached to its back, online insects like DARPA's giant flower beetle could be used to run search and rescue missions. However, this research clearly supports its objective to produce remotely controlled soldiers. Seen with this goal in view, DARPA's remotely controlled beetle research portends an ominous possibility for human subjects.

Having begun with implanting BMI interfaces in monkeys, graduating to soldiers, the technology might then be extended to further populations, for example, physicians performing delicate surgery. But why limit BMI technology when it could also be used to improve parenting skills; exponentially expand individual intellects and knowledge bases; and eliminate or greatly reduce accidents on the highways, criminal activities, and, of course, "win the war on terror." In other words, why not make BMI/global brain technologies mainstream.

If this technology were mainstreamed, it would portend new roles for the giant telecoms. Thus, independent service providers for delivery of SyNAPSE services might permit access to the global brain comensurate with how much one could afford to pay. Those who could afford the premium plan might operate in the "fast lane" of this neuvo-net, global information highway, while those who could not, might maximally receive "basic" service.

Given that FISA laws continue to require telecoms to cooperate with government in monitoring all electronic communications passing through its switches, we could expect that the global brain network would be "administered"by the federal government. This would be a post-Orwellian age, an age in which an "internet of things" had morphed into an internet of humans, and humans into a network of peripheral, embodied brains attached to a main brain. Fortunately, this vision is still in the realm of science fiction. But the cyber infrastructure and basic technologies needed to remove it from science fiction and place it in the realm of science are already realities. Indeed, DARPA's BMI technologies have already arrived and can be expected to improve.

Currently, sensors must be situated on the scalp or surgically implanted inside the brain cavity in order to monitor neural brain impulses. In fact, several patents have already been issued, which describe forms of brain machine interfaces. Moreover, patents have been issued that improve the techniques for wireless transmission of the brain patterns intercepted by BMI interfaces. Much of this BMI research has been funded by DARPA, which is likely to continue to make improvements on the methods for intercepting brain activity, coding it, and transmitting it through cyberspace.

It has classically been a mark of paranoia for one to cover one's head with tin foil in order to prevent someone from "picking" one's brain. However, as BMI technologies improve, it is possible that new sensing means for acquiring the cognitive content of one's brain could be developed that allow remote access to the brain, that is, without placing sensors on or inside the skull. If this happens, then it will be possible for subjects to involuntarily have their thoughts monitored, tracked, and (literally) stolen. This might also open the floodgates for involuntarily connecting persons to a global brain network, thereby having one's sensory and motor brain activities remotely controlled by others, notably by the federal government.

Such prospects will likely be perceived by most as very bleak. So unthinkable are such applications of technology that we may conclude that, even if technologically feasible, they will never come to pass. However, this is to ignore the direction of DARPA research. It is also to ignore history, which has had its dark possibilities come to fruition. Ironically, it was IBM that helped the Nazis keep track of Jewish people through the use of punch-card, computing technology, which at the time was innovative. So it would not be shocking if, in the present century, the same company were to come to the aid of a government with totalitarian leanings by constructing a formidable form of TIA technology such as that conceived under the DARPA/IBM global brain joint venture.

A culture of control will not come to fruition overnight. It is a gradual process commensurate with changes in technology. Evidently, future technologies such as BMI and SyNAPSE technologies will present a challenge to the survival of privacy in the twenty-first century, and beyond. It is not viable to simply hope either that we will not use these emerging monitor-and-control technologies for oppressive purposes (for example, we will just stick to using BMIs to help paralyzed people move a prosthetic limb, or we will just restrict RFID technology to keeping track of inventory), or that the technologies in question will simply not work. The stakes are just too high to not react—and indeed overreact—to these dangerous possibilities.

15

Reality and the Politics
of Power

On the morning of June 4, 1987, thousands of students filled Tiananmen Square to protest against the oppression of the Chinese Communist Party. But that evening the People's Liberation Army rolled in with tanks, opening fire, killing thousands of students, and injuring thousands more.

This actually happened, and there were eyewitnesses. Nevertheless, the Chinese government has refused to admit that the massacre even occurred. The event is not mentioned in Chinese textbooks; Internet police patrol the Internet and block access to information about the massacre; Chinese media, which are state run, are forbidden from reporting about it; and the government arrests dissidents who attempt to speak out against what really happened. Instead, the Chinese government claims that the event was merely "a political disturbance" of "counter-revolutionary hooligans"; that civilians incited the violence; and that deaths were few.[1]

The sad truth is that, in a culture of control (of which Communist China is an example), the government and its mainstream media accomplices have power over what passes as reality. In such a culture, it is not facts but rather politics that defines reality. "We control matter because we control the mind," said a foot soldier of Big Brother in Orwell's *1984*. "Reality is inside the skull.... There is nothing that we could not do. Invisibility, levitation—anything. I could float off this floor like a soap bubble if I wish to. I do not wish to, because the Party does not wish it."[2]

And the possibilities for state-controlled reality are likely to increase with new technologies. We are now entering an age of virtual reality where facts existing outside human consciousness may not be readily distinguishable from those purely inside the mind. Currently, there exist virtual reality (VR) Web sites that allow people to build a "second life" for themselves where they can interact with others in a virtual world. For example, one such site called Keneva claims that it "blurs the line between the offline and online world in a 3D virtual world where the virtual you is an extension of the real you."[3] As VR technologies continue to expand the virtual experience to encompass all the senses so that the qualitative experience becomes indistinguishable from being in the offline world, the VR subject may eventually lose track of the distinction altogether.

In such a world, those who control the VR technologies will, like Orwell's Party, hold mastery over "reality" while the rest of us will be manipulated like puppets. This idea can be gleaned from sources as ancient as Plato's Allegory of the Cave, and it has been popularly expressed in the film, the Matrix, in which a cyber-intelligence keeps the minds of human beings occupied and trapped inside a virtual world while it lives off the heat of their bodies in seeking dominion over the offline world.

The idea of the state keeping its citizens focused on a make-believe world while they are exploited for purposes of world domination is not at all far-fetched. In fact, this has already happened, albeit in the low-tech world of cable and network news. For example, as was discussed in Chapter 6, the American public has been the target of information and media warfare and "perception management" aimed at selling the war in Iraq.

This program consisted of mainstream media dissemination of phony intelligence claiming that Saddam Hussein possessed weapons of mass destruction. It capitalized off of the 9/11 attacks by falsely linking Hussein to these attacks. It staged phony events such as the toppling of the statute of Hussein in Baghdad (staged by American troops, not Iraqi citizens) to symbolize an American victory;[4] and a morale-boosting, heroic tale of the capture and escape of Private Jessica Lynch from an Iraqi hospital, which turned out to be a PR stunt, compliments once again of the Rendon Group.[5] This was not virtual reality; nor was it reality. But, for the average American, it *seemed* real.

Building such bogus public perception may become an easier task with the advent of new delivery technologies. Thus, in the future, VR technologies may make it possible for consumers of news and information to be inserted into a news event and experience, in three-dimensions, being an eye-witness to, or a participant in taking out a Taliban military installation by remote controlling a predator drown. Indeed, virtual reality war games used to train military already exist and a logical extension of this may be to integrate them into a digital "news" package.

In fact, new digital technologies go beyond virtual reality to include "augmented reality," which is a hybrid between offline reality and virtual reality. Recently Lockheed Martin received a contract from DARPA to develop a set of lenses that would be capable of augmenting real objects with virtual images as well as data. For example, a soldier wearing these lenses would be able to mark an object with a number and other soldiers wearing the lenses would also be able to see the number superimposed on the object.

If such technology becomes mainstream, just how reality is transfigured will depend on who is behind the controls. Matrix-like worlds are in the offing. In the hands of a megalomanical government, "information warfare" and "perception management" can take on new and chilling meanings.

Mediated Reality

It is not technology per se that is moving us toward a culture of control, for technology does not have to be used to undermine autonomy. It can (and should) be used to enhance it. For example, in 1877, the establishment of the Bell Telephone Company marked a milestone for human communication that would change the face of business and interpersonal communications forever. However, few if any would have thought that this company would be implicated in helping government spy on the phone calls of millions of people throughout the world in the twenty-first century. For, while telephony could be adapted for such a purpose, this use was parasitic on its primary communications function.

To be sure, technology is a factor in this degenerative trend but that is because of an underlying voracious appetite for money and power. What giant media companies publish as news and information is largely determined by their bottom lines; and what governments enact as law is largely determined by corporate lobbies, politico-corporate quid quo pro, campaign finances, and the desire to stay in office. These politico-corporate factors tend to shape the reality that Americans see and hear on network and cable news shows.

Advertisers do not care to advertise on a network or cable TV station if they will not stand to reach enough people to make the high costs of advertising worthwhile. Thus, news and information must be assembled in a manner that will keep viewers' attention, and cater to their values and interest, including their political views. Thus, attitude fitting is an important part of the news.

At the same time, media companies walk a tight rope with the federal government. In November 2004, right before Americans went to the polls to cast their votes for a new president, a headline that read "Bush Lied about Warrantless Wire Tapping of All Private Conversations" would have certainly gotten the attention of millions of Americans, and might have changed the course of American history; however, such a headline would have angered a lot of power brokers atop Capital Hill. Consequently, in 2004, no such headline saw the light of day, even though the *New York*

Times was aware of Bush's unlawful surveillance program prior to the 2004 presidential election.[6]

A popular assumption of mainstream media is that the average consumer of news and information has a low IQ and short attention span. Thus, for the sake of holding their attention (ultimately for the sake of maximizing advertising profits), what passes for reality on mainstream media stations is a "dumbed down" piecemeal rendition of reality.

The happenstance renditions of reality depicted by mainstream news media are also an important part of herding Americans into blind conformity. A constant, 24/7 line of news feeds on cable networks such as Fox and CNN would suggest that Americans are being kept well-informed; however, by any reasonable standard of what it means to be informed, this assumption is false.

What one gets when one tunes into mainstream network and cable news is a simplistic stream of reports about disconnected events in the world with little or no attempt to explain them. As Michael Parenti expressed, "Instead we are left to see the world as do mainstream pundits, as a scatter of events and personalities propelled by happenstance, circumstance, confused intentions, bungled operations, and individual ambitions—rarely by powerful class interests.[7] Being adequately informed requires *understanding* these events. However, whatever underpins or supports such knowledge has been removed. Thus,

> we read or hear that "fighting broke out in the region," or "many people were killed in the disturbances," or "famine is on the increase." Recessions apparently just happen like some natural phenomenon ("our economy is in a slump"), having little to do with the constant war of capital against labor and the contradictions between productive power and earning power.[8]

Such lifting out of context also makes it possible for mainstream media to spin reality to the beat of a particular political agenda. Thus, being told that the "Insurgents killed ten American troops" leaves out the fact that the so-called "insurgents" were motivated to defend their homeland against invaders—not unlike what motivated the Americans themselves to attack British invaders during the Revolutionary War. Here, the absolutistic notion that there is only one side to a story—the American side—is fortified with emotionally charged pejorative language ("insurgent"). This further emotional import manipulates rather than informs.

Headlines are also a common ground for placing emotively charged language aimed at manipulating support for a given political agenda. When America invaded Iraq, the mainstream corporate media ran the headline, "Shock and Awe," as though the dismembered bodies of innocent civilians—many women and children lying in heaps on residential streets—were not human lives; and as though the experience of bombs and mortar fire was not really "terrorizing" those whom the U.S. government claimed to be liberating. Mainstream media concealed from the public this gruesome reality about death and destruction while focusing instead on the staged scene of a statue of Saddam being toppled. And now, under the Obama administration, mainstream media is still not providing Americans an accurate and complete accounting of deaths related to the U.S. invasions of Iraq and Afghanistan.[9]

The Control of Higher Education

Higher education in America is perhaps the most stable bastion of democracy. However, it is presently under attack by right-wing conservative organizations, which are attempting to use the banner of "student rights" to propagate its own right-wing agenda. One such organization is Students for Academic Freedom (SAF). The announced purpose of the SAF is to serve as "a clearing house and communications center for a national coalition of student organizations whose goal is to end the political abuse of the university and to restore integrity to the academic mission as a disinterested pursuit of knowledge."[10]

In fact, the SAF is far from "disinterested." It is a branch of the David Horowitz Freedom Center founded in 1988 by conservative activist David Horowitz. This center has received support from such right-wing organizations as the Bradley Foundation and the Sarah Scaife Foundation, the latter of which had ties to the Project for the New American Century.[11] The political agenda of the Horowitz Center has included stances against affirmative action, reparations for slavery, support for escalating a war on terrorism, and the doctrine of preemption.[12]

Thus, what it construes as ending the political abuse of the university and restoring integrity to academia can be read as an attempt to establish a foothold in the universities, which have been the most ardent critics of its own political agenda.

This center, acting through its SAF, has spearheaded attempts to pass legislation giving legal teeth to its "Student Bill of Rights." According to this document,

> Curricula and reading lists in the humanities and social sciences should reflect the uncertainty and unsettled character of all human knowledge in these areas by providing students with dissenting sources and viewpoints where appropriate. While teachers are and should be free to pursue their own findings and perspectives in presenting their views, they should consider and

make their students aware of other viewpoints. Academic disciplines should welcome a diversity of approaches to unsettled questions.[13]

On the surface, there is obviously nothing wrong with "diversity of approaches to unsettled questions." However, the obvious question is who decides what these viewpoints are and where they are "appropriate." Should an anthropology professor be required to teach creationism along with evolution? Should American history courses include the view that "Black Africans and Arabs were responsible for enslaving the ancestors of African-Americans" (a view that Horowitz himself entertained)?[14] Should a sociology professor be required to teach the view that affirmative action for minorities is based on a lie since "African-Americans are failing because they are not prepared by their families and their culture to succeed" (another view that Horowitz has held)?[15]

In fact, proposed legislation for such a student bill of rights would authorize students to file suit against their professors for failing to satisfy their expectations. Far from promoting academic freedom, such legislation would have the effect of intimidating professors into offering views that they themselves would deem inappropriate for inclusion in their courses.[16]

Such extreme subjectivism is paradigmatic of the Orwellian concept that "reality is inside the skull" and that, therefore, descriptions of external reality can be melded to whatever one desires. This is the incipient seed that permits the rewriting of reality to fit one political agenda over another. And this hidden political agenda can thereby be dressed up in the garb of student rights and academic freedom whereas it is just the opposite.

The danger is that indoctrination will be substituted for critical thinking in the name of education. Some views are simply not respectable and do not deserve to be taught. Thus, the claim that racism did not prevent the advance of blacks in America flies in the face of empirical evidence. (Who can rationally deny that Blacks did not receive an inferior education in segregated America?) And while creationism may be grist for the mill of a religion course, the attempt to pass it off as science is plainly out of gear with the large body of scientific evidence that contradicts the claim that the earth was formed about 6,000 years ago.

Also, while ethics is replete with hard cases and room for disagreement, basic human rights cannot be dismissed as merely relative. When the Chinese government killed thousands of student protestors in Tiananmen Square, an atrocious violation of human rights was committed. And when, in America, blacks and whites lived in segregated quarters, drank from separate water fountains, used separate bathroom facilities, and received separate educations, the injustice could not be covered up under the banner of "separate but equal."

Such atrocious violations of human rights in our own backyard should remind Americans that they are not immune to being indoctrinated to accept great iniquity under some slogan or cover for oppression in the form of law. Reality can be misrepresented in such ways. However, a bogus claim or idea, no matter how artfully it may be dressed up to look like truth, is still counterfeit.

Surveillance Video Cameras in the Classroom

The attempt to control curricula at institutions of higher education becomes more disconcerting when it is coupled with a growing trend to install surveillance video cameras on college campuses. Allegedly for security purposes, at some universities, such as the University of Texas at Austin, cameras have been installed in classrooms, which can monitor in real time professors' lectures and class discussions. The University of Texas also successfully lobbied the Texas Legislature to change existing law to permit it to keep information on its surveillance activities from the public. This means that university administrators can legally monitor students and faculty without their knowledge or consent.[17]

As bastions of democracy, colleges and universities are supposed to be free from abridgments of academic freedom; however, a consequence of such monitoring is to intimidate both students and faculty from freely expressing their views. The trend to install surveillance cameras, especially in classrooms, therefore threatens to undermine the culture of autonomy existing on college campuses and to morph this democratic forum into a burgeoning culture of control.

An increasing number of public elementary and high schools in the United States and Great Britain[18] are also being fitted with surveillance cameras, allegedly for security purposes. For example, in Biloxi, Mississippi, each of its eleven public schools has had surveillance cameras installed in every one of its classrooms.[19] Moreover, some cameras have also been purchased with federal money (such as ones in Canton, Mississippi), raising the specter of federal monitoring of students' activities.[20]

As a rule, state laws do not regulate the use of surveillance cameras in schools, hence increasing the possibility that surveillance cameras will be used for purposes other than maintaining security. However, some states have attempted to address at least some aspects of the lack of regulation. For instance, in 2009, legislation was introduced in the state of Washington (pending at the time of this writing) requiring that notice be posted outside public school rooms and buildings stating that occupants may be subject to video monitoring.[21] Unfortunately, such a proposal fails to address the more fundamental issue of purposes of monitoring.

If the recent FISA amendments are to serve as a model for prospective laws governing monitoring of students inside their schools, then the "significant purpose" of such monitoring may be touted as maintenance of security while also permitting monitoring for purposes unrelated to this purpose. And, as with FISA, unless there are provisions made for oversight—such as monitoring the monitors—it is unlikely that such laws will safeguard against abuse of information gleaned from classroom surveillance, for example, the firing of instructors based on their political views.

In chapter 13, it was seen how surveillance cameras with interfaces to federal agencies have already been installed in private as well as public zones of major cities in the United States and Britain. It is, therefore, not surprising that such cameras are now starting to be used in schools. A logical step in this movement toward a culture of control is to attach school surveillance cameras to the massive total information network infrastructure already being operated by the federal government. If and when this happens, there is the real and serious possibility that education in the United States will become little more than state indoctrination, monitored and controlled by federal agencies.

Unless the trend to use surveillance cameras in schools is stopped, it can reasonably be predicted that this use will continue to expand. In fact, in one recent case, without knowledge or consent of its students, a school district in Philadelphia had allegedly gone so far as to install software in school-issued laptops, which permitted school officials to remotely activate the computers' webcams and to spy on the students *in their homes*.[22] The School district allegedly claimed that it had installed the software in the computers for purposes of recovering lost or stolen computers. However, at the time of this writing, a federal class action lawsuit against the school district is pending, which in part argues that, pursuant to the Fourth Amendment, the students' reasonable expectation of privacy with respect to the use of such computers had been violated.[23] The outcome of this legal case will set a major precedent. If the right to privacy is permitted to be overridden for such purposes as keeping track of school equipment, then this will be tantamount to having no reasonable expectations about privacy, even in one's own home.

Common Confusions about Freedom and Democracy

The monitoring and controlling of education is a breeding ground for religious intolerance and an opportunity to proselytize and indoctrinate students to share a common faith. In this context, it is often automatically assumed by the extreme right in America that God exists and that this God is the one embraced by Christians. Ironically, despite such intolerance, many members of this group still rate themselves as champions of freedom and democracy. The reason for this paradox appears to lie in a fundamental semantic confusion about the meaning of "democracy" in relation to other terms of political economy, such as "capitalism," "socialism," "communism," and "fascism." While Karl Marx proclaimed religion to be the opium of the people, and capitalism as a system of exploitation of workers aimed at the destruction of a free and democratic society, these individuals have gone to the opposite extreme of placing God and capitalism as the grounds of freedom and democracy. Here, the distinction between "democracy" and "theocracy" has been ignored along with separation of church and state. And the definition of "a free nation" has somehow morphed into the idea of a "free market," albeit one that is controlled by just a few behemoth corporations.

Having built a corporate dynasty on slave labor and the stifling of fair competition, retail giants, such as Walmart, have become the symbol of the free world, and many Americans have supported this new symbolism by becoming faithful patrons. Thus, many Walmart shoppers neither know nor seem to care about the expense paid in human freedom for this monolithic shoppers' paradise. Some may be too distracted by the savings and the wide array of products displayed on the shelves of a "superstore" to contemplate the gruesome reality behind it all.[24]

In America, colossal health insurance and pharmaceutical companies reap large profits while millions go without adequate health care. Still, many Americans condemn "socialized" medicine because any such social constraints would mean the end of a free-market economy. The "logic" here is black or white. We can be socialists or capitalists (but not both). Since we are capitalists, we must reject socialism. This is precisely the kind of thinking that usurped the possibility of a public option in the recent attempt by the Obama administration to pass healthcare reform.

The consequence of accepting this line of thinking is acquiescence in a politico-corporate system that is markedly antidemocratic, exploitative, and unjust. Instead of condemning this system, many who accept it do so because they think it would be un-American (socialistic, communistic, and even fascistic) to oppose it. Thus, in the name of freedom, they embrace a free-market economy that is anything but free.

Mix into this brew an appeal to the great American tradition of free enterprise; add how un-American and "socialistic" the alternative would be; let the mix be stirred ("authorized") by the president while the mainstream media disseminate the mix and defend it against anyone who might try to provide an antidote; and notice how many millions of Americans fall into a trance of conformity. It is not hard for the politico-corporate media establishment to have this effect when many Americans fail to think for themselves.

Against the dangers of not thinking for oneself, the eighteenth-century British philosopher, John Stuart Mill, admonished, "He who lets the world, or his own portion of it, choose his plan of life for him, has no need of any other faculty than the ape-like one of imitation." We each must do our part in standing firm against the destructive influence of blind conformity. In this post 9/11 era, we can do this by asserting and defending our civil liberties instead of surrendering them; courageously confronting the threat of terrorism instead of caving to government scare tactics and the contrivances of a "war on terror"; cultivating tolerance and respect for others instead of allowing ourselves to be stirred to irrational fear and hatred; keeping ourselves alert and informed despite the failure of the mainstream media to satisfactorily do its job; keeping our faith without becoming dogmatists and fanatics; and living democratically by respecting (indeed defending) the right of those with unpopular viewpoints to be heard; and being an active participant and voice in opposing antidemocratic, oppressive, and dangerous government policies. These things all Americans have a duty to do. They all require thinking for oneself instead of in lockstep.

16

Freedom is Slavery:
Authoritarianism and
Emotional Manipulation in
a Culture of Control

In Orwell's *1984*, a member of the "Inner Party" explains the party's slogan, "Slavery is freedom":

> [P]ower is collective. The individual only has power in so far as he ceases to be an individual. You know the Party slogan: "Freedom is Slavery". . . . the human being is always defeated. . . . But if he can make complete, utter submission, if he can escape from his identity, if he can merge himself in the Party so that he is the Party, then he is all-powerful and immortal.[1]

This is a core idea behind a culture of control, for such a culture relies on the breaking down of individuality in favor of collectivism defined by blind conformity to the will of the state. Such a culture relies on submission as a means of achieving power. If an individual absorbs his identity into the collectivity, into the state, then he has the power and authority of the state behind him instead of against him. For those who submit, this is a psychological payoff.

Authoritarianism

Unfortunately, this sense of power is purchased at a high price; for blind submission to state authority is also a recipe for the dismantling of civil liberties. If citizens submit to state authority when it encroaches on basic rights, it is predictable that the state will continue to escalate its power and control over its subjects. Indeed, in the capacity of government workers and citizens, such authoritarians made the rise of Nazi Germany possible.

Here, "authority" signifies power and those who wield it—the ruling party, a giant corporation, the rich and famous, the influential. Authoritarians are the groupies, yes-men, henchmen, and servants of such authorities, who bask in the association with the powerful.

Now in America, government agents spy on American citizens without a court warrant even if they privately believe that their state is asking them to do something that is probably unconstitutional; workers for the telecoms are willing to oblige; congressional authoritarians (both Democrats and Republicans alike) walk lockstep in eviscerating the Foreign Intelligence Surveillance Act; and citizens whose right to privacy is transgressed have tremendous faith in their government and trust that it will protect them against an invisible enemy who might otherwise strike at any time, without warning, at our cities, schools, financial districts, and transit systems.

Surely such matters, so it is supposed, are best left in the hands of the politicians and national defense agencies. What do ordinary people know about these things anyway? To distrust state authority, to display lack of solidarity with one's nation when its very existence hangs in the balance, is unconscionable. Instead, what is morally incumbent is allegiance to state authority because the state in its infinite wisdom knows best. As for the spies and their corporate accomplices, they are doing their jobs, following orders, ultimately in the service of their nation, for the sake of "national security." Never mind having independent thought and principles, and a conscience. These are for the "surrender monkey," "the liberal," and "the traitor."

Here, there is an analogy between those who would follow an unjust state order and those who would work for an organized crime syndicate. If the illicit act is ordered by the one with authority, then it must be heeded, even if the target is innocent. Seldom are questions asked; for what matters is that one does what one is told. Having absorbed personal individuality into a collective identity, authoritarians always take on and define themselves in terms of the primary values, interests, and goals of the authority, and, accordingly, tend to view their own personal worth in terms of this association and alignment.

It takes an army of such blind conformists to conduct an immoral and senseless war. The authoritarian speaks: "The president said there are weapons of mass destruction in Iraq, so he must know. After all, he is the president." This vacant trust made it possible for the George W. Bush administration to cancel the writ of habeas corpus, operate prison camps that tortured detainees, contravene the Geneva Conventions, issue signing statements that nullified and trivialized the power of Congress, ignore congressional subpoenas, fire federal prosecutors for political reasons not relevant to their performances, deprive citizens of their first amendment rights to free speech and peaceful assembly, and a host of other illegal and unconstitutional actions and policies.

In 2006, when the nonpartisan study group on the Iraq war issued its recommendations to withdraw the troops from Iraq, the president rejected it. Instead, he asked for an increase of troops—up to 200,000 or more over a five-year period. Despite the fact that the military commanders warned against this action, Congress still funded it, and the then newly sworn Secretary of Defense Robert Gates followed his orders obediently. These actions were those of authoritarians, people who follow orders because they come from an authority. To date, there is no clear evidence that this "surge" really had any long-term, positive effect; although, such a critical stance is not one the mainstream media has been willing to stress.

In contrast to the authoritarian are unsung heroes like Richard Barlow. This name is not likely to ring a bell for most Americans, but he is an example of what is sometimes required to overcome authoritarianism. Once a top intelligence officer at the Pentagon who helped to uncover Pakistan's attempt to acquire nuclear weapons, in 1989, Barlow blew the whistle on top-level officials in the George H. W. Bush administration and was fired for it. These officers, including the deputy assistant secretary of defense, were misleading Congress about Pakistan's program, and Barlow told the truth. Stripped of his security clearances, his intelligence career ended along with his marriage. Despite the fact that federal investigators found that he was unjustly fired, he was still unable to collect a federal pension.[2]

Here is an example of someone who defied the government expectation that its officers act as loyal authoritarians, and he paid a price. It is a price, however, that is unfairly borne by the few who, like Barlow, refuse to walk lockstep rather than to surrender their moral integrity. But what if people like Barlow were the rule rather than the exception. This is an ideal not likely to be realized, but there is still the realistic goal of reducing the numbers willing to walk lockstep with what they know or should know to be wrong, and to instead stand on principle.

This is not to disavow the importance of authority or to recommend anarchy as though the only choices were lawless contempt for authority on the one hand and blind conformity on the other. Rather, the realistic choice includes knowing when listening to authority has gone too far, as when one is asked to do what one knows to be wrong. Hitler said "conscience is for Jews" and he proceeded to exterminate them along with others including those who had enough conscience to resist him. The fact is, dictators don't like people of conscience because they make poor puppets. A better world, however, portends more persons of conscience and fewer authoritarians.

Media Authoritarians

This applies to some reporters, particularly those who work in the main-stream. Risking their lives on the battlefield and in other dangerous places in order to get a story only to have the facts twisted and censored by their editors, they should ask themselves if their talents could be better spent else-where. Here, the authoritarianism lies in submission to giant conglomerates that perceive the business of news as just another means for maximizing their bottom lines. A salient example is the case of former *New York Times* reporter, Judith Miller, whose work as an "embedded journalist" during the George W. Bush administration placed her in harm's way to help govern-ment build public support for a dubious war policy.[3] Such journalists would better serve the public by serving independent media organizations not beholden to the government. This is because the job of the Fourth Estate is not to serve the government but to provide a check and balance against government's misuse of power.

Media authoritarians also include "news" pundits and celebrities like Chris Matthews of MSNBC, and former news anchor of CBS, Dan Rather. These are corporate media equivalents of government officers like former Attorney General Alberto Gonzalez who, sworn to execute the law, helped the Bush administration underwrite violations of constitutional law, such as the cancellation of habeas corpus, the use of torture on detainees, and the warrantless spying on American citizens.

Chris Matthews, the host of MSNBC's nightly news show, Hardball, went to bat for George W. Bush and the Iraq war at the height of their popularity but backpedaled when this popularity waned. For example, on September 21, 2006, Matthews stated, "I have been a voice out there against this bullshit war from the beginning."[4] Yet on May 1, 2003, when Bush pro-claimed, "[M]ission accomplished," he was George W. Bush's cheerleader:

> He won the war. He was an effective commander. Everybody recognizes that, I believe, except a few critics. . . . He looks for real. . . . [H]e didn't fight in a war, but he looks like he does. . . . We're proud of our president. . . . Women like a guy who's president. Check it out. The women like this war. I think we like having a hero as our president.

Matthews, therefore, appears to be a "voice out there" for the powers that be, which include the current government administration and his corpo-rate bosses at MSNBC.

Six days after the September 11, 2001, attacks, when former CBS news anchor Dan Rather appeared on the *Late Show with David Letterman* he stated, "George Bush is the president, he makes the decisions," and

"Wherever he wants me to line up, just tell me where. And he'll make the call."[5] As a journalist constitutionally entrusted to holding the feet of the government to the fire, Rather's docility and willingness to "line up" wherever the president wanted him to, was a striking case of authoritarianism. Instead of asking the "toughest of the tough questions" about how the attacks managed to occur in the first place, why the Bin Laden family had been whisked out of the country after the attacks instead of being interrogated, why Bush was more interested in finishing his reading of *The Pet Goat* than to spring into action, and a host of other glaring questions about failed intelligence and botched national defenses, Rather was deferent.

Other authoritarian pundits and celebrities include neoconservatives, such as Bill O'Reilly, Glenn Beck, and Sean Hannity, all of Fox News; and Ann Coulter and Rush Limbaugh, among others. These "neoconservative" authoritarians do not have an allegiance to the state as such, but rather exclusively and narrowly to a state that is based on a particular party politics associated with the extreme right-wing branch of the Republican Party. They tend to be bellicose, mean-spirited, and prone to misstatement of fact and inconsistency.[6]

O'Reilly, whose mantra is "looking out for the folks," advocated a terrorist attack on San Francisco. After a ballot measure was passed by 60 percent of San Franciscans opposing military recruitment at public high schools and colleges, O'Reilly proclaimed, "[I]f Al Qaeda comes in here and blows you up, we're not going to do anything about it. We're going to say, look, every other place in America is off-limits to you, except San Francisco.... You want to blow up the Coit Tower? Go ahead." It is difficult to imagine a more dedicated foot soldier of News Corp (parent company of Fox News) or the Bush administration.

On January 15, 2007, on Fox's *O'Reilly Factor*, O'Reilly discussed the case of Shawn Hornbeck, who had recently been found after having been abducted at the age of eleven. In the four years during which he was held, he was sodomized and tortured. His captor also threatened to kill him if he tried to escape.[7] "There was an element here that this kid liked about his circumstances," said O'Reilly. "The situation here for this kid looks to me to be a lot more fun than what he had under his old parents. He didn't have to go to school. He could run around and do whatever he wanted."[8] Here, O'Reilly's words speak for themselves about his callousness and lack of empathy for the plight of an innocent child.

Fox's Glenn Beck has gone so far as to *groundlessly* accuse Barrack Obama of discriminating against white people, and of being a racist.[9] On *Fox and Friends*, on June 28, 2009, in the context of discussing the Henry Louis Gates case, Beck referred to Obama as "a guy who has a deep-seated hatred for white people or the white culture" and that "This guy is, I believe, a racist."[10]

On April 22, 2009, Sean Hannity, on his Fox News show, discussed water-boarding with his guest, actor Charles Grodin, who asked Hannity if he was for torture. Hannity said he was for "enhanced interrogation," but denied that waterboarding was torture. Grodin asked, "Would you consent to be waterboarded? We can waterboard you?" "Sure," said Hannity, "I'll do it for charity. I'll let you do it. I'll do it for the troops' families."[11] However, after having consented to having it done to him, Hannity never delivered on his promise, despite the fact that MSNBC's Keith Olbermann offered to donate US$1000.00 to charity for every second Hannity withstood waterboarding.[12]

This method of interrogation, which dates back to the Spanish Inquisition, involves strapping the subject down, putting a cloth over the face, and pour-ing water onto the cloth, resulting in the painful sensation of drowning. Since water does in fact enter the lungs, this sensation is that of actually drowning, not a mere simulation.

Although the *Army Field Manual* explicitly forbids waterboarding, and U.S. courts have obtained convictions against individuals who have employed it, the Bush administration used it at least three times on detain-ees, calling it "enhanced interrogation," and refusing to admit that it was torture. So Hannity obediently reiterated the Bush administration's official line, yet his failure to allow himself to be waterboarded betrayed his words.

On October 5, 1995, radio talk show host Rush Limbaugh stated the following:

> There's nothing good about drug use. We know it. It destroys individuals. It destroys families. Drug use destroys societies. . . . And so if people are vio-lating the law by doing drugs, they ought to be accused and they ought to be convicted and they ought to be sent up. What this says to me is that too many whites are getting away with drug use. . . . The answer to this disparity is not to start letting people out of jail because we're not putting others in jail who are breaking the law. The answer is to go out and find the ones who are getting away with it, convict them and send them up the river, too.

However, Limbaugh, who himself illegally obtained thousands of dosages of OxyContin and other painkillers, pleaded "not guilty" to "doctor shop-ping," a third-degree felony punishable by up to five years in prison, and he took his case to the Florida Supreme Court to keep himself out of prison. So, while he was willing to see others "sent up the river" who obtained and used illegal drugs, he was not willing to accept the same fate for himself.

In her book, *Godless: The Church of Liberalism*, Ann Coulter attacked a group of widows who lost their husbands in the 9/11 attacks and who have been critical of George W. Bush's handling of terrorism. Coulter writes, "These broads are millionaires, lionized on TV and in articles about them, reveling in their status as celebrities and stalked by griefarazzis. I've never seen people enjoying their husbands' deaths so much."[13]

Unfortunately, examples like these can be expanded ad nauseam. The lack of attention to evidence, intolerance for alternative perspectives, disrespectful treatment of others, and the refusal to practice what one preaches make such media authoritarians poor role models for a nation priding itself on being democratic. It may be of lesser concern what views they espouse than *how* they reach them; to wit, through mean-spiritedness, false and unwarranted factual claims, intimidation, hatefulness, hypocrisy, and jingoism, all used to sway public opinion.

Anonymous Authoritarianism

Such media authoritarianism can promote cult-like, blind conformity among consumers of news and information. For example, Rush Limbaugh supporters are dubbed "Dittoheads" because they are expected to simply accept and reiterate the views of their media authority. Questioning Limbaugh's authority is thus out of the question. However, not all blindly accepted views in the public arena are sustained by deference to an identifiable media (or government) authority. For, once a view gains popular acceptance, even if it is false or irrational, the mere fact that it *is* popularly accepted can help to sustain it.

According to social psychologist Erich Fromm, there is another form of authoritarianism that has *anonymous* authority. In other forms of authoritarianism, there is always an identifiable authority—the President, the United States government, News Corp., Rush Limbaugh, God. In contrast, in anonymous authoritarianism, there is no identifiable authority.

According to Fromm, in this latter type of authoritarianism, "nobody makes a demand, neither a person nor an idea nor a moral law. Yet we all conform as much or more than people in an intensely authoritarian society would." Here, the authority is a vacuous "It." And what is "It"? It is "profit, economic necessity, the market, common sense, public opinion, what 'one' does, thinks, or feels." Since this "authority" is not overtly identifiable it is unassailable. "Who can attack the invisible? Who can rebel against Nobody."[14]

According to Fromm, anonymous authoritarianism trades on the perceived need to fit in:

> I ought to do what everybody does, hence, I must conform, not be different, not "stick out"; I must be ready and willing to change according to the changes in the pattern; I must not ask whether I am right or wrong, but whether I am adjusted, whether I am not "peculiar," not different. The only thing which is

permanent in me is just this readiness for change. Nobody has power over me, except the herd of which I am a part, yet to which I am subjected.[15]

Here there is the in-group and the out-group—the social outcasts. This simple bifurcation grounds the deductions, "I am not out, therefore I am in" and "I am in, therefore I am not out." What drives such social conformity is fear of rejection by one's compatriots. It is this fear that sets the agenda, not justice or respect for the rule of law. A groundless, destructive war, no less than the rebuilding of New Orleans in the wake of Hurricane Katrina, can receive full public support. For, it is not the relevant facts; nor is it rational argument that decides what is to be backed, but instead fear of being thought an oddball. It is blind emotion that moves this bandwagon.

The Kindling of Fear, Intimidation, and Blind Hatred

In a culture of control, the purpose of the state is to amass power and control. But this goal is unattainable if one values fairness and justice; has love for one's fellow human beings; believes in individual freedom and autonomy; seeks rational solutions to problems of living; and has cultivated one's powers of empathy for others. For, such values will invariably conflict with and get in the way of the amassing of power and control over others. On the other hand, a fitting recipe for one who single-mindedly seeks dominion over others is a callous, even hostile, hateful, uncaring attitude and willingness to breach the rule of law, violate due process, and deprive others of their civil liberties. As George Orwell sums up the look and feel of a culture of control,

> always there will be the intoxication of power, constantly increasing and con-stantly growing subtler. Always, at every moment, there will be the thrill of victory, the sensation of trampling on an enemy who is helpless. If you want a picture of the future, imagine a boot stamping on a human face—forever.[16]

Here, the enemy that gets "trampled" is anyone who refuses to submit to state authority. This can include the peaceful, antiwar protestor; the journal-ist who writes against the administration's war policy; the congressperson on the other side of the isle; the judge who rules against the administration according to settled law; and the whistleblower who exposes the govern-ment's unlawful wiretapping activities. The amassing of power and control, the oppression of other human beings who get in the way, is the ultimate end of a culture of control.

In a budding climate of control, even apparently innocuous expressions of free speech and dissent to state authority can be visited by large-scale, hostile retaliation. For example, on March 14, 2003, about a week before the United States attacked Baghdad, lead singer Natalie Maines of the country/pop group, the Dixie Chicks, said at a London concert that she was ashamed the president came from her home state of Texas. In the aftermath of her remarks, millions of Dixie Chicks CDs were burned throughout America, and the Chicks had also received death threats.[17] Feeding this national "hate fest," a few days after Maimes made her London comment, radio giant Clear Channel (which operates more than 1200 stations throughout the nation) took the Chicks off their play lists "out of respect for the troops."[18] Here, "the enemy" became three musicians from Texas because they were "unpatriotic."

In fact, Clear Channel's role in the uprising against the Dixie Chicks was politically motivated. The vice president of this company was Thomas Hicks, a former business associate of President George W. Bush and a major contributor to the Bush presidential campaigns. The company had also been instrumental in sponsoring pro–Iraq War rallies throughout the United States.[19]

The case of the Dixie Chicks is instructive in showing how blind emotion of the masses can be fired up and used for political advantage, and how this can lead to abridgment of civil liberties—in this case, the First Amendment right to freedom of speech and of the press. Whether the targets are "witches," blacks, Jews, Middle Easterners, or the Dixie Chicks, history is replete with examples of how the blind, destructive passions of large numbers of people can be kindled and manipulated by others who have self-interested purposes.

In fact, what fuels a culture of control is hatred, fear, guilt, intimidation, the desire for approval, and other strong emotions without due regard for fact or logic. Citizens who can be manipulated by appealing to these raw emotions are the backbone of any government administration bent on attaining power and control over others. This is because people acting under the influence of blind emotion can be manipulated to do almost anything, especially when the manipulation is being artfully conducted by a demagogic authority.

Fearmongering

As Plato observed, democracies are most often destroyed from within rather than from without when a self-aggrandizing demagogue stirs up the passions of a gullible, uninformed populace by falsely promising to keep it safe. Blaming others for the woes of state, this self-styled "protector" brings the alleged culprits to justice, winning the trust of the people, and eventually seizing power and becoming a tyrant.

Saddam Hussein was such a bogey man used by the Bush administration to justify the invasion of Iraq. The strategy was classic. Want to support the invasion of a sovereign nation that poses no threat to the homeland? Just get the average citizen to think he might be the next victim of al Qaeda if he fails to jump on the war bandwagon.[20]

Such fearmongering was practiced by the Bush administration in the wake of the 9/11 attacks. When Vice President Dick Cheney claimed knowledge that Saddam Hussein had "an established relationship with al-Qaeda, providing training to al-Qaeda members in the areas of poisons, gases, making conventional bombs," the majority of Americans believed him, and virtually no one in the mainstream media asked for verifiable evidence. No matter that there simply was *no* such evidence for connecting Saddam and al Qaeda. Facts and logic were discarded in the face of blind fear.

Consider the testimony of one Iraq veteran who wrote an anonymous letter to the independent media Web site, Salon.com:

> We now know most of the information given to us by the current administration concerning Iraq, if not all the information, was false. This was information given to the American people to justify a war. The information about weapons of mass destruction and a link to Osama bin Laden scared the American people into supporting the war in Iraq. They presented an atmosphere of intimidation that suggested if we did not act immediately there was the possibility of another attack. Bush said himself that we do not want the proof or the smoking gun to come in the form of a "mushroom cloud." Donald Rumsfeld said, "We know where the weapons are."[21]

As was mentioned in Chapter 10, a 2006 *Washington Post* poll suggested that a majority of Americans would give up their constitutionally protected right to privacy and allow the government to monitor all of their electronic communications and phone calls in the interest of searching for terrorists. With the mention of the words, "terrorist attack," most Americans appear willing, out of fear, to relinquish one of their most important rights.

Well Poisoning

Well poisoning—the manipulative use of negatively charged emotive language—was a prominent fear tactic employed by the Bush administration to manipulate Americans into supporting the invasion of Iraq. On September 20, 2001, when the dust from the 9/11 attacks had not yet settled, Bush pronounced, "You're either with us or against us in the fight against terror." While he was addressing leaders of nations, his message was clear from the start, and it was this message that set the agenda for Bush's war campaign, including his invasion of Iraq. As columnist Gregory Dennis expressed, "I could not help but think his threat was directed, not only at foreign leaders, but at me as well. Is it true that if I disagreed with his actions, I would be no better than the terrorists themselves; that I would be, dare I say . . . "un-American?"[22] One is "un-American," "unpatriotic," and maybe even a "terrorist" or a "traitor" if one does not stand with President George W. Bush. Never mind the simplistic bifurcation of reality into black and white with no shades of grey. One either jumps on the bandwagon or one is with "the enemy."

However, it was not just the average American who was being manipulated. Mainstream media was also swayed by well poisoning. The government manipulated the media by calling it "liberal." Once used to refer to the free and democratic sharing of ideas among citizens, the term "liberal" was converted by neoconservatives into an emotively pejorative term referring to anyone and anything that is "un-American." In this new sense, "liberal" was not unlike "communist," "traitor," or "terrorist," a catchall term used to arouse hatred and fear. As a result, those who used to call themselves "liberal" began to abandon the term and instead called themselves "progressive."

Afraid of being accused of having a "liberal bias," which would translate into lost revenues, the mainstream media allowed itself to be intimated into self-censorship. This is not to say that the mainstream media corporations were not already predisposed toward self-censorship. As was discussed in Chapter 6, predisposing these corporations toward treading lightly on coverage of questionable government practices was their fear of losing lucrative government contracts, tightening of FCC regulations, increased tax burdens, and other penalties.

But not all media corporations needed to be intimidated into cooperating. Most notably, News Corp's Fox New continues to serve as a prominent voice of the extreme right, helping to spread the myth of the liberal media in order to distinguish itself as being the only "fair and balanced" news network, and accordingly to ensure its own popularity among "patriotic" Americans.

The Bush administration also tactically used well poisoning to sway the emotions of the American public. In March 2003, taking a cue from Bush's "with us or with the terrorists," Republican representatives Bob Ney of Ohio and Walter Jones of North Carolina placed a sign at the register of the House cafeteria, stating "Update. Now Serving in All House Office Buildings, 'Freedom Fries.'" They did this after France refused to support the U.S. invasion of Iraq. Many Americans followed the lead, denouncing and mocking the French for their "beret-wearing, wine-drinking, cheese-eating, Jerry Lewis-loving, literature-deconstructing, surrendering-to-the-Germans ways." The New York Post called France and Germany "the axis of weasel," and they ran a front-page photo that grafted giant weasel heads onto the French and German ambassadors to the United Nations.[23]

According to a Gallup poll taken in March 2003, the majority of Americans disliked the French, which represented a reversal of the static trend in the past decade for Americans to think favorably of the French.[24] While most Americans were at least able to see through the silliness of destroying French wine and renaming French fries "freedom fries" and French toast "freedom toast," this reversal in attitude speaks volumes about the dangerous capacity of most Americans to succumb to anonymous authoritarianism backed by well poisoning.

Tempering Hatred and Fear

When blind conformity is so ignited by the flames of irrational passions (hatred and fear), the dangers are inestimable. This is the sort of social mindset that spawns hate groups dedicated to the destruction of others who are "different"—that is, not in the in-group. For those who wonder how such things as ethnic cleansing and holocausts are humanly possible, one need not look beyond the power of blind conformity backed by intense, irrational hatred and fear. Throughout history, megalomaniac governments have found it useful to stir up such emotional juices in its citizens. Hitler used the Jews as the target of blind hatred and fear. The Bush administration aided by mainstream media targeted Muslim extremists who "hate us because we are free." Many Americans have broadened this target to include *anyone* of Middle Eastern descent. Unfortunately, a culture led by blind, indiscriminate emotions instead of by reason is not likely to remain a free, democratic one.

According to the eighteenth century German philosopher, Immanuel Kant, in the throes of such emotions, we lose our capacity for independent, rational judgment. This, he says, is bondage, not freedom at all. For Kant, being free means being *autonomous* (that is, self-determining), which, in turn, means having the power to make a *rational* choice. On this way of thinking, when people let government (or media) pull their emotional strings—for example frighten or intimidate them into submission—without first rationally assessing the matter, they have already surrendered their freedom. They have rendered themselves nonautonomous. They have allowed themselves to become objects of manipulation.

Kant linked being rational and autonomous to being a *person*. For him, the difference between a person and an object is that a person is guided by a rational judgment and an object (or thing) is determined by an external cause. A puppet is an object, because it has no rational capacity and must be manipulated by the hand of another. In a culture of control, government makes objects (and in a sense puppets) of us all by appealing to irrational emotions of hatred and fear instead of reason. In contrast, a democracy is a culture of autonomy, that is, one in which citizens exercise rational self-governance.

This does not mean that one should not have and express emotion. There is an important difference between blind emotions and reasonable ones. The ancient Greek philosopher Aristotle taught that *rational control* over one's emotions and behavior holds the key to living happily and democratically. Extreme emotions and behavior are not rational, however.

Thus, extreme fear is cowardly while not enough is foolhardy. Courage means being led by a rational judgment in the face of danger. An under-standing of this Aristotelian distinction yields realistic concepts of courage and patriotism. A patriotic American has the courage to oppose the unjust policies of an authoritarian government, notwithstanding strong social pressures to conform.

17

An Ethics of Belief for a Free America

In 1958, the Disney Corporation, which now owns ABC, produced a film, "White Wilderness," as part of its "True Life Adventure" series. The film showed lemmings, small mouse-like rodents, supposedly committing mass suicide by leaping into the sea. The narrator, Winston Hibbler, explained, "A kind of compulsion seizes each tiny rodent and, carried along by an unreasoning hysteria, each falls into step for a march that will take them to a strange destiny." Here, in this "true life adventure" lies the source of the common belief that with neither rhyme nor reason lemmings voluntarily, en masse march lockstep to their death.

In fact, the lemming scene in the Disney documentary was a fake. The lemmings in the film were actually thrown off a cliff by the filmmakers. There is no evidence that, in their natural habitats, these tiny survival-seeking rodents are ever moved en masse by blind compulsion to commit suicide.

The case of the lemmings shows how the ability of mass media to deceive the people is largely a function of the willingness of people to believe what they see and hear in the media. Consumers of news and information can play a decisive role in how successful mass media is in disseminating disinformation. The public can guard against being deceived by carefully questioning claims before believing them.

As was discussed in Chapter 6, the primary motivation of corporate media is maximizing profit, not truth as such. As a general rule, only if truth pays will these companies report it. If their cost-benefit analyses routinely included the risk of trying to deceive the discriminating eye of the average viewer, the value of deception would itself be lessened. Unfortunately, the average viewer does not carefully question what the media says, and these corporations know it.

As was also discussed in chapter 6, the deception against which the public must be on guard is a product of an elaborate interplay between military, industrial, political, media, and public relations interests. These are the forces through which news and information get filtered; and censorship, propaganda, and disinformation are the likely products of this interplay.

Clifford's Ethics of Belief

Americans do not need to be helpless victims of the politico-corporate media establishment. However, they can defend against an encroaching culture of control only if they base their judgments about what to believe on evidence. As W. K. Clifford remarked in his famous essay on the *Ethics of Belief*, "It is wrong in all cases to believe on insufficient evidence; and where it is presumption to doubt and to investigate, there it is worse than presumption to believe."[1] In fact, Clifford maintained that each and every one of us (and not just politicians, lawyers, journalists, and others who bear a fiduciary relationship to us) has a duty to question things before we commit them to belief. As he eloquently stated,

> It is not only the leader of men, statesmen, philosopher, or poet that owes this bounden duty to mankind. Every rustic who delivers in the village alehouse his slow, infrequent sentences, may help to kill or keep alive the fatal superstitions which clog his race. Every hard-worked wife of an artisan may transmit to her children beliefs which shall knit society together, or rend it in pieces. No simplicity of mind, no obscurity of station, can escape the universal duty of questioning all that we believe.[2]

So, in the socio-political context of mass media manipulation, how can we manage to avoid being deceived? The short answer is the one that Clifford has given, namely to believe only on sufficient evidence. Presently, there are online independent media and international news sources that make it possible for the public to gather additional information and to corroborate stories before believing them. As was discussed in chapters 7 and 8, there have been significant steps already taken by corporate media and telecom companies working in cooperation with government to turn the Internet into an extension of the mainstream media. If this trend continues, Americans will eventually find little to distinguish net content from what they presently can find on network news. Fortunately, however, the Internet is for the time being a vibrant source for news and information. Americans need to seize the opportunity to reap the benefits of a democratic Internet before it is too late. An informed public sector is the strongest defense against graduating to a culture of control.

However, this response assumes that we are able in the first place to distinguish fact from fiction and sufficient evidence from pseudo-evidence. We must have a sense of what constitutes rational criteria of belief before we can even begin to determine if we have a good reason to commit something to belief. After all, much of what passes as news and information on the net does not come from veridical sources; so we risk exchanging one set of misinformation for another unless we are careful.

This is possible, however, only if we are privy to the sophistical mechanisms the politico-corporate media establishment uses to manipulate and garner support.

For example, it is well-documented that prior to the invasion of Iraq, the George W. Bush administration did not believe that Saddam posed a serious threat to national security. Thus, according to the Downing Street Memo, an official British document that reported a July 23, 2002, meeting between Prime Minister Tony Blair and his inner circle of advisers, seven months before the United States invaded Iraq,

> It seemed clear that Bush had made up his mind to take military action, even if the timing was not yet decided. But the case was thin. Saddam was not threatening his neighbours, and his WMD capability was less than that of Libya, North Korea or Iran.[3]

However, Bush wanted to garner support for invading Iraq and he rightly believed that the American people were feeling insecure enough after the 9/11 attacks to support him if he told them the invasion was necessary to prevent another terrorist attack. So he used this vulnerability to his advantage in getting what he wanted. He manipulated support. "Bush wanted to remove Saddam, through military action, justified by the conjunction of terrorism and WMD. But the intelligence and facts were being fixed around the policy."[4]

The Psychology of Rational Belief

The American people were deceived *insofar as* they believed Bush. The old-fashioned psychology of radical behaviorism would say that there was a cause-and-effect relationship between Bush's claim that we needed to invade Iraq for national security purposes and the majority of Americans going along with him. On this psychology, our response was entirely predictable according to the natural laws governing human behavior. The people really didn't have any choice but to respond as they did. Associate Hussein with the horror of 9/11, and fear supplants the demand for evidence. On this psychology, human beings are complex biological machines that can be programmed or conditioned just by making suitable changes in their environments. On this view, free will does not really exist and, therefore, it is unreasonable to hold people responsible or blame them for their mistakes.

This, however, is an archaic psychology. According to the new behavioral psychology, human beings do indeed have free will and can, therefore, ordinarily be blamed and held responsible for their mistakes. This new psychology is *cognitive* behavioral, not just behavioral. It stresses the human ability to use reason and logic in making practical decisions. It holds that our self-defeating behavior and emotions are largely due to *irrational* thinking. For example, in stereotyping all Arabs as terrorists, one is likely to experience anxiety in dealing with them, and to unfairly discriminate against them. According to this psychology, one can avoid such harmful emotions and behavior by replacing one's stereotype with a more rational belief (do not prejudge anyone on the basis of their race) and then changing one's behavioral response to accommodate the rational belief.

On this view, the American people were under no compulsion to believe Bush. Instead, they had the ability to collect the facts and to draw rational inferences from them. Had they sought evidence first, they might have realized the implausibility that Hussein, a *secular* dictator, was somehow in cahoots with al Qaeda, a radical *sectarian* terrorist group. This fact, in turn, would have led to the demand for more evidence.

How Politico-Corporate Media Manipulation Works

The Bush administration and its corporate media associates encouraged and cajoled mass faulty thinking. Since its war agenda could not be justified rationally, the only way it had to get it through was by sophistical means. It, therefore, resorted to the systematic use of manipulation, including fear mongering (raising and lowering the terrorism alert level), well poisoning (calling people who oppose the war "un-American" or "traitors"), making threats (threatening to jail journalists who published "classified" government leaks), propagation of prejudice (media stereotypes of Arabs as terrorists and suicide bombers), claiming a divine inspiration (as Bush did in waging war in Iraq), jingoistic appeals (positioning the American flag behind network news anchors), disseminating government propaganda through the news networks (using "embedded" journalists as Defense Department mouthpieces); injecting fake news stories into network affiliate news, pressuring corporate media into self-censorship, and other manipulative devices aimed at short-circuiting rational argument.

Government and media have played on the interests, values, and fears of Americans. Many Americans have been willing to surrender their right to privacy when it was presented as a way to prevent another attack on the homeland. The movement to pass a constitutional amendment defining marriage as between a man and a woman gained support when presented as a way of preventing the desecration of what is holy. The drive to reject stem cell research appealed to "the culture of life." Citizens have been intimidated against protesting against the wars in Iraq and Afghanistan by presenting such dissent as a refusal to "support the troops"; the Iraq war was defended as necessary for "winning the war on terror"; and Obama has employed the same rhetoric to defend the Afghanistan war.

From the Patriot Act to the Clear Skies Act, legislation adverse to common interests of Americans has nevertheless been euphonized with a name that implies support for the very interests it flaunts. Thus, certain provisions of the Patriotic Act are unconstitutional (such as the "sneak and peek" provision) and, therefore, markedly *un*patriotic. Similarly, the Clear Skies Act (proposed in 2003 and 2005) would have relaxed controls on air pollution instead of cleaning it up.

Government and media organizations have formed a symbiotic alliance aimed at amassing incredible amounts of money, power, and control over the lives of Americans. Swayed by carefully contrived manipulation, many Americans have permitted government and its big media helpmates to systematically dismantle the systems of checks and balances against abridgment of civil liberties, including the right to privacy, freedom of speech, and of the press; devalue creativity and independent thinking in education; wage unjust war; build a climate of hate, fear, and bellicosity; dumb-down the mainstream portals of news and information; and take strident steps toward politico-corporate undermining of net neutrality and toward transforming cyberspace into a political weapon.

Bad Faith in America

According to French existentialist philosopher Jean-Paul Sartre, there are no excuses behind which to hide one's responsibility. Thus, the Nazi soldier who proclaimed that he had no other choice but to follow the commands of Hitler is living in "bad faith." He is lying to himself, because there are still other options—in particular, the "ultimate possibilities" of suicide and desertion. The Nazi might prefer serving Hitler to the latter possibilities, but that is still a matter of choice—which accordingly implies freedom and responsibility.

By parity of reasoning, for Americans who live on U.S. soil, pay federal taxes, and receive the benefits of being an American citizen, it is "bad faith" to deny responsibility for U.S. policies, including its war policies. For, there are still other options, such as leaving the nation or refusing to pay the taxes.

In not choosing these options, the war effort becomes one's own, and one is responsible for the war even if one has not declared it. Thus, blaming it entirely on the politicians will not pass muster.

But this responsibility runs deeper than living in this nation, reaping its benefits, and paying taxes that support its destructive policies. This is because, in not exercising our critical powers of independent thought, allowing ourselves to be herded like ignorant cattle, we support a culture of control, and thereby help it to thrive. But should we be sent to the slaughter by our commanders, we are then more complicit than the cow. For, after all, the cow does not support the beef industry.

As emphasized in this book, totalitarian regimes thrive on keeping the masses ignorant. A thoughtful, rational citizenry is to a megalomaniac government what garlic is to a vampire. When the people of a nation are armed with reason, they are not easily manipulated. Accordingly, stopping America from becoming a full-fledged culture of control requires arming ourselves with reason.

This means identifying and abandoning the self-defeating, antiempirical, inauthentic, conformity-oriented styles of thinking by which we have made gullible pawns of ourselves. It also means substituting for these "fallacies," rational, forward-moving, creative styles of thinking. While it is beyond the scope of this book to develop such a democracy-promoting set of critical thinking tools,[5] a logic of this nature must take as its first principle the astute admonition of Clifford that, "it is wrong in all cases to believe on insufficient evidence; and where it is presumption to doubt and to investigate, there it is worse than presumption to believe." A culture based on this sturdy ethics of belief is one least likely to succumb to the sway of a culture of control.[6]

18

Total Information Awareness and the Right to Privacy

As discussed in Chapter 17, a viable ethics of belief prescribes believing things in proportion to the weight of the evidence. Unfortunately, many Americans have uncritically accepted the official government line as to why they should give up their right to privacy and permit warrantless mass surveillance of their personal electronic communications.

But is there truly a rationally defensible *moral* argument for relinquishing this right?

Under both the Bush and Obama administrations, it is clear what the rationale has been for having created and deployed a program of mass, warrantless surveillance. "I wake up every morning thinking about a future attack," said George W. Bush, on February 10, 2006, "and therefore, a lot of my thinking, and a lot of the decisions I make are based upon the attack that hurt us."[1] And on January 22, 2009, President Obama sided with Bush when he urged a federal judge to set aside a ruling on whether a U.S. president can bypass Congress and establish a program of warrantless eavesdropping on Americans.[2]

Clearly, there is a legitimate law enforcement concern about acts of terrorism just as there is about human trafficking, drug smuggling, serial killers, and other illegal activities that pose a danger to others. However, few would argue that mass, warrantless surveillance of American citizens' personal electronic communications should be conducted in order to catch drug smugglers, human traffickers, and serial killers, even if the sum total of the lives these groups destroy, collectively or individually, is more than the sum total of Americans killed in terrorist attacks (which it is). This is because it is a violation of the right to privacy presumed to be guaranteed by the Fourth Amendment of the United States Constitution. So what is the basis of the disparity in treatment?

Utilitarian attempts to justify the TIA Project

The official reason advanced by the Bush and Obama administrations for warrantless mass surveillance is a *utilitarian* one. Utilitarianism is a theory of ethics that says that acts are morally justified according to whether they maximize overall human welfare or happiness. According to this theory, even if trolling through people's personal communications, scanning the full bodies of air travelers, and placing video cameras throughout a city cause inconveniences and delays at airports and offend many, these are relatively minor costs given the greater good these policies serve by protecting human life. However, as appealing as this argument might seem at first sight, utilitarian arguments like the aforementioned one can be used to justify many things that most of us would not agree are moral. Thus, it might be possible to save thousands of lives each year by making speeding on the highways a strictly enforced felony, which carries mandatory jail time. But even if this punitive measure succeeded in its goal of preventing casualties on the roadways, most of us would still object to such a law. This is because we would feel that the punishment was not proportional to the crime, notwithstanding the fact that it could be justified on utilitarian grounds.

And why stop there. Suppose that we could discover cures for diseases that save millions of people by experimenting on a certain few without the consent of these experimental subjects? If all we cared about was the net balance of overall human welfare, then why not simply sacrifice these few experimental subjects for the sake of the many? Never mind that these subjects have not consented to being experimented on. Thus, a major problem with utilitarian arguments is that they can be used to commit great iniquity in the name of maximizing overall happiness.

So it is too with the utilitarian argument that it is okay to eavesdrop on millions of Americans in order to try to catch some prospective terrorists. Even if it worked, it would violate the right of millions of Americans to privacy. And, again, this is assuming that such programs of mass surveillance are actually effective in catching terrorists, which as was discussed in Chapter 2 is highly questionable. Moreover, since such pure utilitarian arguments do not have any side constraints to stop them from justifying too much, there is the problem that they can be used to justify increasingly greater degrees of intrusion. Thus, after the 9/11 attacks, airline passengers were required to submit to having their baggage and personal carryon items searched and having their bodies screened by metal detectors. Now many airports are adding full body scanners that electronically undress travelers. Next, in the offing might be having our brains scanned through Brain Machine Interface technologies to determine if we are entertaining dangerous thoughts. Again, if the goal is airline safety, then why just stop with body scans. This tendency of utilitarian arguments to escalate and justify too much, combined with advancing surveillance technologies, portends serious dangers for a culture with a propensity to spy on its citizens in the name of "national security."

However, the idea of "national security" as understood in terms of protecting against another terrorist attack appears to have been largely a pretext for a broader, hidden agenda. Indeed, if this were the central goal of the Bush administration, it would not have attempted to "make the facts fit the policy" in order to justify invading Iraq.[3]

As discussed earlier, the Bush administration was guided by an imperialistic ideology, which maintained that the world would be best served if America (along with its allies) reigned as its preeminent superpower. This goal itself was to be achieved by fighting multiple, simultaneous wars, including one in Iraq, gaining control over natural resources, such as Middle Eastern oil reserves, and economic globalization attained by feeding the insatiable monetary appetites of giant corporations. The world envisioned by the Bush administration was one in which Western values transfused the Middle East and made them hubs and extensions of the West.

But this vision was myopic and failed to realize the backlash likely to occur when one nation invades another and attempts to redefine this other nation in its own image. The Bush administration failed to take a broader multicultural perspective and to realize that Western religious, social, and economic values were not likely to take root in a culture that was hostile to these values. Hence, the Bush administration's broad utilitarian calculus was likely to fail from the start.

The warrantless mass surveillance program was born of such myopic vision and intolerance. As unconstrained utilitarian arguments tend to do, this program expanded its scope to include targeting certain journalists and antiwar protesters, and was used to conduct "information warfare" to neutralize stories that might have undermined the Bush administration's plans and policies. The enemy to be watched, thus, became anyone who was against these policies, especially the war effort. Like any totalitarian, bellicose regime, it fed on a paranoid or near-paranoid drive to be "all knowing" while being itself as opaque and secretive as possible. The Patriot Act breached the constitutional boundaries between criminal investigations and intelligence gathering. Documents that had before been declassified became classified and unlawful to possess. FBI rules were revised to permit racial profiling as a basis for spying on Americans. The press was kept on a short leash, with "embedded" reporters turned into government puppets. These and many other attempts to unilaterally control the flow of information were put into practice. And all this was done in the name of "national security."

This is why there is need for ethical constraints on what can be done in the name of "national security" (or the "the common good"). And it is here that recognition of the right to privacy is essential for the preservation of a free and democratic society. Ignore this right long enough and the political thirst for power and control, coached in terms of national security, will intrude further and further into the affairs of citizens and eventually undermine freedom, democracy, and human dignity.

The Right to Privacy

A right exists when there is an interest and a rule such that the said rule forbids others from interfering with the said interest. Thus, one has a right to life insofar as there is a rule that forbids others from taking one's life. A *legal* right exists when there is an interest that is protected by a legal rule. The rights of Americans to be protected, "in their persons, houses, papers, and effects, against unreasonable searches and seizures," and not without a warrant based on probable cause, are legal rights because the Fourth Amendment protects the stated areas of interest against encroachment by government. But these rights (involving searches and seizures of persons or their property) are also *moral* rights insofar as the Fourth Amendment also expresses a moral rule.

The right to privacy is a moral right that is (or at least is supposed to be) legally protected. This right is related to the right to liberty (as included in the Fourteenth Amendment's protection against any person being deprived of "life, liberty, or property") in that one's liberty or freedom can be diminished when personal information about oneself is shared with others. For example, disclosure of the fact that one has received psychiatric care could affect how one is treated by others and impede one's career goals.

However, the right to liberty is logically distinct from the right to privacy, which has to do with the acquisition of personal information. The right to privacy signifies the right not to have one's personal information shared with others. Such information includes the most intimate facts about oneself. Not only does it include such facts as one's medical history, bank records, and credit history; it also includes personal beliefs, preferences, and desires, such as one's social and political views, religious convictions, sexual preference, sexual desires, fantasies, hopes, dreams, aspirations, and deeply held moral convictions. Such information thus largely serves to define one's individuality, that is, the person one is. Therefore, violations of one's privacy can constitute violations of one's individuality or personhood. The rule that forbids others from invading this personal space is thus a moral rule.

Unlike legal rules, moral rules, as such, are not backed by sanctions (penalties for noncompliance) applied by an authority that has an organized means of enforcement, such as a police force. This is why international laws (laws existing between nations) are sometimes claimed to be moral rules rather than legal ones—because they require an organized means of enforcement, which assumes a world government with power of enforcement.

Nevertheless, some moral rights apply to basic, universal, human interests and, therefore, ought to be protected by the legal machinery of the state. Such rights, known as *human rights*, are often said to arise out of what it means to be a human being and not simply out of some concept of net utility.

The Right to Privacy as a Human Right

A theory of human rights of this kind was formulated by the eighteenth century philosopher, Immanuel Kant. As was discussed in Chapter 16, according to Kant, people have an inherent worth or value that does not depend on their utility. This is in contrast to physical objects, which only have value in relation to their utility. For example, if one's pen ran out of ink and could no longer be used to write, and if no other use could be found for what remained of the pen, then it could be discarded, thrown out for want of any worth or value. In contrast, human beings are not to be discarded or thrown away (killed or destroyed) if we cannot find a use for them. This is because their worth, said Kant, is a constant and can never be diminished (or augmented) by their usefulness for some desired end that others may intend. This is what makes it morally objectionable to treat the poor, the disabled, and the elderly as "throwaway" or second-class citizens—they still retain their human worth. They belong, said Kant, to a "community of ends" and as such deserve to be treated with the respect that any other person receives.

This human worth or dignity, according to Kant, derives from the fact that human beings can make claims on others. This is because they are autonomous beings. That is, they are capable of using their rational capacity to decide for themselves. This is in contrast to physical objects, which are always under the control, and are determined by others.

Therefore, the treatment owed to persons must be distinguished from objects. To manipulate, deceive, cajole, or otherwise thwart the rational self-determination of a person is to treat a person as an object. This is a logical mistake as well as a moral one. Persons and objects are not the same and the treatment of the one should not be confused with the other.

According to Kant, utilitarianism engenders this general confusion between persons and objects, for this theory discounts or weighs up and subtracts the values of human beings as though they were physical things to be tallied. Thus, sacrificing some human beings to maximize overall happiness is to use or treat some people as means to the happiness of others. It is to treat them as expendable commodities. However, Kant admonishes us to "always treat humanity, whether in your own person or in the person of any another, never simply as a means, but always at the same time as an end."[4] Utilitarianism treats persons "simply as a means" (objects) instead of as "ends" (persons) and is, therefore, unacceptable.

Thus, on this theory, all human beings have a right to be treated as persons and not as mere objects. They have human rights. These rights derive from the self-determining nature of human beings. The right to privacy is such a right. Human beings have a right not to have their personal, private space invaded by others. This is to treat them as nonautonomous beings, that is, as mere objects or things. Warrantless, mass surveillance of Americans' private phone calls, e-mail messages, and Internet activities is in violation of this human right.

In response, it might be argued that the American people had the right to waive their right to privacy by giving their consent to the government's warrantless mass surveillance program. Thus, when it became known in 2005 that the Bush administration was monitoring Americans' electronic communications, many Americans said they were willing to accept this program for the sake of national security. However, this "consent" was lame, because it was after the fact. The program was already in effect, and Americans were not given a choice.

So what would valid consent have looked like, that is, consent that would have treated Americans as "ends"?

First, such consent would have treated the American people as autonomous agents by having provided them with a choice. Insofar as the government was claiming to be invading their privacy on paternalistic grounds (that is, for their own good), Americans should have been free to have accepted or rejected it. This condition of valid consent could have been fulfilled by the federal government's having presented alternative national security options to the American people in advance by opening up public debate on these options (say via the Internet), taking national surveys, and even by permitting state-by-state public referenda. Not only were such public forums absent; the program operated in total secrecy and not even Congress (the presumptive representative of the people) was given a voice.

Second, the American people would need to have been adequately informed. This means providing relevant and true information about the nature and extent of the surveillance. Unfortunately, even when the

New York Times broke the story, the full extent of surveillance was not revealed. Basing its report on government officials, the *Times* said that the National Security Agency (NSA) had been monitoring without warrants the *international* telephone and e-mail messages *of hundreds or possibly thousands* of people inside the United States. In fact, the NSA was also monitoring all *domestic* phone calls, e-mail messages, as well as Internet activities, and the number of people being monitored was in the *millions*. So, even after the fact, Americans were not given all the facts, and some of what they were told was false, misleading, or inaccurate.[5]

Third, frightening the American people into compliance by evoking the chilling image of the burning twin towers under siege (a popular device used by the Bush administration with the help of the mainstream news networks) was to manipulate the consent of Americans; whereas valid consent needs to be *freely* given.

So, the "consent" that was obtained by the government was neither informed nor freely given, nor did it respect Americans as autonomous agents by giving them a choice. Accordingly, on Kantian standards, the government contravened a basic human right of the American people (to be treated as persons) when it systematically invaded their privacy.

A utilitarian Justification of the Right to Privacy

However, even if the Kantian doctrine of human rights is rejected, the legal enforcement of a rule that protects the privacy of Americans against government encroachment can still be defended on utilitarian grounds. For unless such a rule is in force, it is inevitable that state power will eventually be used for narrow political purposes by a power-seeking government. The right against government encroachment of one's personal and private space is an essential check in a functional system of checks and balances against the rise of a totalitarian government regime that will oppress the people and destroy their potential for a satisfactory life in common.

The human interest in privacy is essential to human happiness. To see this, imagine a state in which whatever you think or say becomes public knowledge. You wish someone dead and it shows up in a government registry. You have sexual desires for another and the desire is immediately public knowledge. You tell your attorney something that might incriminate you and it is immediately sent to opposing counsel. Your physician sends the positive tests results of an HIV test to your employer. You have diarrhea and it is all over the Internet. In short, suppose all private information about you, regardless of whether it is potentially defamatory, damaging, confidential, or highly embarrassing, becomes fodder for public examination. Such a world would be one in which all or at least most of us would not wish live.

True, different people have different priorities about what kinds of personal information are acceptable to share with others. For example, some consider age or weight to be highly personal information, which they do not care to share. But clearly, every competent human being would want at least *some* personal information kept private. In a bona fide culture of control, all personal information would in principle be subject to examination by the state. In such a culture, no one would have his or her interest in privacy protected.

The creeping decline of privacy in America should, therefore, concern all of us. Those who say they do not care if the state monitors their personal e-mail messages, phone calls, and Internet activities have as much to fear as those of us who find such wholesale violations of privacy unacceptable. As the technological means continues to escalate, even to the degree of being able to directly tap people's personal thoughts, there is no limit to how intrusive government surveillance will become.

This does not mean that the right to privacy is absolute. Thus, there are always possible exceptions to a moral rule. For example, lawyer-client confidentiality is a very strong privacy protection. Nevertheless, the American Bar Association's confidentiality of information rule permits disclosure of confidential client information by an attorney to an appropriate third party without the consent of the client "to prevent reasonably certain death or substantial bodily harm."[6]

So it may be asked, does the government's alleged grounds for abridging the right to privacy of American citizens constitute a legitimate exception to the moral rule protecting the privacy of personal information?

Why the TIA System Wrongfully Violates the Moral Right to Privacy

W.A. Parent has offered the following standards or guidelines for determining wrongful invasion of privacy:[7]

1. For what purposes is the undocumented [unpublished] personal knowledge being sought?
2. Is this purpose a legitimate and important one?
3. Is the knowledge sought through invasion of privacy relevant to its justifying purpose?
4. Is invasion of privacy the only or the least offensive means of obtaining the knowledge?
5. What restrictions or procedural restraints have been placed on the privacy-invading techniques?

6. What protection is to be afforded the personal knowledge once it has been acquired?

Unfortunately, taking the six, abovementioned standards into account, the Total Information Awareness project fails to provide a legitimate and over-riding reason for invading the privacy of millions of Americans.

For what alleged purpose is the government invading the privacy of millions of Americans? According to both Bush and Obama administrations, this purpose is to prevent another terrorist attack. So, is this purpose *legitimate and important*?

Clearly, preventing another terrorist attack can be a legitimate and important purpose for mass invasions of privacy *only if* the TIA system actually works efficiently to achieve such an end. However, as was discussed in Chapter 2, the technology has technical problems. It requires construction of algorithms sufficient to identify and distinguish patterns of terrorist behavior from that of innocent people. However, in contrast to consumer shopping habits and financial fraud patterns, terrorist activities do not occur frequently enough to construct an adequate model for predicting them. Moreover, when they do occur, which is one or two events every few years, their patterns of preparation and planning tend to be distinct, thereby making it impossible to divine a predictable pattern. Consequently, "The one thing predictable about predictive data mining for terrorism is that it would be consistently wrong."[8] As such, this disposes such data mining engines to false positives, which in turn, not only violates the privacy of innocent persons, but also exposes them to the possibility of false arrest and detainment.

Is the knowledge government seeks through the invasion of privacy *relevant* to preventing a terrorist attack? Unfortunately, the Patriot Act has allowed that a *significant purpose* rather than *the purpose* of surveillance be the collection of foreign intelligence. This means that such mass dragnets of electronic information are permitted to capture information that is entirely *irrelevant* to the purpose at hand—that of capturing foreign intelligence. Thus, the program fails to satisfy the third standard.

Is invasion of privacy the *only* or *the least offensive* means the government has of obtaining foreign intelligence? The 1978 FISA Act had also provided for warrantless surveillance for foreign intelligence gathering but it had to be sought as the primary purpose, not merely a significant purpose for a wiretap; and it could not target American citizens without a warrant. However, government could conduct surveillance of electronic communications involving an American citizen in the absence of a warrant for up to 72 hours in an emergency situation, and could subsequently apply for a warrant, thus allowing for situations where there was not enough time to apply for a warrant in advance. Thus, the earlier protections allowed acquisition of the same information without the necessity of a mass dragnet and violation of privacy. Accordingly, the TIA system is not the only and least offensive means the government can have for acquiring foreign intelligence.

What restrictions or procedural restraints has the government placed on its privacy-invading techniques? Unfortunately, as was discussed in Chapter 3, the FISA Amendments Act of 2008 has eviscerated the role of the FIS courts to largely reviewing the procedures in place for protecting against unjustified invasions of privacy. However, the government does not have to provide details, such as the names of persons and their addresses to be placed under surveillance. Such blanket warrants eliminate judicial oversight and permit a mass dragnet, thus allowing virtually unbounded possibilities for invasion of privacy of millions of innocent Americans. Moreover, as was also discussed in Chapter 3, the new FBI rules permit racial profiling, thus opening up the floodgates for further racially motivated invasions of privacy. As such, the program of warrantless mass surveillance fails to satisfy standard 5 not only by having inadequate legal procedures in place to safeguard personal information, but by adding provisions that increase the likelihood of unjustified violations of privacy.

What protection does the TIA system provide for personal knowledge once it has been acquired? There is evidence to suggest that the government has failed to build adequate privacy protection into its mass, warrantless surveillance program. This is true despite the fact that, at the inception of the TIA Project in 2002, under the direction of John Poindexter, DARPA had conducted research into technology that would have safeguarded the privacy of personal information in the TIA databases.

At a 2002 conference in Anaheim, California, sponsored by DARPA, Poindexter stressed the need for a "more systematic" way to protect privacy. Poindexter wanted to create a "privacy appliance" that would conceal identifying information, such as names and addresses, exposing only patterns of data to those having access to the TIA databases. If patterns were discovered that documented that a certain group was planning a terrorist attack, the government could seek a FIS Court warrant to disable privacy protection for the specific identifying information related to the pattern in question, leaving privacy protection in place for all other data. According to a 2003 congressional report on TIA, "The idea is that this device, cryptographically protected to prevent tampering, would ensure that no one could abuse private information without an immutable digital record of their misdeeds." Moreover, according to the report, the details of use of the privacy appliance would be made available to the public.[9]

Unfortunately, when Congress allegedly defunded TIA in 2003, and components were transferred to the NSA's Advanced Research and Development

Activity (ARDA), research on the privacy appliance, which had been ongoing at Xerox's Palo Alto Research Center, was cancelled. Consequently, the NSA's warrantless mass surveillance program, which came to light in 2005, included no such privacy safeguards.[10]

It is, therefore, evident that, in the end, the government perceived protecting the privacy of millions of Americans as expendable. It was not that the government did not have an idea about how to safeguard its massive data warehouses. It simply decided not to continue to fund the research. Moreover, given that the operation of such a safety appliance would have been made available to the public had it existed, it is evident that the Obama administration has not to date created a privacy appliance to safeguard the stores of information it continues to collect on millions of American citizens. Instead, the Obama administration has embraced the 2008 FISA Amendments Act enacted under the Bush administration. This act makes no software provisions for protecting the privacy of Americans. Indeed, if the U.S. government insists on amassing private information of its citizens, it should at least build into FISA "minimization standards"(standards that require government to take reasonable precautions not to target American citizens) the provision of a privacy protection appliance.

Hence, based on Parent's six standards, the TIA project wrongfully invades the right to privacy of millions of Americans. The moral imperative is, therefore, to legally enforce the moral right to privacy. Presently, the legal force of this right has been abridged by FISA reform, the Patriot Act, and related legal reform, which remove the safeguards instituted by the 1978 FISA Act in concordance with the Fourth Amendment of the U.S. Constitution. Without the legal enforcement of this right as a side constraint on utilitarian attempts to justify increasingly greater abridgments of privacy, America is destined to cross the point of no return, where the concept of a free and democratic America will be yet another farce chiseled in the minds of suggestible Americans by government and its corporate media representatives.

19

Change We Can Believe In

As the Total Information Awareness (TIA) project continues to gather steam, government will continue to increase its ability to control those subject to it, and America will eventually be transformed into a full-fledged culture of control. This is not speculation. It is an inductive inference and a matter of probability based on the information presented in the chapters of this book.

Like a cancer that continues to spread, there will be a point of metastasis when the infection can no longer be treated. Advances in surveillance technologies will help to circulate this infection inside every corpuscle through every capillary, vein, and artery, and to every organ of the state body; so that its constitution, along with its protective capacities, will eventually rot away. This process has already begun with the evisceration of the Fourth Amendment; and it is wishful thinking that there will be a spontaneous remission. Something needs to be done, and soon. So what is to be done?

What Americans Can Do

Complacency of the American public with the status quo is part of the disease. Referring to the masses of Oceana, the protagonist in Orwell's *1984* declared, "Until they become conscious they will rebel, and until after they have rebelled they cannot become conscious." Unless Americans become conscious of their dwindling civil rights, the signs and symptoms of this decline, and the seriousness of this disease, they will remain in a state of complacency, and the cancer will continue to spread.

Orwell's protagonist continued,

> If there was hope, it *must* lie in the proles [the citizens], because only there in those swarming disregarded masses, 85 per cent of the population of Oceania, could the force to destroy the Party ever be generated. . . . [I]f only

they could somehow become conscious of their own strength, they would have no need to conspire. They needed only to rise up and shake themselves like a horse shaking off flies. If they chose they could blow the Party to pieces tomorrow morning. Surely sooner or later it must occur to them to do it? And yet—![1] (Italics mine)

The power of Americans lies in their ability to organize and pool their numbers. When a massive earthquake devastated Haiti, Americans joined a common cause to raise millions for the Haitian relief fund. Here, there was consciousness of a need, and Americans took action.

The loss of basic rights over time is more insidious than a natural disaster. It is more like a silent cancer that spreads below the skin. It may not readily be noticed until it is too late. The mainstream corporate media is also part of this disease inasmuch as it has helped to conceal the signs and symptoms of our diminishing privacy by censoring and downplaying its imminent dangers. Nevertheless, the effect will be to undermine the fabric of democracy in America. This is harm worthy of joining together to prevent.

Public consciousness is essential. In the absence of a reliable mainstream media, Americans need to look elsewhere to obtain their information about government malfeasance. At this juncture, there are still competent, independent, online sources that can fill the mainstream void. The appendix to this book includes selected online government, media, and corporate watchdog organizations that keep their ears to the ground, and can be useful in providing information about government activities, notably TIA and related activities, that have not been adequately covered by the mainstream corporate media. All of the listed organizations actively advocate for change or otherwise provide the facility to make one's voice heard. The activities supported by these organizations include filing lawsuits, filing Freedom of Information Act requests, creating petitions, sponsoring conventions, organizing students to engage in investigative reporting, planning peaceful demonstrations, and other constitutional and democratic measures for affecting change. Americans who want to become a part of the movement to end TIA should become actively involved in some of the key issues and causes that are addressed by these organizations.

In addition to these and other activist organizations, there are presently many competent independent online news sources, which can provide perspectives not found in the mainstream media. A list of some of these outlets can be found on the Project Censored Web site.[2] Americans can thereby supply themselves with information and work toward having their collective voice heard. They can focus on governmental and corporate organizations (including media and telecom corporations) that are presently aiding and abetting transformation from a culture of autonomy to one of control.

Americans who have become conscious of this impending danger should pass this knowledge on to others. It is crucial that the public be informed.

A public that is informed cannot easily be seduced and manipulated into surrendering its civil rights. As discussed in Chapter 17, an antidote to government programs of "information warfare" and propagandizing is that of believing only on the basis of evidence. This means looking underneath the superficiality of a government spokesperson quoted on the evening news or on the CNN or Fox Web sites. It means giving up blind obedience to a politico-corporate machine that has profited from taking away our personal privacy and liberty. It requires building a new democratic ethics of belief based on the quest for information, real information.

This quest is not just a recommendation. As W. K. Clifford made clear,[3] all of us have a duty to question all that we believe. This universal duty includes holding our representatives' feet to the fire. In particular, President Obama was elected on a platform of "change we can believe in." However, a necessary condition of any such change must be transparency in government, not clandestine operations aimed at mass, warrantless spying on Americans. This platform of candor to the public cannot include sending thousands of troops to Afghanistan in order to create the conditions favorable for big oil companies like Amoco to build an energy pipeline.

Transparency of government also requires candor in the way of ideological commitment. What is Obama's view about the ratification of the International Criminal Court? Does he favor a global tax? Does he think that a North American Union is a good idea? What particular powers should be delegated to the United Nations and what powers should be set by nations? In the end, questions such as these, which relate to the place of America in a global economy and to the status and future of American sovereignty, should be debated and discussed in an open public forum, not behind a veil of secrecy and mainstream media censorship.

The Obama administration should also affirm its claimed commitment to transparency by filling the Privacy and Civil Liberties Oversight Board established by Congress in 2007 to monitor protection of civil liberties. This oversight board was supposed to be an *independent* arm of checks and balances on government with full subpoena power to investigate possible civil liberties violations by the executive branch. However, to date, the Obama administration, like its predecessor, the Bush administration, has failed to nominate even a single member to serve on the five-person board. Nor has an office or Web site for the Board been established.[4] The Obama administration should, therefore, honor its claimed commitment to the protection of civil liberties by taking appropriate and overdue actions to constitute this Board.

Obama has also claimed to support protection of net neutrality, so presumably he values the opinions of Americans. The Internet could be a useful venue for the free expression of ideas about how America is to define itself in relation to a globalized digital age. Such active participation of Americans in a public forum and exchange between the government and citizens of the United States about issues that matter to us all, or should matter, is the lifeline of a culture of autonomy. On the other hand, confining these big issues to an inner circle of government officials, media moguls, corporate executives and other power brokers is a mark of a culture of control.

In an age in which new digital technologies have the potential to change the face of human existence, from brain machine interfaces to an Internet of things—and even an "internet of people" plugged into a surveillance system, a democratic and free culture cannot remain democratic and free for long by secretly developing and plotting to deploy such technologies in the name of "national security." The right to privacy is a fundamental moral right and as such must be protected from such encroachment by government.

Americans and indeed all other citizens of the world have a right not to be tagged, chipped, or otherwise electronically branded, tracked, traced, or monitored. Yet we are becoming increasingly more accustomed to being watched. Few seem to mind when the electronic eye of a video camera stares blankly at them on a city street. Many claim not to mind that their personal e-mail and phone messages and Internet activities are being monitored. Most do not question the necessity, or the wisdom, of having their credit card purchases, bank records, health records, and other personal information stored in a government database. Few have become outspoken critics of the new body-scanning technologies being used at airports. It is now acceptable practice for companies like Google to store cookies on our computers for purposes of acquiring our behavior patterns. Few are protesting inclusion of their fingerprints, retinal images, or DNA in the FBI's biometric database. Few of us are even aware that every newborn child now has a sample of his or her DNA stored in a government lab.[5] Of course, all of these things have been defended by government—or by private companies—on the grounds of being for our own good.

So, what will we be prepared to accept next? What about subcutaneously implanting RFID chips inside everyone's body? Implantation of such track and trace devices is already becoming more prevalent. And why stick to reading our e-mail messages when government can read our brains directly? The technology still needs to be refined but it is now a reality. Likewise, what about remotely controlling our emotions, thoughts, and deeds? After all, DARPA is now looking into making such automata out of our military. And surely all of these things might also be defended on grounds of "national security" and as necessary to "fighting a war on terror."

Ending the Pseudowar on Terror

"Fighting a war on terror" must cease to be accepted by the American public as a trump card to override fundamental human rights. The Obama administration has both a moral and a legal obligation to protect the right to privacy against capricious and needless abridgement, and all Americans have a duty to insist on it.

So, what measures might this administration (or a subsequent one) take to close down an unrealistic attempt to stop terrorism by waging an Orwellian style "war"?

To its credit, the Obama administration has indicated its determination to invest in alternative renewable, energy sources. However, it needs to get beyond its rhetoric to take serious steps to resolve its energy problems through development of such sources. Instead of pandering to the far right and to big oil interests by keeping up the charade that such interests had nothing to do with invading Iraq and Afghanistan, the Obama administration should be candid about past history, and denounce preemptive wars aimed at seizing sovereign nations' natural resources.

Only by denouncing preemptive war altogether, as being in violation of international law, can the United States hope to avoid the outward appearance of having such untoward motives. The appearance (and reality) of conflict of interest might further be circumvented by replacing members of the old guard, such as Secretary of Defense Robert Gates, who are aligned with the Bush administration's doctrine of preemption. Nor should those who lead the Department of Defense have documented ties to military contractors. The Obama administration should shut down the military-industrial revolving door, which has played a significant role in the spawning and perpetuation of the TIA project.[6]

The Obama administration should also unequivocally denounce development of biological and chemical weapons. This denouncement must candidly speak to its own efforts and not merely the efforts of other nations dubbed "rogue" nations. By *secretly* conducting its program of bio defense,[7] the Obama administration has risked becoming a catalyst to a biological and chemical arms race among nations distrustful of the United States' true intentions. The United States cannot consistently hope to secretly grant itself special prerogatives to do that for which it would condemn other nations. In the process of attempting to defend itself against terrorism, it must not itself become one.

The Obama administration should discontinue the development of anti-ballistic missile systems because they are destabilizing. They encourage the buildup of nuclear arms by other nations in an effort to defeat these inherently less-than-bulletproof systems. Other nations become "sitting ducks" for nations guarded by such defenses. Thus, they are encouraged to build up their arsenals for self-protection.

Antiballistic missile systems also provide a first strike incentive and advantage for any nation that feels threatened by a nation guarded by such a system. Since the shield provided by the system is not bulletproof, other nations can gain an advantage by attacking the shielded nation first before it attacks them. If a nation attacks the shielded nation first, before it is attacked and loses some of its ballistic missile capability, it has the best chance of getting some of its missiles through the enemy's shield to destroy its arsenal before its own arsenal is destroyed.

This also means that so-called "strategic defenses" must be part of an offensive posture that includes ballistic missiles. A major function of an antiballistic missile system is to guard a nation's ballistic missiles from being destroyed during a first strike by another nation. Consequently, the United States cannot at once stand for nuclear nonproliferation while building weapons systems that encourage both the proliferation and the use of nuclear weapons.

The United States should alternatively join multilateral attempts at reaching diplomatic solutions to international disagreements, or work toward the imposition of economic sanctions (where necessary); and, as a last resort, work in concert with the United Nations Charter to reach military solutions.[8] To its credit, the Obama administration has expressed the need for diplomacy. Unfortunately, its rhetoric has largely been overshadowed by fighting a preemptive, perpetual "war on terror." The latter is antithetical to world peace, security, and freedom.

The Obama administration should draw a clear distinction between defending cyberspace against cyber attacks and an offensive posture aimed at policing and controlling it. Clearly, a program of warrantless, mass (global) surveillance goes beyond defending cyberspace against cyber attacks.

Obama should also align his rhetoric with the terminology that preceded the George W. Bush administration. This would require consistently referring to terrorists as *criminals*. Such a change in terminology would have important legal significance, for it would rule out military tribunals (still a part of the Obama administration's treatment of detainees) and restore the criminal justice system as the appropriate legal venue for adjudicating alleged crimes involving terrorism.

The Obama administration should dispense with the idea of "prolonged detention," which is de facto the punishment of detainees for crimes they have not yet committed.

It should decentralize intelligence. By according the Director of National Intelligence (DNI) authority over all other intelligence agencies—CIA, FBI,

NSA, etc.—and by making the DNI answerable directly to the president, the Bush administration established the infrastructure for unitary executive authority. Agencies need to share intelligence, but they should not be constrained by the president acting through the DNI. This gives the executive branch unchecked power to control intelligence and opens the floodgates for abuse of power.

Legal changes we can believe in

FISA Reform

The FISA Amendments Act of 2008 should be revisited by Congress and replaced by a FIS Act that, pursuant to the 1978 FISA Act, makes it illegal to conduct warrantless, mass surveillance of Americans' electronic communications. This new act should also cancel the 2008 FIS Act's granting of retroactive and future legal immunity to telecom corporations, thereby allowing American citizens a legal avenue for redressing abridgment of their Fourth Amendment right to privacy by these giant corporations. FIS Courts must also be restored to their traditional role of having judicial oversight instead of virtual rubber stamps for the DNI and the Attorney General (AG).

This means that certifications made to the FIS Court must provide incontrovertible evidence that the procedures adopted for conducting surveillance satisfy appropriate minimization standards for protecting the privacy of American citizens. Such evidence should include the algorithm being used to conduct the surveillance. It should also include particular information, such as names, addresses, places, and other details. The court should retain independent individuals with expertise in adequately assessing the surveillance software for conformity to approved minimization standards, and periodic court ordered audits should be conduct to make sure that the software actually being used is that for which a certification has been granted by the FIS Court.

At the time of this writing, H.R. 3846, the FISA Amendments Act of 2009, has been proposed to "provide additional civil liberties protections, and for other purposes." This bill has provisions for repealing retroactive immunity to telecommunication corporations and a provision on "prohibition on bulk collection under FISA Amendments Act."[9] These measures move in the right direction. The Obama administration should break its concordance with the Bush administration's program of mass, warrantless surveillance, and, pursuant to the Fourth Amendment, support a viable reform bill.

Retraction of FBI Racial Profiling

The Obama administration should also retract any FBI rule that permits racial profiling as it is a violation of the equal protection clause of the United States Constitution.

PATRIOT Act Reform

Congress should revisit Section 18 of the PATRIOT Act, which eliminates Provision 104(7)(B) of the 1978 FISA Act requiring that *the purpose* (not "a significant purpose") of conducting a warrantless electronic surveillance be to obtain foreign intelligence information. The legal barrier between intelligence gathering and criminal investigations that is required by the Fourth Amendment must be reinstated. FBI should not be able to acquire admissible criminal evidence against an American citizen without warrant or probable cause under the pretext of conducting a terrorism investigation unrelated to the criminal investigation.

In contravention of the Fourth Amendment, Section 213 of the PATRIOT Act (The "sneak and peek" provision) allows law enforcement officers to search the homes or businesses of private citizens without their knowledge or permission. Because such searches can be conducted without giving the subject of the search an opportunity to challenge the validity and extent of the search warrant, this provision gives unchecked power to government to intrude on citizens' personal space. It should, therefore, be cancelled. Similarly, Section 215 of the PATRIOT Act, which gives the FBI the warrantless power to access the books, records, papers, documents, and other "tangible things" through the issuance of National Security Letters (NSL), gives unchecked power to government to abridge the right to privacy. Such authority to access personal property should require a search warrant based on evidence showing probable cause; and those subject to the search should be notified.

Unfortunately, far from so amending this provision, the Obama administration has reinstituted it, unchanged. On February 25, 2010, the U.S. House of Representatives passed without modification. H.R. 3961 to extend for one year, beginning on March 1, 2010, expiring provisions of the PATRIOT Act.[10] On February 27, 2010, President Obama signed this bill just when the questionable provisions of the PATRIOT Act were due to expire.

These provisions included PATRIOT Act sections 206, regarding FISA court orders for multipoint or "roving" wiretaps, and 215 (as discussed above); and Section 6001(a) of the Intelligence Reform and Terrorism Prevention Act of 2004 concerning "lone wolf" terrorists (individuals acting alone with no connection to a foreign power).

In fact, on November 5, 2009, the House Judiciary Committee favorably reviewed an alternative bill, H.R. 3845, sponsored by Rep. John Conyers (D. MI),[11] which would have strengthened privacy protections under Section 15 of the PATRIOT Act by requiring the government to justify that the records it was seeking (business, library, or bookseller records) in counterterrorism investigations were relevant to the said investigation. It would have also required the government to notify recipients of a nondisclosure ("gag") order of their right to challenge the said order in court.

The bill would have also let the "lone wolf" provision expire—a case that did not belong under the FIS Act in the first place; and it would have required the government to describe its "roving target" in sufficient detail for a judge to distinguish the prospective target from any other possible individual who might get caught in a multipoint surveillance net. However, H.R. 3845 was never considered by the full House and none of these protections made it into the bill that Obama signed. Thus, the same unconstitutional provisions of the PATRIOT Act that were passed in haste by Congress in the immediate aftermath of the 9/11 attacks now remain intact under the Obama administration, at least until March 1, 2011. Regarding the PATRIOT Act, the Obama administration, therefore, has another chance in 2011 to deliver change we can truly believe in.

Getting Rid of Military Commissions

In October 2009, President Obama signed the Military Commissions Act of 2009 into law. This act, which replaced the Military Commissions Act of 2006, has made some important improvements on the earlier Act. For example, the 2006 Act gave the president the power to interpret the Geneva Conventions, including Article 3 concerning what constitutes torture. "The President," it said, "has the authority for the United States to determine the meaning and application of the Geneva Conventions."[12] The 2009 Act does not contain such a provision. The 2006 Act also suspended habeas corpus. However, pursuant to the 2008 Supreme Court ruling in *Boumediene v. Bush,* the 2009 Act does not contain such a blatantly unconstitutional provision.

Nevertheless, the core of the 2006 Act remains intact. While the earlier Act authorized the president to establish military commissions for "unlawful enemy combatants," the 2009 Act authorizes the president to establish military commissions for anyone declared an "unprivileged enemy belligerent." The differences between "unlawful enemy combatant" and "unprivileged enemy belligerent" are largely cosmetic.[13] As defined by the 2009 Act, an "unprivileged enemy belligerent" is an individual who "(A) has engaged in hostilities against the United States or its coalition partners; (B) has purposefully and materially supported hostilities against the United States or its coalition partners; or (C) was a part of al Qaeda at the time of the alleged offense under this chapter."[14] As for the definition of "hostilities," it means "any conflict subject to the laws of war." However, what constitutes "the laws of war" is left undefined; and given that the Obama administration has followed the Bush administration in extending the meaning of "war" to cover "hostilities" perpetrated anywhere and everywhere (including in someone's living room), "the law of war" can mean virtually anything anyone wants it to mean.

Like the Bush administration's 2006 version, Obama's 2009 version equates one who "supports" hostilities with one who actually engages in them. This opens the floodgates to try individuals under military commissions who have not, themselves, engaged in acts of terrorism. The assumption that supporting hostilities (whatever exactly that is) is equivalent to participation in hostilities has, in fact, already been rejected by several federal judges.[15]

Further, the purpose of the 2009 Act is held to be "to try *alien* unprivileged enemy belligerents for violations of the law of war and other offenses triable by military commission" (emphasis added). This is in contravention of the equal protection clause of the Fourteenth Amendment since it clearly establishes a double standard—one for citizens and another for noncitizens. And if the military tribunal standards cannot be consistently applied to everyone, then there is reason to believe it should not be applied to anyone.[16]

Such inconsistencies cannot be covered up by changing "unlawful" to "unprivileged" or "combatant" to "belligerent." The problem is due to an inherently flawed and contradictory legal scheme. To render the system consistent, military commissions must be abandoned along with the pretext of fighting a war on terror (or a "war on al Qaeda"), and federal courts must be consistently used to prosecute crime, which is what terrorism really is. Obama's adoption of Bush's confusion of crime with war has led him deeper into a legal quagmire. The consequence has been to continue on a path toward a culture of control in which individuals who have not committed acts of terrorism are treated the same as those who have, and the commission of "hostilities" according to "the law of war" can be used as a pretext to deprive selected individuals of their right to equal protection of the law.

Changing the Corporate Landscape

Steady creep of globalization has changed the political realities. Giant corporations spanning the globe now have the ability to influence decisions, worldwide, made at the highest state levels. At the same time, these companies have no moral conscience and will do what's in their best financial interest, including helping government create and operate the machinery for systematically violating human rights. The TIA network, whose tentacles span continents, demonstrates what such cooperation can do.

Telecommunication companies such as Comcast and AT&T now have legal mandates to provide the infrastructure and facility for the NSA along with its sister federal agencies to "immediately provide the Government with all information, facilities, or assistance necessary to accomplish the acquisition."[17]

At the time of this writing, Comcast has struck a deal with General Electric to take control of NBC, including its newsroom. Comcast's cable and Internet services already reach 30 percent of American homes; and it is now attempting to acquire NBC Universal's assets, including 26 TV stations in the largest U.S. markets, the NBC network, some of the highest–rated cable TV networks, and the Universal film library.[18]

The United States Justice Department is conducting a review of the impending merger, and the outcome of this review as well as whether the merger will be approved by the Federal Commerce Commission (FCC) is not presently known. Nevertheless, the dangerous probability of a merger of this nature eventually coming to pass should not be underestimated.

As was discussed in Chapter 7, the Supreme Court's 2005 decision in *Brand X* has cleared the way for cable companies like Comcast to control the flow of information by keeping competitors from using their cables. If Comcast acquires NBC, it will increase its ability and financial incentive to favor its own programming and to exclude other cable networks from having their programming carried on its cable system. Media Access Project's Andrew Jay Schwartzman has admonished the Senate Judiciary Committee,

> There are scores of cable networks which have been unable to obtain carriage on Comcast and other cable systems. I'm here, and they are not, because some of these companies have told me that they are afraid of retaliation. Indeed, over the last several years numerous programmers such as NFL Network, WealthTV and the Tennis Channel have unsuccessfully pursued carriage complaints at the FCC.... Acquisition of NBC's stable of cable networks will greatly exacerbate the imbalance of power.... The existing legal framework already gives Comcast every incentive to favor its own programming over independently produced cable channels. This can include refusal to carry competitors, paying them far less for carriage or placing them on a lesser watched program tier.[19]

The obvious consequence of this will be that the American people will receive less independent programming. Instead, Comcast will increase its power to control what Americans see and hear over its cable lines.

In the case of news, this can further diminish the waning ability of mainstream media to keep the people informed. For example, it would be wishful thinking to suppose that Comcast's NBC would inform the people that it is working with government to intercept their phone calls and e-mail messages; or that it is using its electronic equipment to monitor the communications of journalists or to spy on its competitors. It takes only a little creativity to imagine how serious the consequences of this conflict of interest could be.

The Comcast/NBC merger also portends grave harm for net neutrality. If the merger succeeds, then Comcast will increase its control over the content of the Internet. As discussed in Chapter 7 (on net neutrality), the very real danger is that mainstream media will gain a dominating foothold on the Internet. As gatekeeper of the cables, Comcast's foray into controlling a major slice of the mainstream media would be a major step toward bringing the Internet and mainstream media under one common owner. This would make the Internet an extension of mainstream media and would, as such, mark the end of a democratic, free Internet. The fate of the Internet is, therefore, now largely in the hands of the FCC, which will soon decide whether to approve this merger.

The Disposition of the TIA Network

To date, the Obama administration has walked lockstep with the Bush administration in attempting to seal up the ability of the American people to seek redress from the Telecoms, such as Comcast and AT&T, for having unlawfully violated their right to privacy. The retroactive immunity granted by the 2008 FISA Amendments Act to telecoms against civil and criminal liability and state investigations prevents the people from taking legal action against these companies. So far, the Obama administration has not taken any initiative in supporting the passage of FISA reform such as the 2009 FISA Amendments Act, which would subtract such retroactive immunity.

Further, in 2009, the Obama Justice Department argued that the government could not be sued even for unlawful spying on Americans pursuant to Section 223 of the U.S. PATRIOT Act, which says, "Any person who is aggrieved by any willful violation" of the PATRIOT Act or of the Foreign Intelligence Surveillance Act of 1978 "may commence an action in United States District Court against the United States to recover money damages."[20] However, since no "willful violation" occurred according to the intended meaning of this term, argued the Obama administration, the American people cannot sue the government for spying on them.[21]

If the Obama administration wants to honor its promise to respect the constitutional rights of Americans, including their Fourth Amendment rights, then it should not continue to use legal gymnastics to trump serious constitutional rights. In the larger context of constitutional law, it is doubtful that such an interpretation of Section 223 of the PATRIOT Act will hold up. For if this is what this provision really means then *it*, not the Fourth Amendment, should be declared unconstitutional.

Clearly, the fate of the TIA project depends on the legal climate in which it operates. Unfortunately, in the current legal climate under the Obama administration, it is not likely this project will cease any time soon. Americans must, therefore, be vigilant in attempting to change the law by making their collective voice heard. For if this project continues to make progress amid burgeoning technologies that have the capacity for increasingly more intrusive modes of monitoring, tracing, tracking, and control, then the outlook for the survival of the free world looks rather bleak.

Toward a System of Universal Privacy Protection

The 1978 FISA Act included so-called "minimization standards," which were also retained by the 2008 FISA Amendments Act. According to these standards, specific procedures had to be adopted that were "reasonably designed in light of the purpose and technique of the particular surveillance to minimize the acquisition and retention, and prohibit the dissemination of nonpublicly available information concerning unconsenting United States persons."[22] Clearly, the present TIA system has not adopted procedures reasonably designed to minimize acquisition and retention, and prohibit dissemination of the personal information of millions of Americans. Instead, this system is one that seeks *total* information, not minimized acquisition of such information; such information is retained for an indefinite amount of time; and there is no prohibition on its dissemination.

These procedures also require that "no content of any communication to which a United States person is a party shall be . . . retained for longer than twenty-four hours unless a court order . . . is obtained or unless the Attorney General determines that the information indicates a threat of death or serious bodily harm to any person."[23] Clearly, storage of the personal information of millions of Americans for an indefinite amount of time in massive databases without their express permission is in violation of this FISA provision.

To satisfy the said minimization standards, there would at least need to be safeguards built into the TIA system that would bar unrestricted acquisition and dissemination of stored personal information pursuant to a court warrant. Technological means of fulfilling this function are possible and would be an important step toward respecting privacy. As was discussed in Chapter 18, when the TIA project was first conceived in 2002, DARPA had conducted research into creation of such a "privacy appliance" that would have safeguarded the privacy of personal information in the TIA databases.

This appliance would have permitted applications of algorithms to locate behavioral patterns indicative of possible terrorist plots but would have also used encryption to lock out access to personally identifying information, such as names and addresses of particular American persons; it would have left an electronic trail of any unauthorized attempt to gain access to the stored identifying information; and it would have only made personally identifying information available to government pursuant to a court warrant. Unfortunately, the research to develop such privacy protections was discontinued, and there is presently no reason to believe that a device of this nature will be added to the TIA system.

No computer system is invulnerable to hacking, and there is no guarantee that the TIA system would not still be abused by government if such a privacy appliance were installed in it. Indeed, the most reliable safeguard against government abuse of the people's right to privacy is the dismantling of the TIA system altogether. The government simply does not need this massive system of stored data to gather foreign intelligence and to conduct lawful wiretaps. In fact, as discussed in Chapter 2, such a system is not even effective in finding terroristic behavioral patterns and it tends to produce false positives.

However, in the absence of dismantling this system, there is no rational basis for arguing against developing and installing a security appliance to protect the right to privacy of anyone—both Americans and non-Americans alike—whose personal data is being stored in this massive data network. For, such privacy appliances can be constructed to protect *everyone's* privacy, not just Americans.

The TIA system is transnational, capturing, storing, and searching the personal data of persons worldwide. At the same time, the right to privacy is a universal right, and not simply the right of Americans. It is everyone's right. Therefore, all people throughout the world have a right to the protection of their privacy.

As such, it is the right of all people of all nations to insist that their personal information be safeguarded and protected against government abuse. Since it is not only possible to harness technology to invade privacy, but also to protect it, technologies that invade privacy should not be permitted to proceed in the absence of technologies that protect it.

A surveillance system protected by such privacy-protecting technology would at least have the following functionality:

1. Prevention of access to all personally identifying data, whether that of an American or non-American person.

2. Pursuant to new intelligence laws, a federal surveillance court warrant required to access personally identifying data.
3. All surveillance warrants based on probable cause established on the basis of an electronically detected behavioral pattern indicating a terrorist activity.
4. All surveillance warrants restricted to personally identifying information related to such an electronically detected behavioral pattern.
5. No access granted to any data not electronically flagged as relevant to such an electronically detected behavioral pattern.

An information system equipped with such privacy safeguards is no panacea given the serious potential for abuse inherent in the very existence of such a vast network of personal information under centralized control. Moreover, such systemic change does not even begin to address the challenge to freedom of speech and of the press posed by corporate media consolidation, globalization, and the dangers inherent in control of the world's wealth and political power by a relatively few giant multinational corporations. Nevertheless, a system that incorporated such functional privacy protection would be a step toward slowing the steady, metastatic spread of cancer now infecting democracy.

Presently, no such privacy protection is operative, and all of us are vulnerable to the exploitation and abuse of government power. As technologies with the capacity to track, trace, monitor, and control become increasingly more intrusive, the ability of government (perhaps world government) to exploit and abuse us all will exponentially increase. Unless we all begin to speak out, *now,* against the systematic and global violation of the right to privacy, we will have written the epitaph of democracy.

Appendix

Selected Organizations that Advocate for Constructive Change

All of the following online organizations strive to promote and safeguard conditions essential to the existence and flourishing of a culture of autonomy in a digital age, especially privacy; being kept informed about government, mass media, and corporate activities that threaten to undermine freedom and democracy; and the public interest in shaping government policy. All people throughout the world can do their part in helping to stop the steady, oppressive, and transformative march toward a culture of control as described in this book by supporting suitable, peaceful activities sponsored by these or other reputable organizations dedicated to the same mission.

American Civil Liberties Union (ACLU, www.aclu.org)

Works through the courts, legislatures, and communities to protect individual rights and liberties guaranteed by the Constitution and laws of the United States.

Center for Digital Democracy (CDD, www.democraticmedia.org/)

Seeks to protect the public interest in digital communications. Works to promote net neutrality; universal access to the Internet; diverse ownership of new media outlets; and privacy. Activities include outreach to the press and policymakers; writing reports, and blogs; conducting investigative research; and organizing campaigns.

Common Cause (www.commoncause.org)

Seeks to help citizens make their voices heard in the political process and to hold their elected leaders accountable to the public interest; and empowers members, supporters, and the general public to take action on major policy issues.

CorpWatch (www.corpwatch.org)

Through investigative research and journalism, advocates for multinational corporate accountability and transparency; exposes multinational corporations that profit from war, fraud, environmental, human rights, and other abuses; and keeps the public informed about such matters.

Electronic Frontier Foundation (EFF, www.eff.org)

Defends free speech, privacy, innovation, and consumer rights pertaining to digital technologies. Primary vehicles of change are the courts, where it brings and defends lawsuits; mobilization of concerned citizens to oppose unacceptable legislation; advising policymakers; and educating press and public.

Electronic Privacy Information Center (EPIC, http://epic.org/)

Public interest research center for protection of privacy, the First Amendment, and constitutional values in issues arising from use and development of electronic information technologies. Publishes an e-mail and online newsletter, reports, and books about privacy, open government, free speech, and other topics related to civil liberties.

Fairness and Accuracy in Reporting (FAIR, www.fair.org)

National media watch group working with both journalists and activists to expose media bias and censorship; advocates for greater diversity in the press; defends muzzled journalists; advocates for structural reform in the media; and encourages the public to become media activists rather than passive consumers of news.

Free Press (www.freepress.net)

National media organization working to reform the media. Through education, organizing and advocacy, seeks to promote diverse and independent media ownership, strong public media, quality journalism, and universal access to communications.

Media Access Project (MAP) (www.mediaaccess.org/)

Represents the public interest in communications and technology issues before the Federal Communications Commission (FCC), other policy-making bodies, and in the courts. Advocates for open, diverse media; equitable access to media and to telecommunications services; and for public discourse on social issues.

Open Congress (www.opencongress.org)

Seeks to make what is really going on in Congress accessible to the public and to give the public a voice by merging official government data with news, blogs, social networking, and public participation tools, such as ways to contact Congress and an open platform for individuals and organizations to organize online communities around their political interests. Sponsors Open House and Open Senate Projects aimed at identifying ways in which the Congress can open up and allow greater public access to congressional activities.

OpenInternet (http://openinternet.gov/index.html)

This Web site is government-run—by the Federal Communications Commission (FCC). However, it provides an open forum to post ideas about Internet freedom. This can be a way to have the FCC hear your ideas about protecting Internet neutrality against encroachment by giant telecommunication corporations and government agencies that seek to monitor, monopolize, and control it.

Project Censored (www.projectcensored.org/)

Teaches students and the public about the role of a free press in a free society and brings significant news to light that has not been covered by the mainstream media. Journalists, scholars, librarians, students, and concerned citizens around the world submit stories to Project Censored staff and students from Sonoma State University, who review the submissions and select the top 25 stories, which are then ranked in order of importance and published in a yearbook.

Prometheus Radio Project (www.prometheusradio.org/)

Builds, supports, and advocates for community radio stations. Primary goal is to build low-power FM (LPFM) community radio stations in order to democratize the media. Supports community groups at every stage of the process of building community radio stations; facilitates public participation in the FCC regulatory process, and sponsors events promoting media democracy and LPFM radio.

Public Citizen (www.citizen.org)

Consumer advocacy organization representing consumer interests in congress, the executive branch and the courts. Advocates for government accountability; consumer rights to seek redress in court; clean, safe, sustainable energy sources; just trade policies; affordable healthcare; and environmental protections.

Notes

Introduction

1. George Orwell, *1984* (London: Secker and Warburg, 1949). Available online at http://www.msxnet.org/orwell/print/1984.pdf.

Chapter 1

1. This nationalistic movement toward world domination is examined in Chapter 9.
2. Public Law 95-511, 92 Stat. 1783, October 25, 1978. Accessed on February 25, 2010 from http://www.cnss.org/PL%2095-511.pdf.
3. HR 3162, October 24, 2001. Accessed on February 25, 2010 from http://epic.org/privacy/terrorism/hr3162.html.
4. American Civil Liberties Union, "Surveillance under the U.S. PATRIOT Act," ACLU Web site, April 3, 2003. Accessed on February 25, 2010, from http://www.aclu.org/national-security/surveillance-under-usa-patriot-act.
5. However, in 2007, a lower court ruled that the gag order provision of the PATRIOT Act was unconstitutional and the Obama administration did not appeal the decision to the Supreme Court. See ACLU, "Obama Administration Will Not Ask Supreme Court to Take up National Security Letter 'Gag Order' Decision," May 18, 2009. Accessed on February 20, 2010 from http://www.aclu.org/national-security/obama-administration-will-not-ask-supreme-court-take-national-security-letter-gag-.
6. Charlie Savage, "Battle Looms Over the PATRIOT Act," *New York Times,* September 19, 2009. Accessed on February 25, 2010, from http://www.nytimes.com/2009/09/20/us/politics/20patriot.html. See also Associated Press, "Obama Signs One-Year Extension of PATRIOT Act," *New York Times,* February 27, 2010. Accessed on February 28, 2010, from http://www.nytimes.com/aponline/2010/02/27/us/politics/AP-US-Obama-Patriot-Act.html. And see also Chapter 19.
7. Marbin Miller, "Police Showdown Over Schiavo Averted," *Miami Herald,* March 26, 2005. Retrieved online on June 12, 2009, from http://www.commondreams.org/headlines05/0326-03.htm.
8. However, Qwest was subsequently forced to cooperate. On August 22, 2008, a three-member Foreign Intelligence Surveillance (FIS) Court of Review granted

a motion by the Bush administration compelling it to participate in the warrantless surveillance program. See Foreign Intelligence Surveillance Court of Review, In re Directives [redacted text] Pursuant to Section 105B of the Foreign Intelligence Surveillance Act, No. 08-1, August 22, 2008. Accessed on February 25, 2010, from http://www.fas.org/irp/agency/doj/fisa/fiscr082208.pdf.

9. U.S. Supreme Court, Syllabus, Citizens United v. Federal Elections Commission. Accessed on January 22, 2010, from http://www.supremecourtus.gov/opinions/09pdf/08-205.pdf.
10. John Paul Stevens, Minority Opinion, Citizens United v. Federal Elections Commission, Accessed on January 22, 2010 from http://www.supremecourtus.gov/opinions/09pdf/08-205.pdf.
11. Adam Liptak, "Justices, 5 to 4, Reject Corporate Spending Limit," *New York Times,* January 21, 2010. Accessed on January 22, 2010 from http://www.nytimes.com/2010/01/22/us/politics/22scotus.html?hp.
12. One exception to this, however, is his retention of the terms "war on terror" and "war on al-Qaeda," which, as will be discussed in Chapter 10, illegitimately extends the concept of war.
13. President Barrack Obama, Remarks by the President on National Security, National Archives, Washington, D. C., May 21, 2009. Accessed on February 24, 2010, from http://jerusalem.usconsulate.gov/pdfs/obama_speechen052109.pdf.
14. Military Commissions Act of 2006, Public Law 109-366, Sec. 948a(1) Accessed on February 24, 2010, from http://frwebgate.access.gpo.gov/cgi-bin/getdoc.cgi?dbname=109_cong_public_laws&docid=f:publ366.109.
15. See Chapter 10.
16. See "Obama: Time to Look Forward, but Bush Aids aren't above the Law," USA Today, January 11, 2009. Accessed on February 24, 2010, from http://content.usatoday.com/communities/theoval/post/2009/01/61177294/1.
17. See Chapter 19.
18. Project for the New American Century, Rebuilding America's Defenses: Strategy, Forces, and Resources for a New Century, 2000. Accessed on February 24, 2010, from http://www.newamericancentury.org/RebuildingAmericasDefenses.pdf.
19. DARPA, Memo on Brain Machine Interface, September 17, 2001. Accessed on February 25, 2010, from http://dart.stanford.edu:8080/sparrow_2.0/pages/teams/DARPABrainMachineInterface.html.
20. Alan Rudolf, Brain Machine Interfaces, Defense Sciences Office, DARPA Web site, March 6, 2003. Accessed on February 25 from http://web.archive.org/web/20030306155324/http://www.arpa.mil/dso/thrust/biosci/brainmi.htm.
21. Antonio Regalato, Brain-Machine, MIT Technology Review, February 1, 2001. Accessed on February 25, 2010, from Interface http://www.technologyreview.com/InfoTech/12261/.
22. Amanda Onion, "The No-Doze Soldier: Military Seeking Radical Ways of Stumping Need for Sleep," ABCNews.com, December 18, 2003. Accessed on February 25, 2010, from http://www.sleepnet.com/tech7/messages/625.html.

Chapter 2

1. Niccolo Machiavelli, *The Prince*, Ch. 3. Accessed on February 25, 2010, from http://www.gutenberg.org/files/1232/1232-h/1232-h.htm.
2. United States Department of Defense, News Transcript, "Secretary of Defense Rumsfeld Media Availability en Route to Chile," November 18, 2002. Retrieved on line on June 9, 2009, from http://www.fas.org/sgp/news/2002/11/dod111802.html.
3. See Chapter 6.
4. John Markoff, "Chief Takes Over New Agency to Thwart Attacks on U.S.," *New York Times,* February 13, 2002. Retrieved online on June 9, 2009, from http://www.ratical.org/ratville/JFK/JohnJudge/linkscopy/PoindyToIAO.html.
5. American Civil Liberties Union, Action Alert, Accessed on June 9, 2009, from http://ga1.org/aclu_sc_action/alert-description.html?alert_id=4132.
6. The definitions of technologies assembled here are adapted from DARPA, IAO Web site. Accessed on June 9, 2009, from http://web.archive.org/web/20021003045334/www.darpa.mil/iao/programs.htm.
7. Jason Ethier, "Current Research in Social Network Theory." Retrieved online on June 9, 2009, from http://www.ccs.neu.edu/home/perrolle/archive/Ethier-SocialNetworks.html.
8. Ellen Nakashima, "Lockheed Secures Contract to Expand Biometric Database," *Washington Post,* Wednesday, February 13, 2008. Accessed on February 25, 2010, from http://www.washingtonpost.com/wp-dyn/content/article/2008/02/12/AR2008021202777.html.
9. Ryan Singel, "Whistle-Blower Outs NSA Spy Room," *Wired,* April 7, 2006. Accessed on February 25, 2010, from http://www.wired.com/science/discoveries/news/2006/04/70619.
10. Bewirt, "All About NSA's and AT&T's Big Brother Machine, the Narus 6400," *Daily Kos,* Friday April 7, 2006. Accessed on February 25, 2010, from http://www.dailykos.com/storyonly/2006/4/8/14724/28476.
11. In September 2004, William Crowell, a former Deputy Director of the NSA and the DARPA Task Force on Terrorism and Deterrence, joined the Board of Directors of Narus. See "Narus Appoints Former Deputy Director of the National Security Agency to Its Board of Directors," Narus Web site, September 29, 2004. Accessed on February 25, 2010, from http://web.archive.org/web/20050206184639/narus.com/press/2004/0929.html.
12. See, for example, John Searle, *Minds, Brains, and Science.* (Cambridge: Harvard University Press, 1984).
13. This is not to say that the Arar lease was discovered through the use of TIA technology. It is not clear how the lease was obtained. But electronic surveillance was used in investigating Arar prior to his deportation to Syria, and it is not unlikely that it helped build the (false) case against him. See, Robert Fife, "Foreign spies may have stolen Arar document, Minister can't explain how else U.S. agents obtained lease paper," CanWest News Service. Accessed on February 25, 2010, from http://circ.jmellon.com/docs/html/foreign_spies_may_have_stolen_arar_document.html.

14. Jeff Jonas and Jim Harper, "Effective Counterterrorism and the Limited Role of Predictive Data Mining," *Policy Analysis*, No. 584, December 11, 2006. Accessed on February 25, 2010, from http://www.cato.org/pubs/pas/pa584.pdf.
15. Ibid.
16. Ibid.
17. CBS News, "Al-Awlaki May Be Al Qaeda Recruiter," *CBS News.com*, December 30, 2009. Accessed on February 25, 2010, from http://www.cbsnews.com/blogs/2009/12/30/world/worldwatch/entry6039811.shtml.
18. Mark Hosenball, and Michael Isikoff, and Evan Thomas, "The Radicalization of Umar Farouk Abdulmutallab," *Newsweek.com*, January 2, 2010. Accessed on February 25, 2010, from http://www.newsweek.com/id/229047?from=rss&utm_source=feedburner&utm_medium=feed&utm_campaign=Feed%3A+news week%2FWorldNews+%28UPDATED+-+Newsweek-++World+News%29.
19. "Umar Farouk Abdulmutallab," *New York Times Topics*, February 3, 2010. Accessed on February 25, 2010, from http://topics.nytimes.com/top/reference/timestopics/people/a/umar_farouk_abdulmutallab/index.html.
20. Summary of the White House Review of the December 25, 2009, Attempted Terrorist Attack, White House. Accessed on February 25, 2010, from http://www.whitehouse.gov/sites/default/files/summary_of_wh_review_12-25-09.pdf p. 3.
21. Ibid., p. 5
22. Mark Guarino, "Number of full-body scanners at US airports to triple in 2010," *Christian Science Monitor*, December 30, 2009. Accessed on February 25, 2010, from http://www.csmonitor.com/USA/2009/1230/Number-of-full-body-scanners-at-US-airports-to-triple-in-2010.
23. Agance France-Presse, "travelers to undergo 'enhanced screening' at US airports," The Raw Story, January 3, 2010. Accessed on February 25, 2010, from http://rawstory.com/2009//01/institutes-tighter-longterm-airport-security-rules/.
24. This is not to raise the issue of exposing travelers to increased levels of radiation emitted by these machines. While officials claim that the emissions are negligible, this still fails to address the cumulative effect of such exposure, especially for frequent travelers.

Chapter 3

1. H.R. 6304, FISA Amendments Act of 2008. Accessed on February 25, 2010, from http://www.govtrack.us/congress/billtext.xpd?bill=h110-6304.
2. Executive Order 12333, United States Intelligence Activities, July 31, 2008. Accessed on February 25, 2009, from http://www.fas.org/irp/offdocs/eo/eo-12333-2008.pdf.
3. Reuters, "Proposed new FBI rules draw civil liberties worries," *Reuters.com*, Friday, September 12, 2009.
4. H.R. 6304, Section 702(g)2(B).

5. H.R. 6304, Section 702(b)3.
6. H.R. 6304 Section 802.
7. H.R. 6304, Section 703(e).
8. Fred Lucas, "Left Decries Obama's FISA Vote," *CNS News.com*, July 10, 2008. Accessed on February 25, 2010, from http://www.cnsnews.com/news/print/32152.
9. David Moberg, "Moving Obama Left," *In These Times*, August 25, 2008. Accessed on February 25, 2010, from http://www.inthesetimes.com/article/3859/moving_obama_left/.
10. Jake Tapper, "Obama's FISA Shift," *ABC News.com*, July 9, 2008. Accessed on February 25, 2010, from http://blogs.abcnews.com/politicalpunch/2008/07/obamas-fisa-shi.html.
11. EO 12333, 1.5(a).
12. EO 12333, 1.3.
13. EO 12333, 2.5.
14. EO 12333, 2.5.
15. Statement of the Honorable Patrick Leahey, Hearing on Oversight of the Federal Bureau of Investigation, United States Senate Committee on the Judiciary, September 17, 2008. Accessed on February 25, 2010, from http://judiciary.senate.gov/hearings/testimony.cfm?id=3530&wit_id=2629.

Chapter 4

1. H.R. 6304, Section 702(h)1(a).
2. H.R. 6304, Section 702(h)4(c).
3. FIS Court of Review, In re Directives [redacted text] Pursuant to Section 105B of the Foreign Intelligence Surveillance Act, No. 08-1, August 22, 2008. Accessed on February 25, 2010, from http://www.fas.org/irp/agency/doj/fisa/fiscr082208.pdf.
4. James Risen and Eric Lichtblau, "Court Affirms Wiretapping without Warrants," *New York Times*, January 15, 2009. Accessed on February 15, 2010, from http://www.nytimes.com/2009/01/16/washington/16fisa.html.
5. FIS Court of Review, In re Directives.
6. See also Chapter 3.
7. FIS Court of Review, In re Directives.
8. Risen and Lichtblau, "Court Affirms Wire Tapping without Warrants."
9. Government Defendants' Notice of Motion to Dismiss and For Summary Judgment and Memorandum, Jewel et al. v. National Security Agency et al., Case No. 08-cv-4373-VRW. Accessed on February 25, 2010, from http://www.eff.org/files/filenode/jewel/jewelmtdobama.pdf.
10. See also Chapter 3.
11. Ellen Nakashima and Dan Eggen, "Former CEO Says U.S. Punished Phone Firm," *Washington Post*, Saturday, October 13, 2007. Accessed on February 25, 2010, from http://www.washingtonpost.com/wp-dyn/content/article/2007/10/12/AR2007101202485.html.
12. H.R. 6304, Section 802(a)4(A)i.

Chapter 5

1. Jeff Jonas and Jim Harper, "Effective Counterterrorism and the Limited Role of Predictive Data Mining," *Policy Analysis*, No. 584, December 11, 2006. Accessed on February 26, 2010, from http://www.cato.org/pubs/pas/pa584.pdf.
2. Shane Harris, "FBI, Pentagon pay for access to trove of public records," *Government Executive.com*, November 11. 2005. Accessed on February 26, 2010, from http://www.govexec.com/story_page.cfm?articleid=32802.
3. The history of this company includes breaches in privacy as well as illegal acquisition of personal data. In 2009, ChoicePoint was fined US$275,000 by the U.S. Federal Trade Commission for a data breach in 2008 that exposed personal information of 13,750 people. It failed to protect one of its databases, thereby allowing unauthorized access to personal data such as Social Security numbers and other sensitive information. ChoicePoint was also involved in receiving US$10 million from the U.S. government for an illegally obtained database of personal information of Mexican and Colombian citizens, including such data as passport numbers, physical profiles, birth dates, and marital status.

    In addition, it was responsible for creating the infamous "Florida 'felons list'" during the 2000 Presidential elections, which disenfranchised thousands of blacks and Hispanics, most of whom were Democrats, by erroneously branding them as felons.
4. Sourcewatch, "Richard L. Armitage." Accessed on February 26, 2010, from http://www.sourcewatch.org/index.php?title=Richard_L._Armitage.
5. Leslie Wayne, "Same Washington, Different Office," *New York Times*, March 17, 2006. Accessed on February 25, 2010, from http://www.nytimes.com/2006/03/17/politics/17ashcroft.html.
6. Robert O'Harrow, Jr., "ChoicePoint Finds Wealth in Information: Giant Transforming Itself into a Private Intelligence Service," *MSNBC*, January 20, 2005. Accessed on February 26, 2010, from http://www.msnbc.msn.com/id/6846357/.
7. Martin H. Bosworth, "ChoicePoint-FBI Deal Raises New Privacy Questions," *Consumer Affairs.com*, May 16, 2006. Accessed on February 26, 2010, from http://www.consumeraffairs.com/news04/2006/05/fbi_choicepoint.html
8. See also chapters 2 and 5.
9. "Data Mining & Data Warehousing," SAIC Web site, 2006. Accessed on February 26, 2010, from http://web.archive.org/web/20060209120733/www.saic.com/datamining/data-analysis.html.
10. Shane Harris, "FBI, Pentagon Pay for Access to Trove of Public Records," *Government Executive*, November 11, 2005. Accessed on May 10, 2010 from http://www.govexec.com/story_page.cfm?articleid=32802
11. "AutoTrackXP® and ChoicePoint Online," ChoicePoint Web site, 2003. Accessed on February 26, 2010, from http://web.archive.org/web/20031218085618/www.choicepoint.com/business/public/cbi_1.html.
12. Clear (Consolidated Lead Evaluation and Reporting). Thomson Reuters, July 25, 2009. Accessed on January 17, 2010, from http://www.dcs.state.ok.us/SW_Contracts.nsf/6fe2a5d9256854f886256c63004e411e/

7de5a6efd2e56b5f86257694005adfe3/$FILE/SW804%20CLEAR%20User%20Guide.PDF.

13. Ellen Nakashima, "FBI Prepares Vast Database of Biometrics," *Washington Post*, Saturday, December 22, 2007. Accessed on January 17, 2010, from http://www.washingtonpost.com/wp-dyn/content/article/2007/12/21/AR2007122102544.html.

14. See Chapter 10.

15. See Chapter 7.

16. Andrew Edgecliffe-Johnson, "Thomson Cleared for Reuters Merger," *London Financial Times,* February 19, 2008. Accessed on January 17, 2010, from http://www.ft.com/cms/s/0/33d14772-df29-11dc-91d4-0000779fd2ac.html?nclick_check=1.

17. See Chapter 5.

18. Peter Phillips, "News Bias in the Associated Press," *CommonDreams.org,* July 22, 2006. Accessed on January 17, 2010, from http://www.commondreams.org/views06/0722-21.htm.

19. "Information We Collect and How We Use It," Google Privacy Policy Web site. Accessed on February 26, 2010, from http://www.google.com/intl/en/privacypolicy.html.

20. Andrew Buncombe, "Google Resists Demand to Hand Over Search Records," *The Independent,* Wednesday, March 15, 2005. Accessed on February 26, 2010, from http://www.independent.co.uk/news/world/americas/google-resists-demand-to-hand-over-search-records-469946.html.

21. Eric Mayes, "Google Partners with NSA, CIA on Intelligence Database," Raw Story, March 31, 2008. Accessed on January 17, 2010, from http://rawstory.com/news/2008/CIA_creates_miniGoogle_0331.html.

22. "Social Media," Wikipedia. Accessed on February 26, 2010, from http://en.wikipedia.org/wiki/Social_media.

23. Vanguard.org Web site. Accessed on February 26, 2010, from http://www.thevanguard.org/.

24. "Counsel for National Policy," Sourcewatch. Accessed on February 26, 2010, from http://www.sourcewatch.org/index.php?title=Council_for_National_Policy.

25. See Chapter 11.

26. "The Arpanet," BBN Technologies Web site, 2002. Accessed on February 26, 2010, from http://web.archive.org/web/20020603123655/www.bbn.com/arpanet/index.html.

27. See Chapter 2.

28. Kambiz Foroohar, "CIA Venture Fund Focuses on Spy Gadgets 'Q' Adores (Correct)," *Bloomberg.org,* October 25, 2007. Accessed on February 26, 2010, from http://www.bloomberg.com/apps/news?pid=newsarchive&sid=arSqdOLQVK9g.

29. Matt Marshall, "Spying on Start-ups, CIA Searching Out Technologies to Boost National Security Since the Sept. 11 Terrorist Attacks, The Experimental Venture Capital Firm has Turned into a Fixture in the Valley. The CIA is Scrambling to Make Sense of All the Unstructured Data Floating around

on the Internet and Elsewhere," *Mercury News,* Sunday, November 17, 2002. Accessed on February 26, 2010, from www.siliconbeat.com/entries/ SPYING%20ON%20START-ups.doc.

30. Bob Sullivan, "FaceBook: The End of Secrets?" The Red Tape Chronicles, *MSNBC.com.* Accessed on January 21, 2010, from http://redtape.msnbc. com/2010/01/what-would-a-world-without-secrets-look-like-thanks-to-facebook-we-may-find-out—privacy-experts-continue-to-watch-in-won. html#posts.

31. Electronic Frontier Foundation v. Department of Defense, Central Intelligence Agency, Department of Homeland Security, Department of Justice, Department of Treasury, and Office of the Director of National Intelligence, Complaint for Injunctive Relief, United States District Court for the Northern District of California, San Francisco Division, December 1, 2009. Accessed on February 26, 2010, from http://www.eff.org/files/filenode/social_network/social_ networking_FOIA_complaint_final.pdf.

32. ibid.

Chapter 6

1. At the time of this writing General Electric and Comcast are attempting a merger in which Comcast would gain controlling interest in NBC. See Chapter 19 for a discussion of problems posed by this merger.

2. "From fighters, helicopters and transports to the next generation of unmanned aircraft, GE's military engines provide the necessary power and reliability for any military application. GE's engines are proven in service and continue to operate in critical missions around the world." General Electric Web site. Accessed on February 26, 2010, from http://www.geae.com/engines/military/ index.html.

3. "Military Killer Robots 'Could Endanger Civilians,'" *CommonDreams.org,* Monday, August 3, 2009. Accessed on February 26, 2010, from http://www. commondreams.org/headline/2009/08/03-4.

4. "CIA drone kills al-Qaida operative," *MSNBC.com,* Saturday May 14, 2005. Accessed on February 26, 2010 from http://www.msnbc.msn.com/ id/7847008/.

5. David Barstow, "Behind TV Analysts, Pentagon's Hidden Hand," *New York Times,* April 20, 2008. Accessed on February 26, 2010, from http://www. nytimes.com/2008/04/20/us/20generals.html?_r=2.

6. Daniel Tencer, "Man who Sold Iraq War Vetting Imbedded Journos: Report," Raw Story, August 24, 2009. Accessed on February 26, 2010, from http:// rawstory.com/08/news/2009/08/24/iraq-war-salesman-now-vetting-journos/.

7. "Profile: NBC," History Commons. Accessed on February 26, 2010, from http://www.historycommons.org/entity.jsp?entity=nbc.

8. "Major Bob Bevelacqua Answers Your Questions," *FoxNews.com.* Accessed on February 26, 2010, from http://www.foxnews.com/story/0,2933,83192,00.html.

9. "Recap of Nov. 22: Dow 10,000? Get Saddam!," *FoxNews.com,* Monday, November 24, 2003. Accessed on February 26, 2010, from http://www.foxnews.com/story/0,2933,103929,00.html.

10. David Barstow and Robin Stein, "Under Bush, a New Age of Prepackaged TV News," *New York Times,* March 13, 2005. Accessed on February 26, 2010, from http://www.nytimes.com/2005/03/13/politics/13covert.html?_r=1&hp&ex=1110776400&en=c0b6bad84e5bf46a&ei=5094&partner=homepage.

11. Mark Mazzetti and Borzou Daragahi, "U.S. Military Covertly Pays to Run Stories in Iraqi Press," *CommonDreams.org,* Wednesday, November 30, 2005. Accessed on February 26, 2010, from http://www.commondreams.org/headlines05/1130-07.htm.

12. Jeffery Kan, "Postmortem: Iraq War Media Coverage Dazzled but It Also Obscured," *UCBerkeleyNews,* March 18, 2004. Accessed on February 26, 2010, from http://www.berkeley.edu/news/media/releases/2004/03/18_iraqmedia.shtml.

13. Daniel Tencer, "Man Who Sold Iraq Now Vetting Imbedded Journos: Report," The Raw Story, August 24, 2009. Accessed on May 10, 2010 from http://rawstory.com/08/news/2009/08/24/iraq-war-salesman-now-vetting-journos/.

14. Judith Miller, "An Iraqi Defector Tells of Work on At Least 20 Hidden Weapons Sites," *New York Times,* December 20, 2001. Accessed on February 25, 2010, from http://www.nytimes.com/2001/12/20/international/middleeast/20DEFE.html.

15. While John Rendon has himself denied connection with the Office of Disinformation, the Rendon Group was contracted by the Pentagon to do what this Office was charged to do—namely, disseminate government propaganda or "disinformation" within foreign media. Hence, his denial may be more a matter of semantics than of fact.

16. Contract Transaction #37266976, FY 2009, extensive detail on transactions, USSpending.gov, Thursday, August 27, 2009. Accessed on February 26, 2010, from http://speakmymindblog.files.wordpress.com/2009/08/rendon-group-federal-contract-details.pdf.

17. Charlie Reed, "Journalists' Recent Work Examined before Embeds," *Stars and Stripes,* August 24, 2009. Accessed on February 26, 2010, from http://www.stripes.com/article.asp?section=104&article=64348.

18. ibid.

19. "Pentagon Terminates Controversial Contract with The Rendon Group," Think Progress, August 30, 2009. Accessed on February 26, 2010, from http://thinkprogress.org/2009/08/30/rendon-terminated/

20. Ibid.

21. James Bamford, "The Man who Sold the War," Rolling Stone, November 17, 2005. Accessed on February 26, 2010 from http://www.rollingstone.com/politics/story/8798997/the_man_who_sold_the_war/3.

22. Ibid.

23. Ibid.

24. Ibid.

25. Shane Harris, "TIA Lives on," *National Journal,* February 23, 2006. Accessed on February 26, 2010, from http://www.nationaljournal.com/about/njweekly/ stories/2006/0223nj1.htm. See also Chapter 2.

26. Ibid. See also Chapter 2.

Chapter 7

1. "Internet Overtakes Newspapers as News Outlet," Pew Research Center for the People and the Press, December 23, 2008. Accessed on February 26, 2010, from http://people-press.org/report/479/internet-overtakes-newspapers-as-news-source.

2. This section is an updated and expanded version of Elliot D. Cohen, "Web of Deceit: How Internet Freedom Got the Federal Ax, and Why Corporate News Censored the Story," Buzzflash.com, July 18, 2005. Available online at http:// www.buzzflash.com/contributors/05/07/con05238.html.

3. National Cable & Telecommunications Assn. v. Brand X Internet Services (04-277) 545 U.S. 967 (2005) 345 F.3d 1120, reversed and remanded. Accessed on February 26, 2010, from http://www.law.cornell.edu/supct/html/04-277. ZS.html.

4. *AT&T Corporation vs. Portland* US Ct of Appeals for 9th Circuit, No. 99-35609, June 6, 2000. Accessed on February 26, 2010, from http://www.fcc.gov/ogc/ documents/opinions/2000/99-35609.html.

5. *Chevron U.S.A., Inc. v. Natural Resources Defense Council, Inc.,* 467 U.S. 837, decided June 25, 1984. Accessed on February 25, 2010, from http://www.law. cornell.edu/supct/html/historics/USSC_CR_0467_0837_ZS.html.

6. *National Cable & Telecommunications Assn. v. Brand X Internet Services.*

7. Ibid.

8. *AT&T Corporation vs. Portland* US Ct of Appeals for 9th Circuit.

9. See Chapter 6.

10. Julius Genachowski, "Preserving a Free and Open Internet: A Platform for Innovation, Opportunity, and Prosperity," The Brookings Institution, Washington DC, September 21, 2009. Accessed on February 26, 2010, from http://openinternet.gov/read-speech.html.

11. Peter Svenssen, "Comcast Blocks Some Internet Traffic," *MSNBC,* October 19, 2007. Accessed on February 26, 2010, from http://www.msnbc.msn.com/ id/21376597/.

12. Ibid.

13. Martin Bosworth, "House Introduces Internet Freedom Preservation Act," Consumer Affairs.com, August 1, 2009. Accessed on February 26. 2010, from http://www.consumeraffairs.com/news04/2009/07/internet_freedom. html#ixzz0Tgh5oKV5.

14. David Worthington, "GOP Moves to Block Net Neutrality," Techologizer, September 21, 2009. Accessed on February 26, 2010, from http://technologizer. com/2009/09/21/gop-moves-to-block-net-neutrality/.

15. House Resolution 30, January 7, 2009. Accessed on February 26, 2010, from http://www.govtrack.us/congress/billtext.xpd?bill=hr111-30.
16. Owen Fletcher, "China Orders Google to Suspend Foreign Site Searches," *PC World*, June 19, 2009. Accessed on February 26, 2010, from http://www.pcworld.com/businesscenter/article/166996/china_orders_google_to_suspend_foreign_site_searches.html?tk=rel_news.
17. Wang Xinyuan, "Baidu Expects Last Year's Revenue Growth to Repeat," Global Times, February 11, 2010. Accessed on May 14, 2010 from http://business.globaltimes.cn/industries/2010-02/505233.html
18. "Clash on the Great Firewall," *Wall Street Journal*, January 14, 2010. Accessed on May 14, 2010 from http://online.wsj.com/article/SB10001424052748704586504574655232889222954.html.

Chapter 8

1. Project for the New American Century, "Rebuilding America's Defenses: Strategy, Forces and Resources for a New Century," 2000. Accessed on February 26, 2010, from http://www.newamericancentury.org/RebuildingAmericasDefenses.pdf.
2. Ibid.
3. Secure Computer, "Special Report: Secure Computing Corporation and Network Support," Local Netter, Vol. 14, No. 12, 1994.
4. "U.S. corporations massively read employee e-mail, Help Net Security," May 20, 2008. Accessed on February 26, 2010, from http://www.net-security.org/secworld.php?id=6149.
5. Christopher Ketcham, "Israeli Spying in the United States," Counterpunch. org, March 12, 2009. Accessed on February 26, 2010, from http://www.counterpunch.org/ketcham03122009.html.
6. "Code Name Echelon," CyberCity Café. Accessed on February 26, 2010, from http://www.cybercitycafe.com/explore/echelon.html.
7. Peter Goodspeed, "Echelon: Online Surveillance," *National Post*, Saturday, February 19, 2000. Accessed on February 26, 2010, from http://fire.net.nz/echelon.htm.

Chapter 9

1. George Orwell, *1984* (London: Secker and Warburg, 1949), Ch. 17, p. 112. Available online at http://www.msxnet.org/orwell/print/1984.pdf.
2. Ibid., p. 117.
3. "Budget of the United States Government: Browse Fiscal Year 2010," GPO Access. Accessed on February 26, 2010, from http://www.gpoaccess.gov/usbudget/fy10/browse.html#budget.
4. "Citizen's Guide to the Federal Budget," GPO Access. Accessed on February 26, 2010, from http://www.gpoaccess.gov/usbudget/fy99/guide/guide02.html#C22.

5. Remarks by the President on Iraq, Cincinnati Museum Center—Cincinnati Union Terminal, Cincinnati, Ohio: October 7, 2002. Italics added. Accessed on February 26, 2010, from http://www.informationclearinghouse.info/article3711.htm.
6. The National Security Strategy of the United States of America, White House, Washington, D.C., September, 2002. Italics added. Accessed on February 26, 2010, from http://www.globalsecurity.org/military/library/policy/national/nss-020920.pdf.
7. Charter of the United Nations, Chapter 7, especially arts. 39, 41, 42, and 51. Accessed on March 25, 2009, from www.un.org/aboutun/charter.
8. Hermann Goering at Nuremberg Trials shortly before he was sentenced to death. Accessed on February 26, 2010, from http://www.allgreatquotes.com/war_quotes.shtml.
9. "Excerpts From Pentagon's Plan: 'Prevent the Re-Emergence of a New Rival,'" *New York Times*, March 8, 1992. Accessed on February 26, 2010, from http://www.nytimes.com/1992/03/08/world/excerpts-from-pentagon-s-plan-prevent-the-re-emergence-of-a-new-rival.html?pagewanted=1.
10. Ibid.
11. George W. Bush, "A Period of Consequences," Citadel, South Carolina, Thursday, September 23, 1999. Accessed on February 27, 2010, from http://www.citadel.edu/pao/addresses/pres_bush.html.

Chapter 10

1. Barrack H. Obama, Remarks at the State Department, January 22, 2009. Accessed on February 27, 2010, from http://www.gpoaccess.gov/presdocs/2009/DCPD200900014.pdf.
2. "Text: Obama's Speech on National Security," *New York Times,* May 21, 2009. Accessed on February 27, 2010, from http://www.nytimes.com/2009/05/21/us/politics/21obama.text.html.
3. Lolita C. Baldo, "Obama Abandoning 'War On Terror' Catchphrase," *Huffington Post,* January 31, 2009. Accessed on February 27, 2010, from http://www.huffingtonpost.com/2009/01/31/obama-abandoning-war-on-t_n_162804.html.
4. "Your complacency will only aid and abet our national suicide. Remember, they wouldn't dare bomb Pearl Harbor, but they did. They wouldn't dare drive two planes into the World Trade Center, but they did. They wouldn't dare pilot a plane through the most sophisticated air defenses in the world and crash into the Pentagon, but they did. They wouldn't dare pass the largest spending bill in history, in open defiance of the will of the people, but they did." Glenn Beck Show, April 10, 2009. http://crooksandliars.com/david-neiwert/becks-version-thomas-paine-compares.
5. "War on Terror Update: 50% Now Say U.S. is Winning War on Terror," Rasmussen Reports, Wednesday, February 24, 2010. Accessed on February 27, 2010, from http://www.rasmussenreports.com/public_content/politics/mood_of_america/war_on_terror_update.

6. See Chapter 6 for details on how the Bush administration managed to carry out this "information warfare."

7. Michael Walzer, *Just and Unjust Wars* (New York: Basic Books, 1977), p. 137.

8. Project for the New American Century, Rebuilding America's Defenses: Strategy, Forces and Resources for a New Century, 2000. Accessed on February 27, 2010, from http://www.newamericancentury.org/RebuildingAmericasDefenses.pdf.

9. Ibid.

10. Ibid.

11. Barrack H. Obama, "The American Moment: Remarks to the Chicago Council on Global Affairs," Chicago, IL, April 23, 2007. Accessed on February 27, 2010, from http://www.barackobama.com/2007/04/23/the_american_moment_remarks_to.php.

12. Barrack H. Obama, "The War We Need to Win," The Woodrow Wilson International Center for Scholars, Washington, DC, August 1, 2006. Accessed on February 27, 2010, from http://www.americanrhetoric.com/speeches/barackobamawilsoncenter.htm.

13. Barrack Obama, *The Audacity of Hope: Thoughts on Reclaiming the American Dream* (New York: Random House, 2006), p. 479.

14. See also Chapter 6 for a discussion of Gate's involvement with TIA technologies.

15. Project for the New American Century, "Rebuilding America's Defenses."

16. "Obama's Remarks on Missile Defense Strategy," *New York Times,* September 17, 2009. Accessed on February 27, 2010, from http://www.nytimes.com/2009/09/18/us/politics/18shield.text.html?_r=1.

17. Project for the New American Century, "Rebuilding America's Defenses."

18. "Biological and Chemical Weapons," The Center for Arms Control and Non-Proliferation. Accessed on February 27, 2010, from http://www.armscontrolcenter.org/policy/biochem/.

19. Project for the New American Century, "Rebuilding America's Defenses."

20. Obama, *The Audacity of Hope,* pp. 308–9.

21. Project for the New American Century, "Rebuilding America's Defenses."

22. Donna Miles, "Gates Establishes New Cyber Subcommand," United States Department of Defense Web site, June 24, 2009. Accessed on February 27, 2010, from http://www.defenselink.mil/news/newsarticle.aspx?id=54890.

23. Mark Hosenball, "Paranoia Watch: Ultrasecret NSA has Conspicuous Role in New Federal Cybersecurity Center," *Newsweek,* Friday, October 30, 2009. Accessed on February 27, 2010, from http://blog.newsweek.com/blogs/declassified/archive/2009/10/30/paranoia-watch-ultra-secret-nsa-has-conspicuous-role-in-new-federal-cyber-security-center.aspx.

24. Ibid.

25. See Chapter 8.

Chapter 11

1. Barack H. Obama, "First Speech before the United Nations General Assembly," New York, NY, September 23, 2009. Accessed on February 27,

2010, from http://www.americanrhetoric.com/speeches/barackobama/barackobamafirstunitednationsspeech.htm.

2. See Chapter 1 for further discussion of this decision.

3. David Rockefeller, *Memoirs* (New York: Random House), p. 405.

4. Paul Joseph Watson, "Leaked Agenda: Bilderberg Group Plans Economic Depression," Prison Planet, Wednesday, May 6, 2009. Accessed on February 27, 2010, from http://www.infowars.com/leaked-agenda-bilderberg-group-plans-economic-depression/.

5. Obama initially picked Senate Democrat leader Tom Daschle, who is also a Bilderberg member. Daschle later withdrew, however.

6. Bilderberg Group Members List. Accessed on February 27, 2010, from http://darkhorsetrader.wordpress.com/2009/02/14/bilderberg-group-members-list/.

7. Judi McCleod, "Bilderberg Boys Will Decide Who's Obama's "Chosen" Veep," *Canada Free Press,* June 6, 2008. Accessed on February 27, 2010, from http://www.canadafreepress.com/index.php/article/3395.

8. Paul Joseph Watson, "World Bank President Admits Agenda for Global Government," Wednesday, April 1, 2009. Accessed on February 27, 2010, from http://www.prisonplanet.com/world-bank-president-admits-agenda-for-global-government.html.

9. Council on Foreign Relations (list). Accessed on February 27, 2010, from http://www.nndb.com/org/505/000042379/.

10. Kurt Nimmo, "Obama Appoints Top Notch CFR, Bilderberg Members," Prison Planet, Friday, January 23, 2009. Accessed on February 27, 2010, from http://www.prisonplanet.com/obama-appoints-top-notch-cfr-bilderberg-members.html.

11. Jerome R. Corsi, "Bush Sneaking North American Super-state Without Oversight?" June 13, 2006. Accessed on February 27, 2010, from http://www.wnd.com/news/article.asp?ARTICLE_ID=50618.

12. Ibid.

13. Ibid.

14. "The SPP is Dead. Let's Keep It That Way," rabble, September 24, 2009. Accessed on February 27, 2010, from http://rabble.ca/news/2009/09/spp-dead-lets-keep-it-way.

15. "Security and Prosperity Partnership of North America," SPP.gov. Accessed on February 27, 2010, from http://www.spp.gov/.

16. Council on Foreign Relations, "International Institutions and Global Governance Program, World Order in the 21st Century, A New Initiative of the Council on Foreign Relations," May 1, 2008. Accessed on February 27, 2010, from http://www.cfr.org/content/thinktank/CFR_Global%20_Governance_%20Program.pdf.

17. Ibid.

18. Ibid.

19. Sissela Bok, *Lying: Moral Choice in Public and Private Life* (New York: Vintage Books), 1999.

20. James P. Tucker, Jr., "Bilderberg Pushing World Tax," *American Free Press,* May 6, 2002. Accessed on February 27, 2010, from http://www.denverpatriot community.org/AmericanFreePress/AFPNewsMay02.htm#anchor14968.

21. "Global Taxes are Back, Watch Your Wallet," CFIF.org. Accessed on February 27, 2010, from http://www.cfif.org/htdocs/freedomline/un_monitor/in_our_opinion/global_taxes.htm.
22. Cliff Kincaid, "Obama's Global Tax Proposal Up for Senate Vote," Accuracy in Media, February 12, 2008. Accessed on February 27, 2010, from http://www.aim.org/aim-column/obamas-global-tax-proposal-up-for-senate-vote/.
23. James P. Tucker, "Bilderberg Split on Iraq War," *American Free Press,* May 26, 2002. Accessed on February 27, 2010, from http://www.prisonplanet.com/bilderberg_split_on_iraq_war.html.
24. "The Peru FTA after One Year," Public Citizen. Accessed on February 27, 2010, from http://www.citizen.org/trade/index.cfm/trade/newnaftas/.
25. "About the Organization," Trilateral Commission webpage. Accessed on February 27, 2010, from http://www.trilateral.org/about.htm.
26. Zbigniew Brzezinski, stated while National Security Advisor to President Carter. Accessed on February 27, 2010, from http://contenderministries.org/UN/globalismquotes.php.
27. Alec MacGillis, "Brzezinski Backs Obama," *Washington Post,* Saturday, August 25, 2007. Accessed on February 27, 2010, from http://www.washingtonpost.com/wp-dyn/content/article/2007/08/24/AR2007082402127.html.
28. Yaakv Lappin, "Obama Advisor Raises Concerns," Y Net News.com, September 16, 2007. Accessed on February 27, 2010, from http://www.ynet.co.il/english/articles/0,7340,L-3449954,00.html.
29. See Chapter 8 for further discussion of PNAC.
30. Bilderberg Membership List.
31. This term has been applied to the politic of Henry Kissinger, Secretary of State under Nixon. Kissinger is also a member of Bilderberg.
32. David Rockefeller, September 23, 1994. Accessed on February 27, 2010, from http://contenderministries.org/UN/globalismquotes.php.
33. Project for the New American Century, Rebuilding America's Defenses. Accessed on February 27, 2010, from http://www.newamericancentury.org/RebuildingAmericasDefenses.pdf.
34. Rockefeller, June 5, 1991, Bilderberger meeting in Baden Baden, Germany. Accessed on February 27, 2010.
35. Bilderberg Membership List.
36. See Chapter 14.
37. "International Criminal Court," Wikipedia. Accessed on February 27, 2010, from http://en.wikipedia.org/wiki/International_Criminal_Court.
38. Responses from Barrack Obama on International Criminal Court, Citizens for Global Solutions. Accessed on February 27, 2010, from http://globalsolutions.org/politics/elections_and_candidates/questionnaire/2004?id=20.
39. James P. Tucker, Jr., "Bilderbergers Own President Obama," *American Free Press,* May 15, 2009. Accessed on February 27, 2010, from http://www.thecitizen.com/~citizen0/node/36810.
40. Philosopher Immanuel Kant has argued similarly. "A federal union of free and independent states," he argued, "is still to be preferred to an amalgamation of the separate nations under a single power which has overruled the rest and

created a universal monarchy." Such "universal despotism," he said, would end "in the graveyard of freedom." Kant, Perpetual Peace, quoted in "World Government," Stanford Encyclopedia of Philosophy. Accessed on February 27, 2010, from http://plato.stanford.edu/entries/world-government/.

Chapter 12

1. George Orwell, *1984*, (London: Secker and Warburg, 1949), Chapter 1, p. 10. Available online at http://www.msxnet.org/orwell/print/1984.pdf.
2. Scott Shane, "Cheney is Linked to Concealment of C.I.A. Project," *New York Times*, July 11, 2009. Accessed on February 27, 2010, from http://www.nytimes.com/2009/07/12/us/politics/12intel.html.
3. SEC. 501(a)(1). Accessed on February 27, 2010, from http://intelligence.senate.gov/nsaact1947.pdf.
4. Joby Warrick, "CIA Assassin Program was Nearing New Phase," *Washington Post*, Thursday, July 16, 2010. Accessed on February 27, 2010, from http://www.washingtonpost.com/wp-dyn/content/article/2009/07/15/AR2009071503856.html.
5. Shane, "Cheney is Linked to Concealment of CIA. Project."
6. Sec. 1102(d).
7. See Chapter 14.

Chapter 13

1. "New York City Police Department Releases Draft of Public Security Privacy Guidelines for Public Comment," NYPD Web site, Wednesday, February 25, 2009. Accessed on February 27, 2010, from http://www.nyc.gov/html/nypd/html/pr/pr_2009_005.shtml.
2. These license plate readers may also be used to implement a plan to charge motorists a fee when they enter Manhattan below eighty-sixth Street.
3. "Mayor Bloomberg and Police Commissioner Kelly Announce $24 Million In Homeland Security Funding for Expansion of Lower Manhattan Security Initiative To Midtown," NYPD Web site, Sunday, October 4, 2009. Accessed on February 27, 2010, from http://www.nyc.gov/html/nypd/html/pr/pr_2009_028.shtml.
4. Steven Josselson, "New York's 'Ring of Steel,'" Gotham Gazette, September 4, 2007. Accessed on February 27, 2010, from http://www.gothamgazette.com/article/issueoftheweek/20070904/200/2278.
5. Kelly Arena and Carol Cratty, "FBI Wants Palm Prints, Eye Scans, Tattoo Mapping," CNN, Monday, February 4, 2008. Accessed on February 27, 2010, from http://www.cnn.com/2008/TECH/02/04/fbi.biometrics/index.html.
    See also "FBI Preps $1bn Biometric Database, 'Next Generation Identification' awaits you," The Register, December 24, 2007. Accessed on February 27, 2010, from http://www.theregister.co.uk/2007/12/24/fbi_database_biometrics/.

6. "Mayor Bloomberg and Police Commissioner Kelly Announce $24 Million in Homeland Security Funding for Expansion of Lower Manhattan Security Initiative to Midtown," NYPD Web site, Sunday, October 4, 2009. Accessed on February 27, 2010, from http://www.nyc.gov/html/nypd/html/pr/pr_2009_028.shtml.
7. Mark Townsend and Paul Harris, "Security Role for Traffic Cameras," *The Observer*, Sunday, February 2003. Accessed on February 27, 2010, from http://www.guardian.co.uk/politics/2003/feb/09/terrorism.transport.
8. Ibid.
9. Ibid.
10. Steven Josselson, "New York's Ring of Steel."
11. Michael M. Grynbaum, William K. Rashbaum and Al Baker, "Police Seek Man Taped Near Times Sq Bomb Scene," *New York Times*, May 2, 2010. Accessed on May 14, 2010, from http://www.nytimes.com/2010/05/03/nyregion/03timessquare.html.
12. Jim Dwyer, "Police Video Caught a Couple's Intimate Moment on a Manhattan Rooftop," *New York Times*, December 22, 2005. Accessed on February 27, 2010, from http://www.nytimes.com/2005/12/22/nyregion/22rooftop.html?_r=1&scp=10&sq=surveillance%20cameras,%20police,%20abuses&st=cse.
13. "Seeing through Walls. Engineers Develop Technology to See through Walls," *Science Daily*, July 1, 2007. Accessed on February 27, 2010, from http://www.sciencedaily.com/videos/2007/0706-seeing_through_walls.htm.
14. Declan McCullagh and Robert Zarate, "Scanning Tech a Blurry Picture," Wired, February 16, 2002. Accessed on February 27, 2010, from http://www.wired.com/politics/law/news/2002/02/50470.
15. Keven Bonsor and Ryan Johnson, "How Facial Recognition Systems Work," howstuffworks.com. Accessed on February 27, 2010, from http://electronics.howstuffworks.com/gadgets/high-tech-gadgets/facial-recognition3.htm.

Chapter 14

1. Associated Press, "Justice Dept. Wants Phone Locales without Warrant," *New York Times*, February 12, 2010. Accessed on February 23, 2010, from http://www.nytimes.com/aponline/2010/02/12/business/AP-US-TEC-Cell-Phones-Surveillance.html.
2. Communications Assistance for Law Enforcement Act H.R.4922, 1994. Accessed on February 27, 2010, from http://epic.org/privacy/wiretap/calea/calea_law.html.
3. Declan McCullagh, "Perspective: E-tracking through your cell phone," cnet news, February 13, 2006. Accessed on February 27, 2010, from http://news.cnet.com/E-tracking-through-your-cell-phone/2010-1039_3-6038468.html.
4. "FDA clears RFID chip for Humans," Drug Researcher, October 18, 2004. Accessed on February 27, 2010, from http://www.drugresearcher.com/Tools-and-techniques/FDA-clears-RFID-chip-for-humans.

5. Julia Scheeres, "Tracking Junior with a Microchip," Wired, October 10, 2003. Accessed on February 27, 2010, from http://www.wired.com/science/discoveries/news/2003/10/60771.

6. "VeriChip Tagging Soldiers," RFIDNews.org, March 17, 2007. Accessed on February 27, 2010, from http://www.rfidnews.org/2007/03/17/verichip-tagging-soldiers.

7. Brian Brady, London Independent, "Prisoners 'to be chipped like dogs,'" January 13, 2008. Accessed on February 27, 2010, from http://www.infowars.com/articles/bb/rfid_uk_prisoners_chipped_like_dogs.htm.

8. "Radio Frequency Identification (RFID)," Electronic Frontier Foundation. Accessed on February 27, 2010, from http://w2.eff.org/Privacy/Surveillance/RFID/.

9. Chillingly, such a program appears to have already been proposed by the Bilderberg Group. See Chapter 11.

10. 9/11 Commission Report Implementation Act of 2004 S2774. Accessed on February 27, 2010, from http://www.theorator.com/bills108/s2774.html.

11. Bill Christensen, "RFID Mates with Surveillance Cameras," Technovelgy. Accessed on February 27, 2010, from http://www.technovelgy.com/ct/Science-Fiction-News.asp?NewsNum=1088.

12. Defense Advanced Research Projects Agency (DARPA), "DARPA-BAA-09-55: Persistent Stare Exploitation and Analysis System (PerSEAS)," FedBizOpps.gov, September 18, 2009. Accessed on February 27, 2010, from https://www.fbo.gov/index?s=opportunity&mode=form&id=f0144cfa4fb1ebbd4ac95f43a3a24540&tab=core&_cview=0.

13. DARPA, "DARPA-BAA-09-55 Persistent Stare Exploitation and Analysis System (PerSEAS) Broad Agency Announcement (BAA) for Information Processing Techniques Office (IPTO) Defense Advanced Research Projects Agency(DARPA)." Accessed on February 27, 2010, from http://www.darpa.mil/IPTO/solicit/baa/BAA-09-55_PIP.pdf.

14. Defense Advanced Research Projects Agency (DARPA), "DARPA-BAA-09-55: Persistent Stare Exploitation and Analysis System (PerSEAS)."

15. "IBM's Global Brain, Machines Like Us," October 30, 2008. Accessed on February 27, 2010, from http://machineslikeus.com/news/ibms-global-brain.

16. Dharmendra Modha, "IBM Seeks to Build the Computer of the Future Based on Insights from the Brain" (Video), YouTube. Accessed on February 27, 2010, from http://www.youtube.com/watch?v=1y0NOa-yjr8&feature=player_embedded.

17. Bruce Falconer, "Defense Research Agency Seeks to Create Supersoldiers," National Journal, November 10, 2003. Accessed on February 27, 2010, from http://www.ratical.org/ratville/CAH/superSoldier.html.

18. Alan Rudolph, "From the DARPA Website: Brain Machine Interfaces." Accessed on February 27, 2010, from http://www.infowars.com/print/ps/brain_machine_darpa.htm.

19. Emily Singer, "The Army's Remote-Controlled Beetle," Technology Review, Thursday, January 29, 2009. Accessed on February 27, 2010, from http://www.technologyreview.com/computing/22039/?a=f.

Chapter 15

1. Jamie Dean, "The Tiananmen generation," *Worldmag.com,* June 6, 2009. Accessed on February 28, 2010, from http://www.worldmag.com/articles/15447.

2. George Orwell, *1984,* (London: Secker and Warburg, 1949), Chapter 20, p. 153. Available online at http://www.msxnet.org/orwell/print/1984.pdf.

3. "Discover Our 3D Virtual World," Kaneva Web site. Accessed on February 28, 2010, from http://www.kaneva.com/3-d-world.aspx.

4. Jon Elmer, "Army Report Confirms Psy-ops Staged Saddam Statue Toppling," *The NewStandard,* July 3, 2004. Accessed on February 28, 2010, from http://newstandardnews.net/content/?action=show_item&itemid=641.

5. "The Story of Private Jessica Lynch, a Heroine of Propaganda," Voltairenet, June 3, 2004. Accessed on February 28, 2010, from http://www.voltairenet.org/article30097.html.

6. Christine Bowman, "Did the NYT Help Bush Win the 2004 Election by Sitting on the Illegal NSA Wiretapping Story at the Request of Jane Harman?" Buzzflash, April 30, 2009. Accessed on February 28, 2010, from http://blog.buzzflash.com/analysis/738.

7. Michael Parenti, "Monopoly, Media, and Manipulation," in Elliot D. Cohen, *News Incorporated: Corporate Media Ownership and its Threat to Democracy* (Amhert, NY: Prometheus Books, 2005), p. 107.

8. Ibid.

9. "Battlefield Death Toll Report: 3/26–4/6," Amped Status, Tuesday, April 7, 2009. Accessed on February 28, 2010, from http://ampedstatus.com/battlefield-death-toll-report-326-46.

10. "About SAF," Students for Academic Freedom Web site. Accessed on February 28, 2010, from http://www.studentsforacademicfreedom.org/about/.

11. See Chapter 8.

12. "David Horowitz," Right Web, October 24, 2007. Accessed on February 28, 2010, from http://www.rightweb.irc-online.org/profile/Horowitz_David; See also David Horowitz, "Ten Reasons Why Reparations for Blacks is a Bad Idea for Blacks—and Racist Too," FrontPageMag, Wednesday, January 3, 2001. Accessed on February 28, 2010, from http://97.74.65.51/readArticle.aspx?ARTID=24317.

13. "The Student Bill of Rights," Students for Academic Freedom Web site. Accessed on February 28, 2010, from http://www.studentsforacademicfreedom.org/documents/1922/sbor.html.

14. Horowitz, "Ten Reasons Why Reparations for Blacks is a Bad Idea for Blacks – and Racist Too."

15. David Horowitz, "Alternative to affirmative action?" FrontPageMag, July 23, 1997. Accessed on February 28, 2010, from http://97.74.65.51/readArticle.aspx?ARTID=24401.

16. "From Bad to Worse for David Horowitz," Inside Higher Ed, November 22, 2006. Accessed on February 28, 2010, from http://www.insidehighered.com/news/2006/11/22/tabor.

17. "The Eyes of Texas are Upon . . . YOU!" UT Watch. Accessed on February 28, 2010, from http://www.utwatch.org/security/classrooms.html.

18. "Surveillance Cameras in British Classroom Spark Student Walkout," Student Activism, June 9, 2009. Accessed on February 28, 2010, from http://student activism.net/2009/06/09/surveillance-cameras/.

19. Sam Dillon, "Cameras Watching Students, Especially in Biloxi," *New York Times,* September 24, 2003. Accessed on February 28, 2010, from http://www. nytimes.com/2003/09/24/nyregion/cameras-watching-students-especially-in-biloxi.html?pagewanted=1.

20. Ibid.

21. House Bill 1262, State of Washington, 2009. Accessed on February 28, 2010, from http://apps.leg.wa.gov/documents/billdocs/2009-10/Pdf/Bills/House%20Bills/1262.pdf.

22. Larry Magid, "New Twists in School Webcam Spy Case," *Huffington Post,* February 23, 2010. Accessed on February 28, 2010, from http://www. huffingtonpost.com/larry-magid/new-twists-in-school-webc_b_474127.html.

23. *Blake J. Robbins v. Lower Merion School District et al,* United States District Court for the Eastern District of Pennsylvania, Class Action Complaint. Accessed on February 28, 2010, from http://safekids.com/robbins17.pdf.

24. See especially Robert Greenwald's documentary film, "Walmart: The High Cost of Low Price." http://www.walmartmovie.com/.

Chapter 16

1. George Orwell, *1984,* (London: Secker and Warburg, 1949), chapter 20, p. 153. Available online at http://www.msxnet.org/orwell/print/1984.pdf.

2. Lyndsey Layton, "Share Whistle Blower's fight for Pension Drags On," *The Washington Post,* Saturday July 7, 2007. Accessed on February 28, 2010, from http://www.truthout.org/docs_2006/070707Z.shtml.

3. See Chapter 6.

4. Said when he was a guest on MSNBC's *Imus in the Morning.*

5. Cited in "Are These Guys For Real?" Fairpress. Accessed on February 28, 2010, from http://www.fairpress.org/sf0102/editorial924.htm.

6. Former Nixon administration counsel, John Dean, has referred to pundits of this ilk as "conservatives without conscience." See, John W. Dean, *Conservatives without Conscience,* (New York: Penguin, 2006).

   See also Eric Alterman, "Appendix 1: Fact Checking Ann Coulter." Accessed on February 28, 2010, from http://www.whatliberalmedia.com/apndx_1.htm; and "Letterman Appearance, O'Reilly Repeated False Claim That School Changed 'Silent Night' Lyrics," Media Matters, January 4, 2006, Accessed on February 28, 2010, from http://www.mediamatters.org/items/200601040009.

7. Associated Press, "Michael Devlin's Lawyer: Shawn Hornbeck Tried to Stop Abuse of Second Boy," Fox News, Thursday, October 11, 2007. Accessed on February 28, 2010, from http://www.foxnews.com/story/0,2933,301118,00.html.

8. Carol Lloyd, "Is Bill O'Reilly Sorry Now?" *Salon*, October 11, 2007. Accessed on February 28, 2010, from http://www.salon.com/life/broadsheet/2007/10/11/kidnapped/print.html.

9. "Fox Host Glenn Beck: Obama Is a 'Racist' (VIDEO)" *Huffington Post*, July 28, 2009. Accessed on February 28, 2010, from http://www.huffingtonpost.com/2009/07/28/fox-host-glenn-beck-obama_n_246310.html.

10. Ibid.

11. Jason Linkins, "Hannity Offers to Be Waterboarded for Charity (By Charles Grodin!)," *Huffington Post*, April 22, 2009. Accessed on February 28, 2010, from http://www.huffingtonpost.com/2009/04/22/hannity-offers-to-be-wate_n_190354.html.

12. "Keith Olbermann Offers Sean Hannity $1000 for Every Second He Can Endure Waterboarding, (VIDEO)". Accessed on February 28, 2010, from http://videocafe.crooksandliars.com/heather/keith-olbermann-offers-sean-hannity-1000-endure.

13. Cited and discussed in interview with Ann Coulter on "The Situation with Tucker Carlson," June 6, 2007. Accessed on February 28, 2010, from http://www.msnbc.msn.com/id/13184448/.

14. Erich Fromm, *The Sane Society* (New York: Henry Holt & Co., 1990), 152–53.

15. Fromm, The Sane Society, 153–54.

16. Orwell, *1984*, Chapter 20.

17. "Dixie Chicks 'get death threats,'" BBC News, April 24, 2003. Accessed on February 28, 2010, from http://news.bbc.co.uk/2/hi/entertainment/2972043.stm.

18. Michael Fitzgerald, "Dixie Chicks Axed by Clear Channel," *Jacksonville Business Journal*, March 18, 2003. Accessed on February 28, 2010, from http://jacksonville.bizjournals.com/jacksonville/stories/2003/03/17/daily14.html.

19. "Radio Ga Ga," Take Back the Media Accessed on February 28, 2010, from http://www.takebackthemedia.com/radiogaga.html.

20. See, for example, Hermann Goering's enunciation of this basic strategy in Chapter 9.

21. "Letter from an Iraq Vet," *Salon*, August 6, 2005. Accessed on February 28, 2010, from http://dir.salon.com/story/opinion/feature/2005/08/06/vet_letter/index.html.

22. Gregory D. Dennis, "Silencing Dissent," The Tech, Volume 121, Issue 50, Friday, October 12, 2001. Accessed on February 28, 2010, from http://www.tech.mit.edu/V121/N50/col50gregd.50c.html.

23. The NY Post's February 14, 2003, Front Page and Accompanying Article, February 14, 2003. Accessed on February 28, 2010, from http://www.preventtruthdecay.com/mainmiscweasels.htm.

24. "Agenda Setting: France, France's Image Deteriorates after Media Criticism," *MT Journal* Nr. 131, April 2003. Accessed on February 28, 2010, from http://www.agendasetting.com/research/case_studies/eng3.pdf.

Chapter 17

1. W. K. Clifford, *The Ethics of Belief.* Available online at http://ajburger. homestead.com/files/book.htm.
2. Ibid.
3. "The Secret Downing Street Memo," *Sunday Times* (London), May 1, 2005. Accessed on February 25, 2010, from http://www.timesonline.co.uk/tol/news/ uk/article387374.ece.
4. Ibid.
5. I have done so elsewhere. See Elliot D. Cohen, *Critical Thinking Unleashed* (New York: Rowman & Littlefield, 2009).
6. See also Karl Popper, *The Open Society and Its Enemies* (London: Routledge, 2002).

Chapter 18

1. Associated Press, "Bush Defends Spy Program to Republicans," MSNBC, February 10, 2006. Accessed on February 28, 2010, from http://www.msnbc. msn.com/id/11277462/.
2. David Kravets, "Obama Sides with Bush in Spy Case," Wired, January 22, 2009. Accessed on February 28, 2010, from http://www.wired.com/ threatlevel/2009/01/obama-sides-wit/.
3. See Chapter 17.
4. Immanuel Kant, *Groundwork of the Metaphysics of Morals,* trans. H. J. Paton. Reprinted in Elliot D. Cohen, *Philosophers at Work: Issues and Practice of Philosophy* (Fort Worth: Harcourt, 2000), p. 47.
5. James Risen and Eric Lichtblau, "Bush Lets U.S. Spy on Callers without Courts," *New York Times,* December 16, 2005. Accessed on February 28, 2010, from http://www.nytimes.com/2005/12/16/politics/16program.html.
6. American Bar Association, Model Rules of Professional Conduct, Rule 1.6. Accessed on February 28, 2010, from http://www.abanet.org/cpr/mrpc/rule_ 1_6.html.
7. W. A. Parent, "Privacy, Morality, and the Law" in Elliot D. Cohen, *Philosophical Issues in Journalism* (New York: Oxford University Press, 1992), p. 100.
8. Jeff Jonas and Jim Harper, "Effective Counterterrorism and the Limited Role of Predictive Data Mining," 584 Policy Analysis, December 11, 2006. Accessed on January 31, 2010, from http://www.cato.org/pub_display.php? pub_id=6784.
9. Shane Harris and Tim Naftali, "Tinker, Tailor, Miner, Spy: Why the NSA's Snooping is Unprecedented in Scale and Scope," Slate, Tuesday January 3, 2006. Accessed on February 28, 2010, from http://www.slate.com/id/ 2133564/.
10. Ibid.

Chapter 19

1. Orwell, *1984*, (London: Secker and Warburg, 1949), Chapter 7, p. 40. Available online at http://www.msxnet.org/orwell/print/1984.pdf.
2. "Independent News Sources," Project Censored. Available online at http://www.projectcensored.org/censorship/news-sources/.
3. See Chapter 17.
4. Michael Isikoff, "Civil Liberties Board Goes Vacant Under Obama," *Newsweek*, March 2, 2010. Accessed on March 4, 2010, from http://blog.newsweek.com/blogs/declassified/archive/2010/03/02/civil-liberties-board-goes-vacant-under-obama.aspx.
5. Elizabeth Cohen, "The Government Has Your Baby's DNA," CNN Health, February 4, 2010. Accessed on March 1, 2010, from http://www.cnn.com/2010/HEALTH/02/04/baby.dna.government/index.html?hpt=Sbin.
6. See, for example, the discussion of Gates involvement with TIA in Chapter 6.
7. "Obama's Biodefense Approach is Similar to Bush's," HomeLand Security Newswire (HSNW), December 14, 2009. Accessed on February 28, 2010, from http://homelandsecuritynewswire.com/obama%E2%80%99s-biodefense-approach-similar-bush%E2%80%99s.
8. Saying that the United States should relinquish its authority to use force to the UN does not mean that it should relinquish its domestic sovereignty or other international policy authority.
9. FISA Amendments Act of 2009, H.R.3846, October 20, 2009. Accessed on February 28, 2010, from http://www.govtrack.us/congress/billtext.xpd?bill=h111-3846.
10. H.R. 3961, To extend expiring provisions of the USA PATRIOT Improvement and Reauthorization Act of 2005 and Intelligence Reform and Terrorism Prevention Act of 2004 until February 28, 2011. Accessed on March 1, 2010, from http://frwebgate.access.gpo.gov/cgi-bin/getdoc.cgi?dbname=111_cong_bills&docid=f:h3961enr.txt.pdf.
11. H.R. 3845, USA PATRIOT Amendments Act of 2009. Accessed on March 1, 2010 from http://www.govtrack.us/congress/bill.xpd?bill=h111-3845.
12. Military Commissions Act of 2006, Public Law 109–366, 120 Stat. 2600, Oct. 17, 2006. Accessed on February 28, 2010, from http://www.loc.gov/rr/frd/Military_Law/pdf/PL-109-366.pdf.
13. Joanne Mariner, "A First Look at the Military Commissions Act of 2009, Part One," FindLaw, Wednesday, November 4, 2009. Accessed on February 28, 2010, from http://writ.news.findlaw.com/mariner/20091104.html.
14. H.R. 2647-385, Title XVIII–Military Commissions, Sec. V 948(A)7. Accessed on February 28, 2010, from http://www.defense.gov/news/2009%20MCA%20Pub%20%20Law%20111-84.pdf.
15. Joanne Mariner, "A First Look at the Military Commissions Act of 2009, Part One."
16. Ibid.

17. FISA Amendments Act of 2008, H.R. 6304, July 10, 2008, Sec. 702(h)1(a), from http://www.govtrack.us/congress/billtext.xpd?bill=h110-6304.
18. "Testimony of Andrew Jay Schwartzman, President and CEO, Media Access Project To the Subcommittee on Antitrust Competition Policy and Consumer Rights Senate Judiciary Committee," February 4, 2010. Accessed on February 28, 2010, from http://www.mediaaccess.org/file_download/360.
19. Ibid.
20. PATRIOT Act, SEC. 223. Civil Liability for Certain Unauthorized Disclosures. Accessed on February 28, 2010, from http://www.abanet.org/natsecurity/patriotdebates/act-section-223.
21. See also Chapter 4.
22. Public Law 95-511, 92Stat. 1783, Oct. 25, 1978, Section 101(h)1. Accessed on February 28, 2010, from www.cnss.org/PL%2095-511.pdf.
23. Ibid.

Bibliography

Allhoff, Fritz et al., eds. *Nanoethics: The Ethical and Social Implications of Nanotechnology*. Hoboken, NJ: Wiley, 2007.

American Civil Liberties Union. "Surveillance Under the U.S. PATRIOT Act." ACLU Web site, April 3, 2003. http://www.aclu.org/national-security/surveillance-under-usa-patriot-act.

Arena, Kelly and Carol Cratty. "FBI Wants Palm Prints, Eye Scans, Tattoo Mapping." CNN, Monday, February 4, 2008. http://www.cnn.com/2008/TECH/02/04/fbi.biometrics/index.html (accessed on February 27, 2010).

Associated Press. "Bush Defends Spy Program to Republicans." MSNBC, February 10, 2006. http://www.msnbc.msn.com/id/11277462/ (accessed on February 28, 2010).

———. "Justice Dept. Wants Phone Locales without Warrant." *New York Times*, February 12, 2010.

Baldo, Lolita C. "Obama Abandoning 'War On Terror' Catchphrase." Huffington Post, January 31, 2009. http://www.huffingtonpost.com/2009/01/31/obama-abandoning-war-on-t_n_162804.html (accessed March 2, 2010).

Bamford, James. "The Man Who Sold the War." *Rolling Stone*, November 17, 2005.

———. *The Shadow Factory: The NSA from 9/11 to the Eavesdropping on America*. New York: Anchor books, 2009.

Barstow, David. "Behind TV Analysts, Pentagon's Hidden Hand." *New York Times*, April 20, 2008.

Barstow, David and Robin Stein. "Under Bush, a New Age of Prepackaged TV News." *New York Times*, March 13, 2005.

Bilderberg Group Members List. http://darkhorsetrader.wordpress.com/2009/02/14/bilderberg-group-members-list/ (accessed February 27, 2010).

Bok, Sissela. *Lying: Moral Choice in Public and Private Life*. New York: Vintage Books, 1999.

Bonsor, Keven and Ryan Johnson. "How Facial Recognition Systems Work." howstuffworks. http://electronics.howstuffworks.com/gadgets/high-tech-gadgets/facial-recognition3.htm (accessed on February 27, 2010).

Borjesson, Kristina. *Feet to the Fire: The Media after 9/11, Top Journalists Speak Out*. Amherst, NY: Prometheus Books, 2005.

Bosworth, Martin H. "ChoicePoint-FBI Deal Raises New Privacy Questions." Consumer Affairs, May 16, 2006. http://www.consumeraffairs.com/news04/2006/05/fbi_choicepoint.html (accessed on March 1, 2010).

Bowman, Christine. "Did the NYT Help Bush Win the 2004 Election by Sitting on the Illegal NSA Wiretapping Story at the Request of Jane Harman?" Buzzflash, April 30, 2009. http://blog.buzzflash.com/analysis/738 (accessed on February 28, 2010).

Brady, Brian. "Prisoners 'to Be Chipped Like Dogs.'" London Independent, January 13, 2008. http://www.infowars.com/articles/bb/rfid_uk_prisoners_chipped_like_dogs.htm (accessed on February 27, 2010).

Buzzflash. "Elliot D. Cohen Says Question! Be Critical! That's How to Take Back Democracy: A Buzzflash Interview with Elliot D. Cohen." Buzzflash, July 12, 2007. http://www.buzzflash.com/articles/interviews069 (accessed on March 1, 2010).

Bush, George W. "A Period of Consequences." Citadel, South Carolina, Thursday, September 23, 1999. http://www.citadel.edu/pao/addresses/pres_bush.html (accessed on March 1, 2010).

Center for Arms Control and Non-Proliferation. "Biological and Chemical Weapons." http://www.armscontrolcenter.org/policy/biochem/ (accessed on February 27, 2010).

Choicepoint. "ChoicePoint AutoTrackXP®, and ChoicePoint Online." ChoicePoint, 2003. http://web.archive.org/web/20031218085618/www.choicepoint.com/business/public/cbi_1.html (accessed on March 1, 2010).

Christensen, Bill. "RFID Mates with Surveillance Cameras." Technovelgy. http://www.technovelgy.com/ct/Science-Fiction-News.asp?NewsNum=1088 (accessed on February 27, 2010).

Citizens for Global Solutions. "Responses from Barrack Obama on International Criminal Court." http://globalsolutions.org/politics/elections_and_candidates/questionnaire/2004?id=20 (accessed on February 27, 2010).

Clifford, W. K. The Ethics of Belief. Amherst, NY: Prometheus Books, 1999.

Cohen, Elizabeth. "The Government Has Your Baby's DNA." CNN Health, February 4, 2010. http://www.cnn.com/2010/HEALTH/02/04/baby.dna.government/index.html?hpt=Sbin (accessed on March 1, 2010).

Cohen, Elliot D. "America Is Watching You." Truthdig, October 30, 2007. http://www.truthdig.com/report/item/20071030_america_is_watching_you/ (accessed on March 1, 2010).

———. "Bush's Chilling New Definition of 'Unlawful Enemy Combatant.'" Buzzflash, September 30, 2006. http://www.buzzflash.com/articles/contributors/442 (accessed on March 1, 2010).

———. "Bush's Global Mission: His Flawed Logic for Escalating the Iraq War." Buzzflash, January 9, 2007. http://www.buzzflash.com/articles/contributors/694 (accessed on March 1, 2010).

———. Critical Thinking Unleashed. New York: Rowman & Littlefield, 2009.

———. "McBrain Washed: How McCain/Palin are Selling a Phony Image." Buzzflash, September 18, 2008. http://blog.buzzflash.com/contributors/1770 (accessed on March 1, 2010).

———. "Media Mum While Congress Considers Giving Telecoms Blank Check to Eavesdrop." BuzzFlash, October 11, 2007. http://www.buzzflash.com/articles/contributors/1373 (accessed on March 1, 2010).

————— (ed.) *News Incorporated: Corporate Media Ownership and Its Threat to Democracy.* Amherst, NY: Prometheus, 2005.

—————. "President Obama's Orwellian New Category of 'Prolonged Detention.'" Buzzflash, May 23, 2009. http://blog.buzzflash.com/contributors/1978 (accessed on March 1, 2010).

—————. "Save Democracy, Shut Off Chris Matthews." MediaChannel, March 13, 2005. http://bellaciao.org/en/article.php3?id_article=5500 (accessed on March 1, 2010).

—————. "Senate Debates Cheney FISA Bill: Eight Urgent Reasons to Defeat It." Buzzflash, December 17, 2007. http://blog.buzzflash.com/contributors/1477 (accessed on March 1, 2010).

—————. "Senate Judiciary Poised to Pass Total Information Awareness Bill." Buzzflash, November 12, 2007. http://blog.buzzflash.com/contributors/1429 (accessed on March 1, 2010).

—————. "Taking a Page from the Bush Playbook." Truthdig, May 5, 2009. http://www.truthdig.com/report/item/20090505_taking_a_page_from_the_bush_playbook/ (accessed on March 1, 2010).

—————. "The End of Privacy." Truthdig, January 24, 2008. http://www.truthdig.com/report/item/20080124_the_end_of_privacy/ (accessed on March 1, 2010).

—————. "The Fate of a Free Presidential Election in 2008 May Now Depend on the Senate." Buzzflash, November 19, 2007. http://blog.buzzflash.com/contributors/1443 (accessed on March 1, 2010).

—————. "Web of Deceit: How Internet Freedom Got the Federal Ax, and Why Corporate News Censored the Story." Buzzflash, July 18, 2005. http://www.buzzflash.com/contributors/05/07/con05238.html (accessed on March 1, 2010).

—————. "Why Haven't the Mainstream Corporate Media Covered the AT&T/NSA Domestic Spying Program?" Free Press, August 13, 2007. http://www.freepress.net/news/25404 (accessed on March 1, 2010).

Cohen, Elliot D. and Bruce W. Fraser. *Last Days of Democracy: How Big Media and Power Hungry Government are Turning America into a Dictatorship.* Amherst, NY: Prometheus, 2007.

Common Dreams. "Military Killer Robots 'Could Endanger Civilians,'" Common Dreams, Monday, August 3, 2009. http://www.commondreams.org/headline/2009/08/03-4 (accessed on March 1, 2010).

Corsi, Jerome R. "Bush Sneaking North American Super-state without Oversight?" WorldNetDaily, June 13, 2006. http://www.wnd.com/news/article.asp?ARTICLE_ID=50618 (accessed on February 27, 2010).

Council on Foreign Relations. "International Institutions and Global Governance Program, World Order in the 21st Century, A New Initiative of the Council on Foreign Relations." CFR, May 1, 2008. http://www.cfr.org/content/thinktank/CFR_Global%20_Governance_%20Program.pdf (accessed on February 27, 2010).

Council on Foreign Relations Membership List. http://www.nndb.com/org/505/000042379/ (accessed on February 27, 2010).

Dean, John W. *Conservatives without Conscience.* New York: Viking, 2006.

Defense Advanced Research Projects Agency. "DARPA-BAA-09-55 Persistent Stare Exploitation and Analysis System (PerSEAS) Broad Agency Announcement (BAA) for Information Processing Techniques Office (IPTO) Defense Advanced Research Projects Agency (DARPA)." Darpa. http://www.darpa.mil/IPTO/solicit/baa/BAA-09-55_PIP.pdf (accessed February 27, 2010).

———. "DARPA-BAA-09-55: Persistent Stare Exploitation and Analysis System (PerSEAS)." FedBizOpps, September 18, 2009. https://www.fbo.gov/index?s=opportunity&mode=form&id=f0144cfa4fb1ebbd4ac95f43a3a24540&tab=core&_cview=0 (accessed on February 27, 2010).

Dennis, Gregory D. "Silencing Dissent." *The Tech*, Volume 121, Issue 50, Friday October 12, 2001. http://www-tech.mit.edu/V121/N50/col50gregd.50c.html (accessed on February 28, 2010).

Dharmendra Modha. "IBM Seeks to Build the Computer of the Future Based on Insights from the Brain" (Video). YouTube. http://www.youtube.com/watch?v=1y0NOa-yjr8&feature=player_embedded (accessed on February 27, 2010).

Dillon, Sam. "Cameras Watching Students, Especially in Biloxi." *New York Times*, September 24, 2003.

Drug Researcher. "FDA Clears RFID Chip for Humans." October 18, 2004. http://www.drugresearcher.com/Tools-and-techniques/FDA-clears-RFID-chip-for-humans (accessed on February 27, 2010).

Dwyer, Jim. "Police Video Caught a Couple's Intimate Moment on a Manhattan Rooftop." *New York Times*, December 22, 2005.

Edgecliffe-Johnson, Andrew. "Thomson Cleared for Reuters Merger." *London Financial Times*, February 19, 2008. http://www.ft.com/cms/s/0/33d14772-df29-11dc-91d4-0000779fd2ac.html?nclick_check=1 (accessed on March 1, 2010).

Electronic Frontier Foundation. "Radio Frequency Identification (RFID)." Electronic Frontier Foundation. http://w2.eff.org/Privacy/Surveillance/RFID/ (accessed on February 27, 2010).

Elmer, Jon. "Army Report Confirms Psy-ops Staged Saddam Statue Toppling." The NewStandard, July 3, 2004. http://newstandardnews.net/content/?action=show_item&itemid=641 (accessed on February 28, 2010).

Estulin, Daniel. *The True Story of the Bilderberg Group*. Walterville, OR: Tine Day, 2009.

Falconer, Bruce. "Defense Research Agency Seeks to Create Supersoldiers." *National Journal*, November 10, 2003. http://www.ratical.org/ratville/CAH/superSoldier.html (accessed on February 27, 2010).

Fitzgerald, Michael. "Dixie Chicks Axed by Clear Channel." *Jacksonville Business Journal*, March 18, 2003. http://jacksonville.bizjournals.com/jacksonville/stories/2003/03/17/daily14.html (accessed on February 28, 2010).

Fletcher, Owen. "China Orders Google to Suspend Foreign Site Searches." *PC World*, June 19, 2009. http://www.pcworld.com/businesscenter/article/166996/china_orders_google_to_suspend_foreign_site_searches.html?tk=rel_news.

Foreign Intelligence Surveillance Court of Review, In re Directives [redacted text] Pursuant to Section 105B of the Foreign Intelligence Surveillance Act, No. 08-1, August 22, 2008. http://www.fas.org/irp/agency/doj/fisa/fiscr082208.pdf.

Fromm, Erich. *The Sane Society*. New York: Henry Holt & Co., 1990.

Genachowski, Julius. "Preserving a Free and Open Internet: A Platform for Innovation, Opportunity, and Prosperity." The Brookings Institution, Washington DC, September 21, 2009. http://openinternet.gov/read-speech. html (accessed on March 1, 2010).

Goodspeed, Peter. "Echelon: Online Surveillance." *National Post*, Saturday, February 19, 2000. http://fire.net.nz/echelon.htm (accessed on March 1, 2010).

Greenwald, Robert. "Walmart: The High Cost of Low Price." Brave New Films, 2005.

Harris, Shane. "FBI, Pentagon Pay for Access to Trove of Public Records." Government Executive, November 11. 2005. http://www.govexec.com/story_page. cfm?articleid=32802 (accessed on March 1, 2010).

———. "TIA Lives on." National Journal, February 23, 2006. http://www.national journal.com/about/njweekly/stories/2006/0223nj1.htm (accessed on March 1, 2010).

Harris, Shane and Tim Naftali. "Tinker, Tailor, Miner, Spy: Why the NSA's Snooping is Unprecedented in Scale and Scope." Slate, Tuesday January 3, 2006. http://www.slate.com/id/2133564/ (accessed on February 28, 2010).

HomeLand Security Newswire (HSNW). "Obama's Biodefense Approach is Similar to Bush's." December 14, 2009. http://homelandsecuritynewswire. com/obama%E2%80%99s-biodefense-approach-similar-bush%E2%80%99s (accessed on February 28, 2010).

Hosenball, Mark. "Paranoia Watch: Ultrasecret NSA Has Conspicuous Role in New Federal Cybersecurity Center," *Newsweek*, Friday, October 30, 2009. http://blog. newsweek.com/blogs/declassified/archive/2009/10/30/paranoia-watch-ultra-secret-nsa-has-conspicuous-role-in-new-federal-cyber-security-center.aspx (accessed on February 27, 2010).

Isikoff, Michael. "Civil Liberties Board Goes Vacant under Obama." *Newsweek*, March 2, 2010. http://blog.newsweek.com/blogs/declassified/archive/2010/03/02/ civil-liberties-board-goes-vacant-under-obama.aspx (accessed on March 4, 2010).

Jeffers, H. Paul. *The Bilderberg Conspiracy: Inside the World's Most Powerful Secret Society*. New York: Kensington Publishing Corporation, 2009.

Jonas, Jeff and Jim Harper. "Effective Counterterrorism and the Limited Role of Predictive Data Mining." *Policy Analysis*, No. 584, December 11, 2006.

Josselsom, Steven. "New York's 'Ring of Steel.'" *Gotham Gazette*, September 4, 2007. http://www.gothamgazette.com/article/issueoftheweek/20070904/200/2278 (accessed on February 27, 2010).

Kan, Jeffrey. "Postmortem: Iraq War Media Coverage Dazzled but It Also Obscured." UCBerkeleyNews, March 18, 2004. http://www.berkeley.edu/news/media/ releases/2004/03/18_iraqmedia.shtml (accessed on February 26, 2010).

Kaneva. "Discover Our 3D Virtual World." Kaneva. http://www.kaneva.com/ 3-d-world.aspx (accessed on February 28, 2010).

Kant, Immanuel. *Groundwork of the Metaphysics of Morals*. Trans. H. J. Paton. In Elliot D. Cohen, ed., *Philosophers at Work: Issues and Practice of Philosophy*. Fort Worth: Harcourt, 2000.

Katz, Eric, Andrew Light, and William Thompson, eds., *Controlling Technology*. Amherst, NY: Prometheus Books, 2003.

Ketcham, Christopher. "Israeli Spying in the United States." Counterpunch, March 12, 2009. http://www.counterpunch.org/ketcham03122009.html (accessed on March 1, 2010).

Kincaid, Cliff. "Obama's Global Tax Proposal Up for Senate Vote." *Accuracy in Media*, February 12, 2008. http://www.aim.org/aim-column/obamas-global-tax-proposal-up-for-senate-vote/ (accessed on February 27, 2010).

Kravets, David. "Obama Sdes with Bush in Spy Case." Wired, January 22, 2009. http://www.wired.com/threatlevel/2009/01/obama-sides-wit/ (accessed on February 28, 2010).

Lappin, Yaakv. "Obama Advisor Raises Concerns." Y Net News, September 16, 2007. http://www.ynet.co.il/english/articles/0,7340,L-3449954,00.html (accessed on February 27, 2010).

Leahey, Patrick. Hearing on Oversight of the Federal Bureau of Investigation, United States Senate Committee on the Judiciary, September 17, 2008. http://judiciary.senate.gov/hearings/testimony.cfm?id=3530&wit_id=2629 (accessed on March 1, 2010).

Machines Like Us. "IBM's Global Brain." October 30, 2008. http://machineslikeus.com/news/ibms-global-brain (accessed on February 27, 2010).

Magid, Larry. "New Twists in School Webcam Spy Case." Huffington Post, February 23, 2010. http://www.huffingtonpost.com/larry-magid/new-twists-in-school-webc_b_474127.html (accessed on February 28, 2010).

Mariner, Joanne. "A First Look at the Military Commissions Act of 2009, Part One." FindLaw, Wednesday, November 4, 2009. http://writ.news.findlaw.com/mariner/20091104.html (accessed on February 28, 2010).

Marshall, Matt. "Spying On Start-ups, CIA Searching Out Technologies to Boost National Security Since the Sept. 11 Terrorist Attacks," Mercury News, Sunday November 17, 2002. www.siliconbeat.com/entries/SPYING%20ON%20START-ups.doc (accessed on March 1, 2010).

Mayes, Eric. "Google Partners with NSA, CIA on Intelligence Database." Raw Story, March 31, 2008. http://rawstory.com/news/2008/CIA_creates_miniGoogle_0331.html (accessed on March 1, 2010).

Mazzetti, Mark and Borzou Daragahi. "U.S. Military Covertly Pays to Run Stories in Iraqi Press." Common Dreams, Wednesday, November 30, 2005. http://www.commondreams.org/headlines05/1130-07.htm (accessed on March 1, 2010).

McChesney, Robert, and John Nichols. *Tragedy & Farce: How the American Media Sell Wars, Spin Elections, and Destroy Democracy*. New York: New Press, 2006.

McCleod, Julie. "Bilderberg Boys Will Decide Who's Obama's 'Chosen' Veep." Canada Free Press, June 6, 2008 http://www.canadafreepress.com/index.php/article/3395 (Accessed on February 27, 2010).

McCullagh, Declan. "Perspective: E-tracking through Your Cell Phone." CNet, February 13, 2006. http://news.cnet.com/E-tracking-through-your-cell-phone/2010-1039_3-6038468.html (accessed on February 27, 2010).

McCullagh, Declan and Robert Zarate. "Scanning Tech a Blurry Picture." Wired, February 16, 2002. http://www.wired.com/politics/law/news/2002/02/50470 (accessed on February 27, 2010).

Miles, Donna. "Gates Establishes New Cyber Subcommand." United States Department of Defense, June 24, 2009. http://www.defenselink.mil/news/newsarticle.aspx?id=54890 (accessed on February 27, 2010).

Miller, Judith. "An Iraqi Defector Tells of Work on At Least 20 Hidden Weapons Sites." *New York Times,* December 20, 2001.

Nakashima, Ellen. "FBI Prepares Vast Database of Biometrics." *Washington Post,* Saturday, December 22, 2007.

———. "Lockheed Secures Contract to Expand Biometric Database." *Washington Post,* Wednesday, February 13, 2008.

Nakashima, Ellen and Dan Eggen. "Former CEO Says U.S. Punished Phone Firm." *Washington Post,* Saturday, October 13, 2007.

National Cable & Telecommunications Assn. v. Brand X Internet Services (04-277) 545 U.S. 967 (2005) 345 F.3d 1120, reversed and remanded. http://www.law.cornell.edu/supct/html/04-277.ZS.html.

New York Times. "Excerpts From Pentagon's Plan: 'Prevent the Re-Emergence of a New Rival.'" March 8, 1992.

New York Times. "Text: Obama's Speech on National Security." May 21, 2009.

Nimmo, Kurt. "Obama Appoints Top Notch CFR, Bilderberg Members." *Prison Planet,* Friday, January 23, 2009. http://www.prisonplanet.com/obama-appoints-top-notch-cfr-bilderberg-members.html (accessed on February 27, 2010).

NYPD. "Mayor Bloomberg and Police Commissioner Kelly Announce $24 Million In Homeland Security Funding for Expansion of Lower Manhattan Security Initiative to Midtown." NYPD, Sunday, October 4, 2009. http://www.nyc.gov/html/nypd/html/pr/pr_2009_028.shtml (accessed on February 27, 2010).

———. "New York City Police Department Releases Draft of Public Security Privacy Guidelines for Public Comment." NYPD, Wednesday, February 25, 2009. http://www.nyc.gov/html/nypd/html/pr/pr_2009_005.shtml (accessed on February 27, 2010).

Obama, Barrack H. "First Speech before the United Nations General Assembly." New York, NY, September 23, 2009. http://www.americanrhetoric.com/speeches/barackobama/barackobamafirstunitednationsspeech.htm (accessed on February 27, 2010).

———. "The American Moment: Remarks to the Chicago Council on Global Affairs." Chicago, IL, April 23, 2007. http://www.barackobama.com/2007/04/23/the_american_moment_remarks_to.php (accessed on February 27, 2010).

———. *The Audacity of Hope: Thoughts on Reclaiming the American Dream.* New York: Random House, 2006.

———. "The War We Need to Win." The Woodrow Wilson International Center for Scholars, Washington DC, August 1, 2006. http://www.americanrhetoric.com/speeches/barackobamawilsoncenter.htm (accessed on February 27, 2010).

O'Harrow, Jr., Robert. "ChoicePoint Finds Wealth in Information: Giant Transforming Itself into a Private Intelligence Service." MSNBC, January 20, 2005. http://www.msnbc.msn.com/id/6846357/ (accessed on March 1, 2010).

Orwell, George. *1984.* London: Secker and Warburg, 1949. Available online at http://www.msxnet.org/orwell/print/1984.pdf (accessed on March 1, 2010).

Palast, Greg. *Armed Madhouse*. New York: Dutton, 2006.

Parent, W.A. "Privacy, Morality, and the Law." In Elliot D. Cohen, ed., *Philosophical Issues in Journalism*. New York: Oxford University Press, 1992.

Parenti, Michael. "Monopoly, Media, and Manipulation." In Elliot D. Cohen, ed., *News Incorporated: Corporate Media Ownership and Its Threat to Democracy*. Amherst, NY: Prometheus Books, 2005.

Phillips, Peter. "News Bias in the Associated Press." Common Dreams, July 22, 2006. http://www.commondreams.org/views06/0722-21.htm.

Popper, Karl. *The Open Society and Its Enemies*. London: Routledge, 2002.

Prevent Truth Decay. "The NY Post's February 14, 2003 Front Page and Accompanying Article," February 14, 2003. http://www.preventtruthdecay.com/mainmiscweasels.htm (accessed on February 28, 2010).

Project Censored. "Independent News Sources." Project Censored. http://www.projectcensored.org/censorship/news-sources/ (accessed on March 1, 2010).

Project for the New American Century. *Rebuilding America's Defenses: Strategy, Forces, and Resources for a New Century*, 2000. http://www.newamericancentury.org/RebuildingAmericasDefenses.pdf.

Public Citizen. "The Peru FTA after One Year." http://www.citizen.org/trade/index.cfm/trade/newnaftas/ (accessed on February 27, 2010).

Rabble. "The SPP is Dead. Let's Keep It That Way." September 24, 2009. http://rabble.ca/news/2009/09/spp-dead-lets-keep-it-way (accessed on February 27, 2010).

Rasmussen Reports. "War on Terror Update: 50% Now Say U.S. is Winning War on Terror." Wednesday, February 24, 2010. http://www.rasmussenreports.com/public_content/politics/mood_of_america/war_on_terror_uate (accessed February 27, 2010).

Reed, Charlie. "Journalists' Recent Work Examined before Embeds." Stars and Stripes, August 24, 2009. http://www.stripes.com/article.asp?section=104&article=64348 (accessed on March 1, 2010).

Register. "FBI Preps $1bn Biometric Database, 'Next Generation Identification' Awaits You." December 24, 2007. http://www.theregister.co.uk/2007/12/24/fbi_database_biometrics/ (accessed on February 27, 2010).

Reuters. "Proposed New FBI Rules Draw Civil Liberties Worries." Reuters, Friday, September 12, 2009. http://www.reuters.com/article/idUSN1247176820080912.

RFIDNews. "VeriChip Tagging Soldiers." March 17, 2007. http://www.rfidnews.org/2007/03/17/verichip-tagging-soldiers (accessed on February 27, 2010).

Risen, James and Eric Lichtblau. "Bush Lets U.S. Spy on Callers without Courts." *New York Times,* December 16, 2005.

———. "Court Affirms Wiretapping without Warrants." *New York Times*, January 15, 2009.

Rockefeller, David. *Memoirs*, New York: Random House, 2003.

Rudolph, Alan. "Brain Machine Interfaces." DARPA. http://www.infowars.com/print/ps/brain_machine_darpa.htm (accessed on February 27, 2010).

SAIC. "Data Mining & Data Warehousing." SAIC, 2006. http://web.archive.org/web/20060209120733/www.saic.com/datamining/data-analysis.html (accessed on March 1, 2010).

Salon. "Letter from an Iraq Vet." August 6, 2005. http://dir.salon.com/story/opinion/feature/2005/08/06/vet_letter/index.html (accessed on February 28, 2010).

Scheeres, Julia. "Tracking Junior with a Microchip." Wired, October 10, 2003. http://www.wired.com/science/discoveries/news/2003/10/60771 (accessed on February 27, 2010).

Schwartzman, Andrew. "Testimony of Andrew Jay Schwartzman, President and CEO, Media Access Project to the Subcommittee on Antitrust Competition Policy and Consumer Rights Senate Judiciary Committee." Media Access Project, February 4, 2010. http://www.mediaaccess.org/file_download/360 (accessed on February 28, 2010).

Science Daily. "Seeing through Walls Engineers Develop Technology to See Through Walls." July 1, 2007. http://www.sciencedaily.com/videos/2007/0706-seeing_through_walls.htm (accessed on February 27, 2010).

Secure Computer. "Special Report: Secure Computing Corporation and Network Support." Local Netter, Vol. 14, No. 12, 1994.

Shane, Scott. "Cheney is Linked to Concealment of C.I.A. Project." *New York Times,* July 11, 2009.

Singer, Emily. "The Army's Remote-Controlled Beetle." *Technology Review,* Thursday, January 29, 2009. http://www.technologyreview.com/computing/22039/?a=f (accessed on February 27, 2010).

SPP. "Security and Prosperity Partnership of North America." http://www.spp.gov/ (accessed on February 27, 2010).

Stanley, Jay and Barry Steinhardt. "Bigger Monster, Weaker Chains: The Growth of an American Surveillance Society." American Civil Liberties Union, January http://www.aclu.org/FilesPDFs/aclu_report_bigger_monster_weaker_chains.pdf (accessed on March 1, 2010).

Student Activism. "Surveillance Cameras in British Classroom Spark Student Walkout." June 9, 2009 http://studentactivism.net/2009/06/09/surveillance-cameras/ (accessed on February 28, 2010).

Sullivan, Bob. "FaceBook: The End of Secrets?" The Red Tape Chronicles, MSNBC. http://redtape.msnbc.com/2010/01/what-would-a-world-without-secrets-look-like-thanks-to-facebook-we-may-find-out—-privacy-experts-continue-to-watch-in-won.html#posts (accessed on March 1, 2010).

Sunday Times (London). "The Secret Downing Street memo." May 1, 2005 http://www.timesonline.co.uk/tol/news/uk/article387374.ece (accessed on February 25, 2010).

Svenssen, Peter. "Comcast Blocks Some Internet Traffic." MSNBC, October 19, 2007. http://www.msnbc.msn.com/id/21376597/ (accessed on March 1, 2010).

Tapper, Jake. "Obama's FISA Shift." ABC News, July 9, 2008. http://blogs.abcnews.com/politicalpunch/2008/07/obamas-fisa-shi.html (accessed on March 1, 2010).

Tencer, Daniel. "Man Who Sold Iraq War Vetting Imbedded Journos: Report." Raw Story, August 24, 2009. http://rawstory.com/08/news/2009/08/24/iraq-war-salesman-now-vetting-journos/ (accessed on March 1, 2010).

Townsend, Mark and Paul Harris. "Security Role for Traffic Cameras." *The Observer*, Sunday, February 2003. http://www.guardian.co.uk/politics/2003/feb/09/terrorism.transport (accessed on February 27, 2010).

Trilateral Commission. "About the Organization." Trilateral Commission. http://www.trilateral.org/ (accessed on March 1, 2010).

Tucker, Jr., James P. "Bilderbergers Own President Obama." *American Free Press*, May 15, 2009. http://www.thecitizen.com/~citizen0/node/36810 (accessed on February 27, 2010).

———. "Bilderberg Pushing World Tax." *American Free Press*, May 6, 2002. http://www.denverpatriotcommunity.org/AmericanFreePress/AFPNewsMay02.htm#anchor1498 (accessed on February 27, 2010).

———. "Bilderberg Split on Iraq War, American Free Press." Prison Planet, May 26, 2002 http://www.prisonplanet.com/bilderberg_split_on_iraq_war.html. (accessed on February 27, 2010).

United States Congress. House of Representatives. FISA Amendments Act of 2008, 110th Congress, July 10, 2008. http://www.govtrack.us/congress/billtext.xpd?bill=h110-6304 (accessed on March 1, 2010).

———. PATRIOT Act, 107th Congress, October 26, 2001. http://frwebgate.access.gpo.gov/cgi-bin/getdoc.cgi?dbname=107_cong_public_laws&docid=f:publ056.107.pdf (accessed on March 1, 2010).

UT Watch. "The Eyes of Texas are Upon … YOU!" http://www.utwatch.org/security/classrooms.html (accessed on February 28, 2010).

Voltairenet. "The Story of Private Jessica Lynch, a Heroine of Propaganda." June 3, 2004. http://www.voltairenet.org/article30097.html (accessed on February 28, 2010).

Walzer, Michael. *Just and Unjust Wars*. New York: Basic Books, 1977.

Warrick, Joby. "CIA Assassin Program was Nearing New Phase." *Washington Post*, Thursday, July 16, 2010.

Watson, Paul Joseph. "Leaked Agenda: Bilderberg Group Plans Economic Depression." Prison Planet, Wednesday, May 6, 2009. http://www.infowars.com/leaked-agenda-bilderberg-group-plans-economic-depression/ (accessed on February 27, 2010).

———. "World Bank President Admits Agenda for Global Government." Prison Planet, Wednesday, April 1, 2009. http://www.prisonplanet.com/world-bank-president-admits-agenda-for-global-government.html (accessed on February 27, 2010).

White House. Summary of the White House Review of the December 5, 2009 Attempted Terrorist Attack. http://www.whitehouse.gov/sites/default/files/summary_of_wh_review_12-25-09.pdf (accessed on March 1, 2010).

———. The National Security Strategy of the United States of America, Washington, D.C., September, 2002. http://www.globalsecurity.org/military/library/policy/national/nss-020920.pdf (accessed on March 1, 2010).

Worthington, David. "GOP Moves to Block Net Neutrality." Techologizer, September 21, 2009. http://technologizer.com/2009/09/21/gop-moves-to-block-net-neutrality/.

Index